A DECADE OF
DREAMS

Reading Football Club's first 10 years at Madejski Stadium

First published in Great Britain in 2008 by
The Breedon Books Publishing Company Limited
Breedon House, 3 The Parker Centre,
Derby, DE21 4SZ.

A catalogue record for this book is available
from the British Library.

ISBN 978-1-85983-637-8

Printed and bound by Scotprint, Haddington, Scotland.

A DECADE OF DREAMS

Reading Football Club's first 10 years at Madejski Stadium

Written by
Andy West and Mark Bradley

Editorial assistance
thanks to Chris Witcher
and Simon Heggie

Statistical assistance
thanks to Nigel Meek
and Alan Sedunary

Photography
thanks to Richard Claypole,
Jason Dawson, Gareth Davies,
Gary Hynard, Ian Morsman
and Craig Mortimer.

A special thanks also to *Reading
Evening Post* for helpfully providing
us with images for chapters three
and four of this book.

Thanks to PPAUK Agency for
London Irish photos.

breedon books
PUBLISHING

Contents

Chapter 1

In The Beginning...

It started with one man's vision. John Madejski had taken over as Chairman of his ailing local football club in December 1990 with the lofty ambition of guiding his new acquisition – a cash-strapped mid-table Division Three side – into the top flight of English football. But he quickly realised that a major drawback to achieving those goals was the dilapidated state of the Club's creaking Victorian-era ground, Elm Park.

The early 1990s was a period of revolution in terms of football stadia. Hastened by the horrors of the Hillsborough disaster in April 1989 when 96 Liverpool supporters died in a crush on the Leppings Lane terrace, facilities were being renewed, refreshed, redeveloped and rebuilt at a rapid rate. The subsequent Taylor Report into the causes of the disaster decreed that standing terraces should become a thing of the past, and clubs including Huddersfield, Bolton, Derby, Millwall,

Terraces like Elm Park's Tilehurst End were becoming a thing of the past.

Sunderland and Middlesbrough pressed forward with plans to build entirely new grounds, while huge amounts of new-found TV revenue (following the Sky-led launch of the Premier League in 1992) were ploughed into improving existing facilities at famous arenas such as Old Trafford, Highbury, White Hart Lane and, most poignantly, Anfield, where the Kop was converted into seating in 1994.

Reading were in a difficult position. The urban location of Elm Park meant that significant redevelopment of the ground was impossible – there was simply no land to build on. And converting the three existing terraced stands into seating would have reduced the overall capacity to less than 10,000 – clearly insufficient to sustain Premier League, or even Division One, football.

So it did not take John Madejski long to come to a stark conclusion; to take Reading into the Premiership, he needed to build a new ground. Speaking in an exclusive new interview for this book, he reflects:

Fundamentally we knew that, due to the Taylor Report, trying to revamp Elm Park was a complete waste of time and effort, because it was in the wrong place at the wrong time. It was landlocked. It was perfectly good when it was built 100 years ago because people used to walk everywhere and it was easy to get to. But people don't walk anywhere these days. Elm Park was past its sell-by date and we desperately needed to switch to a new environment. We definitely had to move, everyone realised it.

Deciding to move was the easy part, finding a suitable site proved to be more challenging. Although he did widen the search to the outer reaches of Berkshire, Madejski was always keen to build the new ground within the borough of Reading if at all possible, but identifying the required amount of space within the confines of the River

Thames and the M4 was not an easy task. 'The final site wasn't the first place that came along,' says Madejski. 'We looked extensively, all around the county of Berkshire quite frankly. Inside and outside of Reading, there were lots of places we looked at. We needed a big site because I didn't want to go for bog standard. I wanted to produce a stadium we could all be proud of.'

To assist with the process, in 1995 Madejski appointed Nigel Howe to oversee the identification of a suitable site and the eventual construction of the new stadium. The nephew of former Arsenal and England coach Don Howe, Nigel's area of professional expertise lay in property development and he relished the opportunity of fulfilling Madejski's dream. Interviewed for this book, Howe recalls:

When I came to Reading after being introduced to John Madejski by one of the Club's directors, Graham Denton, who I had worked with in the past, I knew very little about what was going to happen…Madejski said that the council had come up with two potential sites some months before – one is the site which we're now on, and the other was where the existing greyhound stadium is and the land around there. At the time I think he felt this was the better site in location terms and when I came along to my first meeting with the council I quickly agreed with that. I felt it had the best

potential access routes. We immediately went into discussions about how we could get into negotiations about acquiring the land from the council and relocating from Elm Park.

It was a mammoth task, but the Club were fortunate to be working with a co-operative council who recognised the potential positive impact of the stadium's construction. Madejski recalls:

We worked very diligently with the local borough council and they came up with the site here. It really caught our imagination. It was a landfill site that was used to throw away millions of plastic rubbish bags, but our overriding thought was 'location, location, location'. The site's proximity to junction 11 of the M4 was overwhelming, we just had to go for it. We knew it would cost millions to get rid of all the

waste and we had to make a sizeable contribution to the building of the A33 relief road, but it was where we wanted to be. It's a very good site – in fact you could argue that it's too good for a football stadium because, commercially, it's very attractive and very viable.

Howe concurs:

My background was property, and the best property developments I've ever done have all been based on location. That applies for this stadium. We're sat just off junction 11 of the M4, 30 miles from London, close to Heathrow, 50–60 miles from Bristol and the M5, close to good links to the south coast, and via the A34 and A404 to the M40 we have an easy run to Birmingham. We have a great network here to get people to and from the stadium quickly for whatever reason, sport or business.

With the site identified, the next step was to agree terms with the council for the purchase of the land. Famously, the Club was asked to cough up a grand sum of £1 but, as Howe explains, it was a more complex deal than that:

The actual contract says it cost £1 and the land is on a 999-year

The vast area of available space was one of the site's main attractions.

lease, so it's a virtual freehold. But obviously the council got a lot back in return and we had to take on a lot of liabilities…For starters we provided £6 million towards the building of the new A33 bypass, and we also had an onerous number of commitments in our section 106 agreement, which was for anything from road improvements to public transport and park and ride schemes which still exist on the site now. So there were a lot of win-win situations for the council. And although the land was sold for only £1, the actual upsides to the council in terms of getting a lot of local infrastructure and amenities developed were great for them.

And then there was the small matter of transforming a former household waste site into a modern football stadium. It was a complicated, costly procedure and provided Howe with a greater scale of work than he had initially envisaged:

When I visited the site for the first time I was surprised. I didn't expect it to be overland fill, I was expecting a lake that had been filled in. I didn't expect to see great big mounds of earth! But actually that made it appeal to me even more, because visually I could see the impact would be even greater. Although construction-wise it was going to present trials in dealing with the landfill, the site was so prominent it meant the stadium would be seen from quite a long distance away and it would be a major landmark building. So that appealed to me and I was very enthusiastic to get on with it.

By the autumn of 1997 the outline shape of the stadium was clearly visible.

The stadium was built on piles of old household rubbish.

'Getting on with it' meant a costly process of remediation work in the first place, ensuring that the site was safe to build on. The new stadium would literally be constructed upon a load of old rubbish, making it very different from a normal building site. There would be a plethora of tests and studies before the first diggers could take up residency, but Howe and Madejski were so convinced by the suitability of the site's location that they were prepared to be patient and do whatever it took. Howe recalls:

The site was about a nine-metre deep existing landfill site – an overland site. In the late 1950s and early 1960s it had just been filled with rubbish, and it was uncontrolled rubbish so nobody really knew what was underneath the site. Its time as a landfill had finished, a very thin cap had been put on top of it, and at the time we took over the site wild horses were grazing on it. We had to deal with a lot of environmental issues and the fact that it was an uncontrolled tip made it even more complicated. The environmental licence which we still have now at the Club means we have to keep continually monitoring the site, making sure the subsoil is OK and insuring it every year.

With an agreement to purchase the land in place and environmental considerations under control, the next obstacle to overcome was financing the work – no mean feat considering the estimated total cost was somewhere approaching the £50-million mark. Clearly, Madejski was going to have to dip heavily into his own personal fortune to provide a large chunk of the investment needed, but financial assistance was also provided by two significant revenue streams – the sale of Elm Park and the development of a new retail park at the site of the new stadium. Howe explains:

Because the Club owned the Elm Park site, we had the opportunity to help the financial side of the move by getting consent for residential housing to be built on the land. We did that and ultimately sold it to Barratt Homes. That was one part of the jigsaw, and another was coming to an agreement with the council that we could sell off part of the new site for retail development – where B&Q, Comet, Pizza Hut and the others are now situated. So we were able to sell that land to a property development company called Salmon Harvester, who then deposited an amount of money into an account, which demonstrated to the council that we had enough to get the stadium built...It wasn't all plain sailing though – putting the commercial development on the site had its own planning issues with the council because it wasn't an area of Reading that was allocated for that form of development. So there was a lot of support required from the council and surrounding businesses to say that they wanted that sort of development in that part of Reading...And then we had to dig this huge great hole out, where we put the retail scheme – Salmon Harvester said that it couldn't sit on the plastic bags and rubbish, it had to be sat on virgin ground.

These muddy wastelands would become a 25,000 capacity football stadium.

got consent in about May 1997 and we started on site a couple of months later. And that left us with effectively a year to build it!

So the work could begin. But what form should the stadium take, what should it look like and how big should it be? From the outset, Madejski had been determined that he did not just want to build a football stadium – after years of being hamstrung by the urban location of Elm Park, the Club now had plenty of space available (66 acres in total) and was spending millions of pounds to build a new facility, so why enforce a self-imposed restriction of only using the stadium on 25 match days a year? Howe explains:

The Chairman felt that the way football is financed, he needed to bring in additional income that

Effectively we dug it out and put it back a few hundred metres away, which lifted the site in parts by another few metres. That's why the stadium itself is a lot higher than B&Q and the other retail outlets on the A33.

With all the necessary hoops finally jumped through, Madejski and Howe were finally able to submit a detailed planning proposal to the council. Howe admits:

By the time we were in a position to hand in the planning proposal, we only had effectively one and a half seasons before we simply had to move. This was because Elm Park would then fail to meet the requirements of the Taylor Report and we'd have to go somewhere to ground share. So we were on a very tight timeframe. We managed to get the planning application in before Christmas of 1996, we

The West Stand begins to take shape.

would help us run the Club and we needed to think about revenue streams that weren't just from football. So we did a deal with Richmond Rugby Club and built the conference centre on the front, which was there right from the start. It was always our intention to build a hotel as well, but that had to wait until a couple of years later…The conference centre was a gamble because we had no idea how successful it would be. I struggled to get a caterer to start with, before a company called Alexander Catering eventually took the contract. They quickly became so successful that people were hearing about this new venue called the Royal Berkshire Conference Centre – which was actually at Madejski Stadium. When the five-year contract was up, the amount of interest we had from major companies such as Sodexho and Compass, who ultimately won it, was phenomenal. And what has always done it for this stadium, hotel and conference centre is our location. The location is so, so good and we were always confident it would work in our favour.

Madejski also had firm ideas about the new stadium's appearance, reflecting 'I always wanted a bowl-type stadium where everybody in the whole arena could see the field of play. Some of the other stadiums you go to, there are pillars in the way or something trapping you from seeing the whole action. But here everyone in the whole arena gets to see everything and that's something we're very proud of.' Howe confirms that the actual design of the stadium was one of the more straightforward aspects of the operation:

Finalising the design was actually quite an easy process because I'd had a good briefing from John Madejski, who had very clear ideas about what he wanted and what he didn't want. He wanted something that was unique, and he wanted something complete. He had in mind that he didn't want four stands or corners missing. He wanted the complete bowl effect. He felt that was very important and it was never really open to question…When we were planning the construction I visited four stadiums that were quite new. I went to Huddersfield, Millwall – which

By the spring of 1998 the Club was able to start marketing the new stadium.

The men who made it happen: director Ian Wood-Smith, chairman John Madejski and chief executive Nigel Howe.

was not considered to have taken on board a lot of the modern ideas – Bolton, which was still under construction when we started, and I also went to Middlesbrough. We were under a lot of pressure to copy Middlesbrough, because the Riverside had been built very economically and that was felt to be the cheap, easy way to get a new stadium built. What I wanted to do here was give a bit more comfort to the fans – there is a bit more leg room here than at some other stadiums. Design-wise, if you go to Middlesbrough now, there is such a lot of steelwork around the outside of the building that it's starting to look a bit tired, whereas we haven't had that problem.

The other issue to be settled was the size of the stadium. With attendances at Elm Park rarely reaching five figures, many supporters and pundits believed it would be foolish and unnecessary to build anything beyond the current Elm Park capacity of 15,000. The phrase 'white elephant' was frequently bandied about, but Madejski and Howe disagreed and were prepared to stick to their guns. Howe says:

We always wanted to get as close as we could to 25,000 seats. We'd carried out research and the results showed that, although during that time we generally had crowds of only 8–9,000 at Elm Park, we felt the area could consistently sustain a much higher level of attendance even if we weren't in the Premier League. We believed that we could get close to a crowd of 25,000 in the Championship at least six or seven times a year. And if we could get to the Premier League we felt we would fill that capacity on a regular basis, and of course with hindsight that's been proved to be right.

So it was all systems go, and the construction of a new stadium started to become reality. But on the pitch the Club was enduring troubled times, giving further fuel to those doubters who questioned the wisdom of investing so heavily in a new state-of-

the-art facility. Terry Bullivant was appointed as manager in the summer of 1997 to succeed Mick Gooding and Jimmy Quinn, but he struggled to keep his team away from the bottom of the Division One table. A succession of injury problems did little to help his cause and, despite a couple of enjoyable Cup runs in the League, it was clear that safety was the most that could be hoped for.

Four miles down the road a new 25,000-capacity stadium was being built and it needed at least Division One football to be cost-effective – Bullivant was under serious pressure to deliver. His team's form picked up slightly around Christmas, including a Boxing Day victory over West Brom, a local 2–0 derby win at Swindon and an impressive 3–0 dismantling of fellow strugglers Manchester City, providing new-found confidence that the disaster of relegation could be avoided. But

Defender Andy Legg visits the half-built stadium.

Elm Park – Reading FC's home for a century.

after that Elm Park success against Manchester City on 24 February, the Royals embarked upon a dreadful run of form that took them deep into relegation territory. With a sequence of results that read 0–1, 1–5, 0–3 and 0–4, time was running out for the affable Bullivant and, after a humbling 3–0 defeat at Oxford United on Tuesday 17 March, Madejski was left with little alternative but to sack his manager.

One of the few shining lights of that season was midfielder Phil Parkinson, who remains saddened that the team was unable to do better for Bullivant. He recalls 'When Bully took over at the start of that season I knew that he had a difficult job. He inherited an ageing squad – players like Trevor Morley, Darius Wdowczyk and Keith McPherson were all coming towards the end of their careers, Michael Gilkes had moved on – and I always expected it to be tough. Unfortunately it didn't work out for Terry but we all liked him and were disappointed that he couldn't bring us success.'

Reserve team boss Alan Pardew took over as caretaker for one game, a 2–0 home defeat to Huddersfield, before former Celtic midfielder and Scotland international Tommy Burns was appointed on a permanent basis just in time to beat the March 1998 transfer deadline day in spectacular fashion by signing no fewer than seven players. Sadly, the capture of the so-called 'magnificent seven' did not have the required effect, and the Royals continued to tumble inevitably and inexorably towards relegation, leaving Madejski to contemplate the fact that his new stadium would struggle to sell even half its total capacity in its opening season in Division Two.

But there was no turning back and the construction of the stadium continued apace. By now the Club had appointed a new stadium manager, Ray Booth, to oversee the nuts and bolts of the facilities at the new ground – to make sure that everything was built properly and that everything worked. With such a short space of time to complete the construction before the start of the 1998–99 season, Ray was immediately

plunged into the deep end and started working day and night to get the new stadium built on time. He recalls:

This was a design and build contract, which means the contractors, Birse Construction, were responsible for designing it as well as building it. A traditional form of contract would be a team of designers who design and detail it, dealing with all the client's requirements and incorporating those requirements into the drawings and specifications. Then a contractor just builds it and doesn't get involved in the design at all…But with this contract the design concept, with the size and appearance, was agreed and then planning consent was obtained by the design consultants. That was put into an employer's requirement document so the contractor had to then design it

in detail in order to build it. We also had a guaranteed maximum price which had been signed, so Birse couldn't actually spend more than the agreed figure, but in the end the project ended up unavoidably costing more than the guaranteed maximum price and we had to go back to the Chairman for some extra money.

Another issue that needed to be resolved was the name of the new

stadium. Various ideas were floated but nothing really stuck, and eventually it was decided to name the new ground after the man who had made it possible. 'Well it wasn't my idea to call it Madejski Stadium, but I am grateful that most journalists can now pronounce my name – in the past nobody ever could!' John Madejski laughs. 'My original idea was to call it the High Tech Stadium and get all the technical companies that base themselves in the M4 corridor on board. The intention was to have all the companies' liveries on the way up to the stadium and exhibit their products, but there wasn't enough interest. So the marketing people felt that Madejski was a very strong name and suggested we call it Madejski Stadium. I thought "well, who am I to argue!".'

As the ill-fated 1997–98 season progressed, the new ground was being built at a rapid rate, looking more and more like an actual football stadium

The underbelly of the East Stand in construction.

with each passing day. One afternoon the players were given a taster of their new surroundings, and midfielder Phil Parkinson recalls a sense of excitement as he toured the shell of the new stadium:

> We all had our hard hats on and walked around the site. One stand was already built at the time and the pitch was being laid, and it was then that the lads realised just how good the new stadium was going to be. We'd just read about it in the papers like everybody else, but when we went up there to have a look it really hit home...From that moment on it was a regular topic of conversation in the dressing room and something we were all quite excited about. We always knew that Reading was potentially a big Club and we couldn't really survive at Elm Park for too much longer – it was a great atmosphere and I loved playing there, especially in night games, but progress had to be made and it was time to move on.

Chairman Madejski was also closely following the progress, and he was given an alternative view of the proceedings:

> I went up to the site a few times to see what was happening. I also went in a helicopter to have a

look from above, and although I was scared stiff it was a tremendous sight to see it taking shape from up there. It was great to see it implemented. You can see photographs, artists' impressions, computer-generated images and so on, but you never know until you see it physically just what it is like. When you see it in the flesh it's so different.

Stadium manager Booth was heavily involved in the nitty-gritty of the process, working closely with construction company Birse on the small but significant details of the build. He says:

> I was mainly answering all the questions that the contractor asked on a day-to-day basis...What colour are the seats? What colour would the steelwork be? Which CCTV system should we choose? Which PA system will we have? How will we do the standby generation

and back-up power supplies? What level of system to choose? How many turnstiles? What's the flow rate of the turnstiles? Then the safety certificate – number of turnstiles, location of turnstiles, how to split the home and away fans, both inside and outside the stadium...there were certainly lots of things to think about!...I have to admit there were some cock-ups along the way! The beer dispensing for instance...we were advised initially by Courage Brewery to only put two lager and two bitter taps in each concourse bar. Alcohol in football concourse bars was a new thing back then – there was no alcohol at Elm Park at all. The concept was new to the football industry and new to the licensing magistrates, so that was another thing we had to do – get an alcohol licence. Everyone was very wary about alcohol in public concourses and we only had one bit of the bar licensed. It was all

Fans invade the Elm Park pitch after the final game.

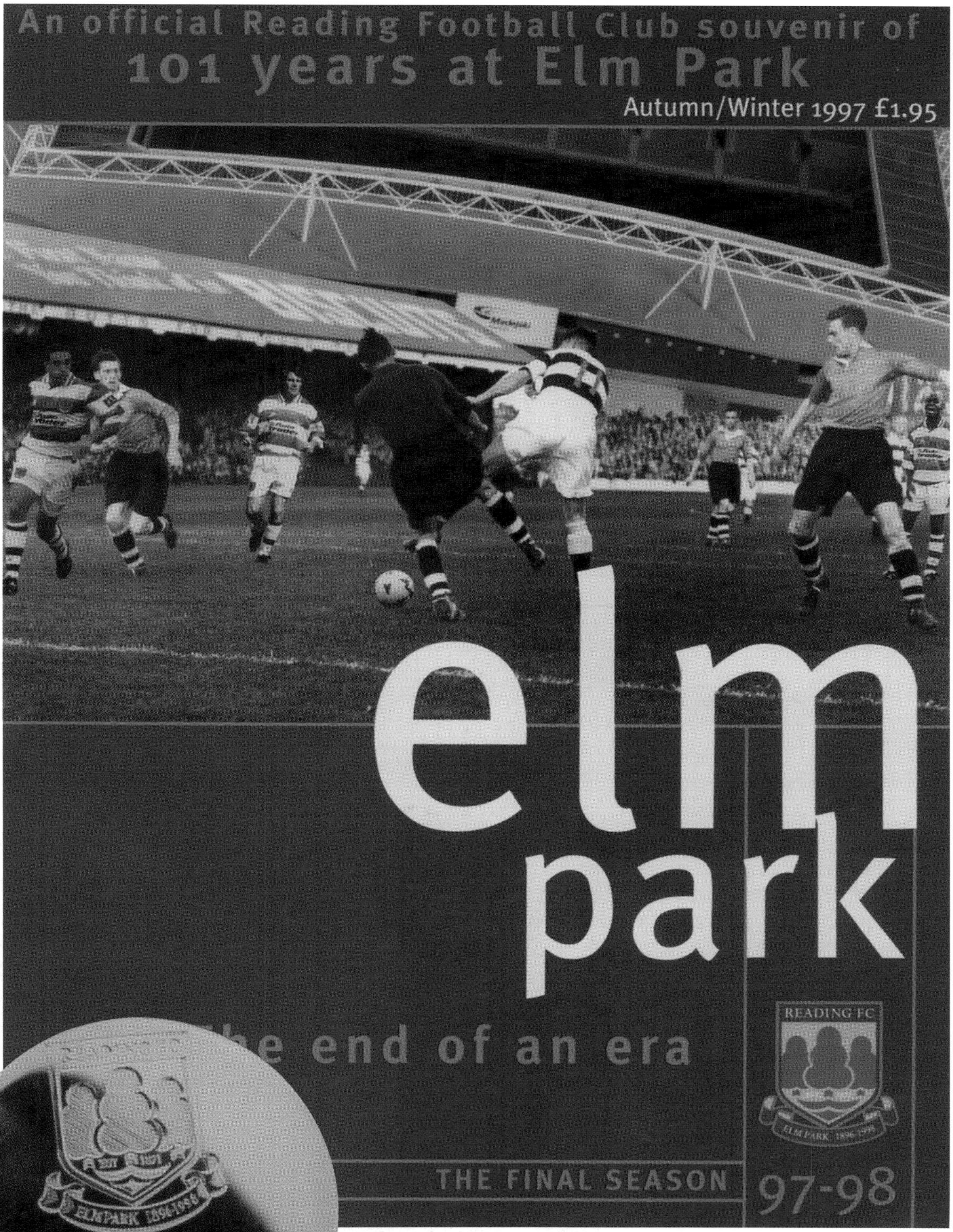
An official Reading Football Club souvenir of
101 years at Elm Park
Autumn/Winter 1997 £1.95
elm
park
The end of an era
READING FC
ELM PARK 1896-1998
THE FINAL SEASON
97-98

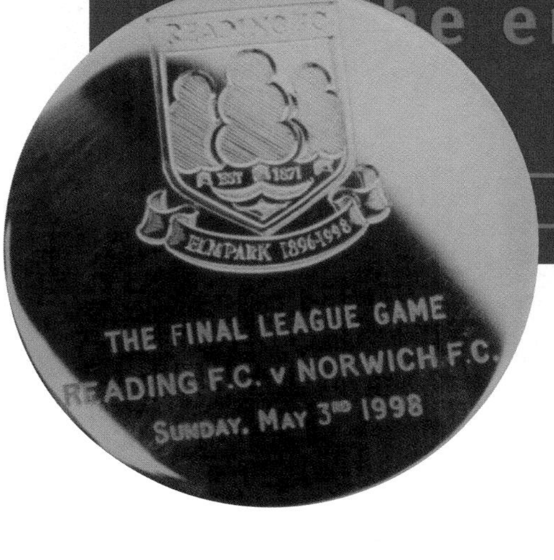
EST 1871
ELMPARK 1896-1998
THE FINAL LEAGUE GAME
READING F.C. v NORWICH F.C.
SUNDAY, MAY 3RD 1998

The Conference Centre takes shape.

very tight and restricted, the police weren't used to it and clearly the demand for alcohol was such that we could never serve it with only two lager and bitter pumps on each bar. So it ended up with us putting pumps in the whole length of the bars and extending it from four taps to the whole bar!

By the summer of 1998, relegation had been confirmed as the Royals ended their hugely disappointing campaign with a 1–0 home defeat against Norwich City in Elm Park's last competitive game (a smattering of friendlies and testimonials took place later). But, despite relegation, there was still an air of anticipation and excitement as the opening of Madejski Stadium loomed ever closer. In fact, for some members of the Club's staff, that move had already taken place, as club secretary Sue Hewett (then assistant to

Andrea Barker) recalls:

I joined the Club in August 1997 and even during my interview process there was a lot of talk about the new stadium — you could tell that everything was being prepared for the move. It was a really exciting time, especially to see the stadium start to take shape…In January

1998 a few of the staff at Elm Park moved permanently to work in portakabins at Madejski Stadium, and there was a constant movement between the two sites. At first you'd be entering a building site, wearing hard hats and wellington boots and everything was covered in mud and gravel, but gradually you could see the stadium and the stands take shape…We were selling season tickets from the portakabins at Madejski Stadium, and there was more interest in season tickets than there ever had been at Elm Park, even though the team had just been relegated. We were literally selling them off hand-drawn plans that were pinned to the walls in the portakabin — it was just pencil marks on a piece of

Construction gathered pace in the early months of 1998.

paper, and at times you did wonder whether these seats would actually exist! It was quite hard to visualise at that time…In the two months leading up to the opening of the stadium it just got busier and busier, and we started to work very long hours — 8am until 11pm most of the time. We were doing things like photocopying and stuffing envelopes, trying to get information to supporters about tickets, bus routes, parking and so on. It felt like you were folding pieces of paper for hours on end! And everyone got involved — I remember the Chairman's daughter, Camilla, used to come in and start stuffing all the envelopes with us. One day even the Chairman himself came in and started scrambling across the floor going through files!

Naturally, the excitement at moving to Madejski Stadium was tinged with sentimental disappointment at leaving the much-loved Elm Park. Supporters recognised that the old ground was

hopelessly outdated and that the facilities available to them at the new stadium would be infinitely better, but there was still a great deal of affection for Elm Park and many accepted the departure with a heavy heart. The Club was well aware that not all supporters were delighted at the prospect of leaving their familiar old ground, and Nigel Howe reflects:

We knew that building a new stadium wasn't unanimously applauded by the fans, interestingly enough. A lot of people felt they were going to lose the traditions of Elm Park. But, to be honest, if you put sentimentality to one side Elm Park was a pile of old rubbish. It was gone as a football venue, it was falling down! But it was in the centre of town, and that was a big reason why a lot of fans liked it, along with the history and atmosphere of the place…We always accepted that it would take three or four months for people to get used to the new stadium, but we were

hopeful that they would also realise how many benefits it was going to bring the Club. The transition from Elm Park to this stadium was a big one for the fans and we were conscious that it was difficult for them. We had a new ticketing system with no cash on the turnstile. Public transport or parking and walking to the stadium was the option rather than walking from your house…but they were changes we had to make for the sake of taking the Club forward. We resisted going back to cash on turnstiles and some of the other things supporters were asking for, because it was a case of wanting to return to the old ways mostly because they weren't used to the new. They were difficult decisions and not universally popular at the time, but they had to be made.

With season-ticket sales progressing rapidly, preparations for the 1998–99 season were almost completely overshadowed by the clamour for information about the new stadium. But Tommy Burns was certainly very active, as he tried to build a squad that could challenge for an immediate return to Division One. His deadline-day signing of seven players was an indication that the Royals had hired a manager who would not be shy in the transfer market, and that trend continued with a flurry of post-season signings.

Many of Burns's captures were

The site neared completion as the opening day beckoned.

complete unknowns to Reading supporters, with possibly the most intriguing arrival being Mass Sarr, a Liberian international winger who had been personally recommended by legendary striker and compatriot George Weah. Burns also snapped up a pair of Dutchmen – giant goalkeeper Peter van der Kwaak and elegant defender Elroy Kromheer. Closer to home, excitement was generated by the signing of two former Manchester United youth stars, attacking midfielder Grant Brebner and centre half Chris Casper, while veteran defender John Polston was also added to provide further experience. A club-record fee of £750,000 was splashed out on a promising young York City winger by the name of Graeme Murty. There was also a significant number of departures, notably striker Trevor Morley, defender Darius Wdowczyk and popular home-grown forward Stuart Lovell, who had remained a huge favourite with the fans despite his infamous penalty miss in the 1995 play-off final against Bolton Wanderers.

Burns's new-look side would begin their campaign with a home fixture against Wrexham – at least, that's what the Football League's fixture computer had decreed. But by now it was apparent there was no way that Madejski Stadium would be ready in time to stage the fixture on the opening date of Saturday 8 August. So, with the League's blessing, the Club was allowed to agree with Wrexham to switch the fixture to north Wales, giving Burns two consecutive away fixtures to start the campaign before Madejski Stadium officially opened its doors with a visit of Luton Town on Saturday 22 August 1998.

From a playing point of view, the season started badly. Very badly. Wrexham ran out 3–0 winners in the rearranged opening fixture at the Racecourse Ground and, if anything, things got slightly worse in the following weekend's 4–1 loss at Bristol Rovers. So the Royals prepared for their opening game at Madejski Stadium with a depressing record of played two, lost two, scored one, conceded seven (along with a League Cup first round first-leg 1–1 draw with Peterborough), but that did little to dampen spirits. The focus was on Saturday 22 August, the visit of Luton Town and Madejski Stadium's first-ever game. After years of planning, the time had finally arrived…a new home for Reading Football Club was ready to open its doors.

JOHN MADEJSKI

It is difficult to write an objective appraisal of John Madejski's time as Reading Chairman without sounding sycophantic. Just how do you analyse the contribution of a man who, without any room for argument, has completely transformed his Club from small-time non-achievers into an organisation that has genuine and credible aspirations of becoming an established Premier League side?

After growing up in Reading and spending the early days of his working career at the *Reading Evening Post*, Madejski amassed a personal fortune by inaugurating the hugely successful *Auto Trader* magazine in the 1970s. Although he freely confesses to never having been an avid football fan, he was attracted to become involved with the Royals after recognising the central role that any football club plays within its local community. Indeed, the theme of 'community, community, community' is one that frequently recurs whenever he is asked to speak about his vision for the Club, and that spirit of inclusiveness runs through all his varied philanthropic interests which include a school, a local history museum and an art gallery.

The first game to take place under Madejski's Chairmanship, on 1 December 1990, was a Division Two fixture against Fulham that resulted in a 1–0 victory thanks to a goal from Stuart Lovell. The game was played in front of 4,073 spectators at Elm Park, leaving the Royals in mid-table comfort in the third tier of English football – a position that more or less encapsulated the Club's unremarkable history; before two seasons in the mid-1980s, Reading had spent an uninterrupted spell of 55 years in the bottom two divisions.

Before long, Madejski was speaking of his vision to take his new acquisition into the top flight and, to be frank, it seemed a quite preposterous idea. In the 119 years since their foundation, Reading Football Club had achieved absolutely nothing of real note – their finest hour was beating Luton Town in the Simod Cup Final – and now their Chairman was talking about competing in the same division as Manchester United and Liverpool? Yet, almost 17 years to the day from that dour struggle against Fulham, Madejski was revelling in his team's 3–1 televised Premier League victory over Liverpool in front of 24,022 spectators in a new state-of-the-art stadium. There were, of course, many important contributory factors in the rise and rise of Reading FC, but there is no doubt that it could not have happened without Madejski's vision.

Like anything that is really worth achieving, it was a struggle and did not happen overnight. The biggest obstacle in taking Reading from nobodies to somebodies was Elm Park, which was simply completely unsuitable for top-flight football. It would have been impossible to sustain a place in the Premier League at the much-loved but outdated and decrepit old ground. As you will read in this book, Madejski displayed all his tenacity and determination to overcome the many

obstacles that were laid in his way. He got Madejski Stadium built and suddenly the Club was transformed into one of real, tangible potential. The infrastructure was in place to accommodate a successful Premier League football club; now he just needed a team to match it.

In accordance with the cruel laws that often seem to govern sport, Madejski's dream was dealt another blow when the move to the new stadium coincided with relegation back into Division Two. Another sizeable mountain had to be climbed before the Chairman's top-flight aspirations could be realised – and, before long, it became apparent that manager Tommy Burns was struggling to lead the Club down the right path. Madejski always loathes to put anyone out of a job – an indication of the loyalty that he shows to the people around him, and the loyalty in return that he inspires in them can be seen in the fact that six of the seven members of his non-football management team have been at the Club for more than 10 years. But on this occasion he came to the sad conclusion that Burns had to go, and he was replaced by Alan Pardew. The rest is history, as Pardew dragged the Club back on track and started the process that his successor, Steve Coppell, was able to finish off in such style. And so in 2006 Coppell and Madejski – for they are very much a team – led the Club into the Premier League for the very first time, smashing all sorts of records along the way.

To many people's surprise, Madejski's first season as a top-flight Chairman was preceded by an

admission that he would be prepared to sell the Club if the right deal came along. He stressed he was in no hurry to get out and that the 'right deal' was not just a financial parameter – Madejski was sticking true to his 'community, community, community' ethos and insisting that a potential buyer had to be somebody who would treat the Club and its supporters in a responsible manner. But a suitable buyer did not arise, and now Madejski finds that he has to do it all over again. After a two-season flirtation with the big guns, last season's relegation means that his Royals find themselves back in the Championship. So Madejski is left with two options: give up and retire gracefully or roll up his sleeves, get stuck into the challenge and continue his quest to establish Reading Football Club as a leading force in English football. No prizes for guessing which option he will take.

Madejski often jokingly tells the tale of his early involvement with Reading Football Club. 'I agreed to become Chairman because the Club badly needed investment and I wanted to put something back into my local community,' he smiles, before pausing to add, 'I didn't realise I'd have to put it all back!' Reading fans will be eternally grateful that he did.

More Than A Game:

From Corporate Catering To Sax And The Soundwaves

Madejski Stadium is not just home for Reading Football Club, its various footballing tributaries and long-term tenants London Irish. Elm Park operated on skeleton staff and remained eerily unused for most working weeks, but such a huge state-of-the-art stadium would be somewhat wasted if it only came alive at kick-off or try time.

An integral part of the stadium design is the Royal Berkshire Conference Centre, currently operated by Compass Group. It boasts the

Princess Suite with a maximum capacity of 700, six more rooms each accommodating 100-plus – the Kennet Lounge, the Loddon Room, the Thames Room, the Premier Lounge, the 1871 Suite and the Royal Suite – as well as 28 smaller executive suites for companies large and small.

Hosting small-scale meetings, huge product launches, sales or training conferences, company exhibitions, weddings, banquets and private parties, the conference centre offers newly renovated hospitality areas to the vast

Thames Valley business base and forms the largest conference venue in Reading – and one of the most accessible venues in the UK. And, in existence since the stadium's opening, the conference facilities have produced revenue that

has helped John Madejski build a successful football club and sustain a thriving business.

The Jazz Café is a live music venue catering for a different customer. It first opened its doors in Henley-on-Thames but relocated to Reading's Madejski Stadium in 2001, renovating and rebranding the existing Shooters bar that had entertained fans since the stadium's opening. Located within the bowels of the East Stand, the restaurant and bar can hold in excess of 300 party-goers until 3am and also acts as a pre-match drinking depository for the Royals season-ticket holders. So Ma-Jazz-Ski Stadium has welcomed the likes of Courtney Pine, Average White Band, Alexander O'Neil, The Commitments, The Real Thing and Shakatak through the back doors.

Staying with the music theme, Reading 107 FM has broadcast a radio station from its purpose-built studio in the south-east corner since 22 October 2002. It started when a consortium submitted their bid for a local commercial station in September 2001, and the licence was awarded the following March. A successful trial week under the guise of New City FM preceded a name change to Reading 107fm, and Tim Grundy went live to Reading at 8am in late October, playing *Listen To The Music* by the Doobie Brothers as the station's first song. Chairman John Madejski had a substantial share in the company from the start, and in December 2005 he took complete control of the station. From its inception, coverage of every Royals game was broadcast to fans who hadn't made it to the match, competing with BBC Radio Berkshire for the football fanbase. In the early days, the Club's media department had a significant hand in relaying every kick back to the studio, but at the end of Madejski Stadium's first decade The Royal Box, hosted by Mark Tompkins, included preview and review shows as well as live commentary alongside former Reading players Michael Gilkes and Barry Hunter.

ITV have rented an office within Madejski Stadium's complex for a number of years too, giving the regional TV station – ITV Thames Valley – a convenient Reading base from which to edit and transmit back to the main studio in Abingdon.

Madejski Stadium has also featured as a filming venue for on-location advertisers and programme makers. *In Deep* saw Nick Berry trip to Madejski Stadium to film part of his BBC police drama, and another ex-*EastEnders* star, Ross Kemp, starred in some *Ultimate Force* action here; filming a scene meant to be at an airport, the players' lounge was converted into an airport lounge and the adjacent toilets into a steam room in 2004. British Airways filmed a sports show for their long-haul in-flight show too, while Robbie Earle shot a piece for *Strictly Come African Dancing*. Channel Five's *Make It Big* headed to Reading and a special short film urging fans to sit down during matches was also shot at Madejski Stadium before being circulated around other clubs for matchday airing. Lucozade, Sony, Orange and MG Rover, along with *What Car?* and *Nuts* magazines, have all filmed or photographed adverts at Madejski Stadium, while MTV filmed an ad campaign against sex trafficking at the Royals' home and footage of Eric Obinna dribbling with the ball featured on a PC World advert. Channel Four's *More Four* advertised their upcoming music shows by parking Metallica's tour bus outside the North Stand for a photoshoot in 2006, but Ford perhaps thrust Madejski Stadium into more homes than anyone else – the car from which ticker tape flies in the pre-match clip ahead of every Sky Super Sunday match is in fact parked in front of Madejski Stadium. The list goes on but you get the picture!

Chapter 2

Opening Day

The big day had finally arrived. Reading were hosting Luton Town in a Nationwide Division Two fixture, but the game of football came a poor second to the occasion – the venue was to be Madejski Stadium, the brand-new home of Reading Football Club. It was a day that had been keenly anticipated for many years – ever since 1983 when the prospect of leaving Elm Park was first mooted. Enthusiasm for the occasion was barely dampened by the team's recent relegation from Division One and poor start to their Division Two campaign, and the decision to build the new stadium was immediately validated, as the opening game attracted an attendance significantly higher than the total capacity of the Club's old Elm Park ground. In fact, the attendance of 18,108 was Reading's highest home gate since a League Cup tie with Southampton in 1978, and the highest for a League game since March 1970 when, coincidentally, Luton were again the opponents.

Behind the scenes the final preparations were frantically taking place, and nobody was busier than stadium manager Ray Booth:

Above and below: Plenty of work still needed completing as opening day beckoned.

When we were getting ready to open, we were working all day and all night. The day before the first game we were still fixing seats, still unpacking furniture…there was a lot that still needed to be done and too little time to do it!…But to be honest I was amazed that we were in a position to open the doors. The stadium had been built in a little over 12 months and I just couldn't believe the build programme when I first saw it. I said there was no way it would only take 12 months and that it wouldn't be open until December or January. And I don't know whether it was Birse or the project manager himself, Kevin Underwood, that made it possible. But we all signed a charter, everyone involved – the management of the Club, the architects,

the planners – and somehow between us all we made it happen on time…I was so surprised and impressed because construction management is my background. I'd worked on civil engineering projects, cliff stabilisation, fuel depots, industrial warehouse schemes and other housing development projects. And the one thing I found working on a site like this for a football club was the determination to make it work from the people that built it. I'd never seen it in the construction industry anywhere else, where you are working with teams of guys who actually want you to open on time! They understood the importance of that date in August, and there was such a desire to get it right on time. They weren't all local builders – there were Manchester City fans, Coventry City fans…you went around the site offices and all the workers had different club badges on their helmets. But there was this desire to do it and get it right on time that you don't get with other builds. I had never seen that before.

To get to this stage, the construction team had initially excavated nearly **500,000 cubic metres** worth of waste to enable the building process to get underway. And, if you like being blinded by science, you will be interested to know that the ground floor comprises a 275 or 300mm power-floated in-situ

reinforced concrete slab on a high-performance methane barrier membrane on 200mm Cordek Ventform units. Naturally, concrete for the ground beams, pilecaps and floor slab is grade C35 with mix proportions suitable to provide resistance to Class II sulfate levels, while terrace units are precast concrete cast in steel moulds with treads at least 100mm thick to accommodate cast-in barrier fixings and also to incorporate a 20mm crossfall for drainage in accordance with FSADC Guidelines. Unless you

are a well-qualified specialist in the building trade, all of that will not mean a great deal. But it does suggest that an awful amount of work had been carried out to turn the wasteland site into a modern, state-of-the-art football stadium. And now the day had arrived…but the work was still continuing as final touches were frantically applied.

The sense of mildly organised chaos that reigned was encapsulated in the new Megastore, where the staff were desperately scrambling to make sure that they had something to sell.

Scott Cowan looks after the queue in his new home.

Merchandise manager Simon Hunt recalls a rather hectic 24 hours:

The new Megastore at the stadium didn't receive its safety certificate until the night before the match. That meant that, with a little over 12 hours until our scheduled opening time, we had no stock, no shelves, no shop fittings – nothing!…So on Friday evening we had to transfer all the stock from Elm Park – hundreds of boxes full of merchandise of every description – and we only had one van to do it with. If I remember rightly, we had to make 23 journeys between Elm Park and Madejski Stadium to transfer it all across. The new tills at the stadium had been fitted but we had no idea whether they would actually work when thousands of people started pouring in – fortunately they did…It was quite a transformation, and when it happened, it happened very quickly. We had been waiting to make the move for months, but now suddenly here we were – one minute we were in, effectively, a broom cupboard at Elm Park and the next we were in this huge cavernous new shop. Once we'd unpacked all the stock and laid it out there still seemed to be so much space! There were only three of us – Scott Cowan, Vinny Bullion and myself – and we worked until 3am trying to get the Megastore ready. Then we slept on the floor to be woken by queues of people already outside the shop before nine o'clock. So we opened the doors, fans rolled in and the queues didn't stop until seven o'clock!

Those supporters who left themselves with sufficient time to go shopping in the brand-new Megastore had done well; by far and away the

A shiny new shop.

Fans await the action on a glorious sunny day.

biggest problem on the day was access to the stadium. The new dual-carriageway A33 relief road was still some months from being completed, meaning that road access for the 18,108 spectators who attended the historic game was extremely basic, and it was not long before the traffic queues started backing up as thousands of people took the unfamiliar journey to their new destination. Chief executive Nigel Howe recalls:

The A33 was still under construction, so we had a basic track – you couldn't really call it a road – of nearly three-quarters of a mile that we had to get people in and out via. We had nearly 20,000 people, all coming here for the first time thinking

they'd have plenty of time and be able to park on-site. There were only 2,000 parking spaces at the stadium and even though we had announced that in advance, it seemed to take people by surprise that they weren't able to just roll up and park within 50 yards of the stadium!

The unfortunate man with the responsibility for looking after traffic and travel issues on the day was stadium manager Ray Booth, who spent most of the day surveying CCTV monitors and making frenetic phone calls. With no small degree of understatement, he concedes:

Traffic that day was a challenge. The A33 didn't exist, it was still

under construction, and the Bennet Road roundabout didn't exist either. Everyone had to come off the Basingstoke Road down the old Bennet Road, around Commercial Road and through the temporary access route which took you through the Greyhound Stadium…It was the route that the works vehicles had used to get to the site and it was only really fit for that purpose, but we didn't have an alternative apart from using Acre Road, across a temporary bit of the A33 and back in through the bottom area. So, to say the least, there were some traffic management issues! We got Reading Borough Council to put traffic light controllers at the ground, and they were pressing buttons to get traffic in and out of the stadium. We also erected temporary signage for the routes in and out of the stadium because a lot of people didn't know exactly where they were going, and a lot of those signs still exist around the town…Getting cars up to the ground wasn't the only issue because we also had delays at the entrances to the car parks – we were charging for car parking and it takes time to charge people and issue a ticket. We moved eventually to season purchases but that wasn't in place for the opening game and it caused a big headache.

Once spectators had managed to negotiate the queues on the roads and the car-park entrances, the next challenge was another queue…for tickets. Most people had purchased their tickets in advance and were able to glide straight into the stadium with relative speed, but the ticket office was besieged by supporters making late purchases and collections. Nigel Howe acknowledges 'We had a lot of issues with people who weren't used to having tickets, they were used to just turning up and paying on the turnstiles at Elm Park. Nobody knew where to go, they'd never been in the stadium before – and don't forget that neither had we! They didn't know how to read their tickets, which gate to go to, where their seats were…so to say it was pandemonium was an understatement.' Booth adds:

It was a massive culture shock for our supporters. At Elm Park you

paid your £10 on the turnstile and in you went. Now, suddenly, you had to buy a ticket in advance. We had massive collection queues – you can put 600 people a minute through the turnstiles, but you can't sell or issue tickets through the ticket office at that sort of pace. We put in some temporary ticket offices to cope with the queues, but we soon had to expand both ticket offices.

It was not just the loyal Royals who were going through the awkward process of familiarising themselves with their new surroundings; club staff had the same problems, especially the many matchday staff who had not been given the opportunity to visit the stadium during the construction process. Booth admits:

Stewarding the stadium was a steep learning curve. We did hold some training days leading up to the first match but we

couldn't have a real ramp-up event in advance – we didn't have time for one. So it was impossible for us to properly prepare for the challenges of stewarding the stadium, simply because we'd not had the chance to go in it! And there were very few people who had the right kind of stadium expertise at that time – it was a relatively new thing because ours was one of the first new stadia to be built.

So patience was a compulsory virtue for Reading fans as they made their way through the queues and the confusion, but once they were inside, it was all worth it. The new stadium was, for many, breathtakingly beautiful. The contrast with Elm Park could not have been greater. The 'complete bowl effect' that Chairman John Madejski had been so keen to create was there for all to see. Many spectators spent their first few minutes inside simply gazing around in awe. Could this really

The wide expanse of the new Princess Suite.

be ours? This sensational brand-new arena – described by *Daily Telegraph* football reporter Bryon Butler as 'heaven on earth' – belongs to little old Reading FC? It seemed too good to be true.

The brand-new hospitality facilities were one of the stadium's many very impressive facets, although Booth recalls that they were not quite at their luxuriant best on the opening day:

Former manager Maurice Evans steps out.

> For the first game we had no kitchens in the hospitality areas – they weren't finished – so we had to set up temporary food cold stores in the corner of the boardroom. We only had refrigeration in there, no cooking facilities, which meant we could only do cold food at first, so all the hospitality rooms only had salads and cold food to start with – just as well it was a hot day! And then of course all the dishes needed washing, which meant they had to be taken away, packaged and boxed and then brought back again.

Aside from the 'prawn sandwich brigade', the rest of the stadium's catering facilities were not exactly up to full speed either. 'We only had one concourse bar, so in the spaces we had where the bars were going to be built we had trestle tables selling sandwich packs and cold drinks,' recalls Booth. 'It was only between August to October that we were able to finish fitting out the concourse bars and the kitchens.' But nobody really cared about the lack of food and drink – they were just glad to be inside their gleaming new home for the first game at Madejski Stadium.

Before the game got underway, the Club had arranged an impressive range of pre-match entertainment for the growing crowd, including parachutists, a marching band, thousands of blue and white balloons and the appearance of a number of former greats such as Maurice Evans, all under the guidance of the day's compère, TV and radio personality Stuart Hall. It was just as well that the supporters who had found their way to their seats were being kept amused, because the road and access issues meant that, somewhat inevitably, kick-off was delayed to give everybody the chance to get inside.

There was a constant buzz of activity as a hive of workers were trying desperately to get everything done. Club secretary Sue Hewett admits that memories of the day are rather hazy:

> It's all just a bit of a blur! It was like a runaway train. We had a very early start but still seemed to be playing catch-up all day. I didn't get to see any of the game, and to be honest I wasn't even aware that the kick-off had been delayed. For most of us, it was the first time that we had actually been inside the stadium, and we were trying to find our way around so we could show other people where they needed to go. So it was a very hard day, but everyone had a huge sense of achievement as well.

Balloons released into the Berkshire sky as Luton warm up.

Another long-serving member of the administration team, Jayne Rapson, reinforces the point that the stadium was new for everybody, not just the fans:

As we got closer to that opening day I had mixed feelings. I felt sad because I had so many wonderful memories from Elm Park, but it was also very exciting because I knew that the Chairman's aim was to get into the Premiership and to achieve that we'd have to go somewhere much bigger. Once we got over to Madejski Stadium it was like a whole new world – just the size of the place! It took a while to get used to being in a completely new environment – it was like moving house. I remember getting lost on several occasions. We all knew every single inch of Elm Park, but the new stadium was completely different, so vast. It was breathtaking.

Eventually, with everybody finally inside and the formalities out of the

The concourse bars open for action.

Unusual delivery method for the matchball.

way, there was a game of football to play. And it was an important one for the Royals, because they badly needed a victory to ignite their campaign. Luton possessed a talented young team that had picked up four points from their opening two games, and they were out to spoil the Royal party.

Reading boss Burns reacted to his team's abject display in the previous week's 4–1 loss at Bristol Rovers by making five changes to his starting line up. He had been very active in the transfer market since taking up his post five months previously, and although injuries denied him the services of three new recruits – Graeme Murty, Chris Casper and John Polston – he had

Grant Brebner and Jim McIntyre (9) celebrate the opening goal.

plenty of options at his disposal. After the deliberations were over, the team selected by Burns to represent Reading in the historic first-ever game at Madejski Stadium lined up in a four-four-two formation as follows: Peter Van Der Kwaak, Andy Bernal, Stuart

Gray, Linvoy Primus, Elroy Kromheer, Grant Brebner, Darren Caskey, Ray Houghton, Mark Reilly, Jim McIntyre, Mass Sarr. That list included five players who were new faces to Reading supporters, having never played for the Club at Elm Park, and it did not take long for one to write his name into the record books as the scorer of Madejski Stadium's first-ever goal. With just 10 minutes on the clock and attacking the South Stand, the Luton defence was unable to clear a loose ball from a Ray Houghton corner, and young Scottish midfielder Grant Brebner, a former Manchester United youth trainee, reacted quickest to smash the ball into the net from 10 yards.

The stadium's maiden goal inspired Burns's men to record a victory that was a little less comfortable than the final 3–0 scoreline would suggest. Luton were hampered by the early withdrawal of two players – Paul McLaren and Dwight Marshall – through injury, and striker Jim McIntyre doubled Reading's advantage early in the second half after being set up by Mass Sarr. The scoring was completed in the final stages, and again it was one of Burns's signings to find the net, as substitute Robert Fleck took advantage of being in a suspiciously offside position to make it a hat-trick of Scotsmen on the score sheet.

The fans went away happy with their new ground and excited by the potential emergence of a new Royals hero. Even though he had not managed to get onto the score sheet, Liberian striker Sarr had produced a stunning performance full of attacking invention to scoop the Man of the Match on his full debut. It is no exaggeration to say that Sarr was sensational, dazzling the bewildered Luton defence with an array of flicks and tricks. Sadly, the promise he displayed on that afternoon was to remain frustratingly unfulfilled throughout the remainder of his

Reading career, but it had been enough to further brighten an already unforgettable afternoon and give the Royals faithful something to talk about other than their awe-inspiring new home. Nigel Howe admits the team's victory brought much relief to the overworked club staff:

I can't even remember how the game went because I spent most of the time worrying about things that were going right or wrong. But the result was very helpful because it left our supporters feeling good about everything and some of those who might have complained didn't. They went home happy. The atmosphere had been amazing and we received some fantastic accolades after that opening fixture. It was obviously a big landmark in the Club's history.

Incongruously, one person who was not able to join in that day of history was the man whose vision had created this exceptional new stadium for Reading Football Club – Chairman John Madejski. He was in Kuala Lumpur, setting up his new Malaysian Motor Trader magazine, but was kept up to date with proceedings by a series of phone calls and was able to reflect, 'Getting into that new stadium was absolutely central to our strategy of rising through the Leagues. It had been a long process but it was all about perseverance and trying to get things right. We hadn't penny pinched, and eventually we delivered a first-class

stadium which is very suitable for the 21st century. Elm Park and Madejski Stadium are complete opposites of the footballing spectrum – chalk and cheese.'

Finally, at the end of a long day, there was some time for staff to celebrate, but not too much because Peterborough United were due to visit for a League Cup tie four days later! Simon Hunt, who had worked tirelessly to accommodate supporters in the new Megastore, recalls: 'When it was all over and the fans had finally gone home, I remember being asked upstairs to the directors' lounge to share a celebratory glass of champagne. Lots of people were still around and there was a real buzz, a true sense of achievement – and relief that everything had gone well! It could have been a disaster and of course there were a few problems along the way, but we overcame them and it was a really memorable day.'

Madejski Stadium was up and running. Now it was time for the focus to return to the football to see whether the team would prove worthy of their new surroundings.

DARREN CASKEY

Reading appearances: 206 (+26)
Reading goals: 45

Darren Caskey arrived at Elm Park in February 1996 with quite a pedigree. The 21-year-old had shot to national prominence three years earlier by leading England's under-18s to a well-publicised European Championship trophy, scoring the winning penalty in the final and captaining a team that also contained Robbie Fowler, Paul Scholes, Sol Campbell, Gary Neville and Nicky Butt. The cultured midfielder was tipped for stardom and initially went on to make steady progress with Tottenham Hotspur, scoring four goals in 32 Premiership appearances – including a last-minute winner against Everton and a full game in a memorable 4–1 victory over Manchester United at White Hart Lane – before surprisingly being deemed surplus to requirements by manager Gerry Francis and sold to Reading for £700,000.

Caskey's Reading career started promisingly enough, with a brilliant volleyed goal that helped to secure a memorable FA Cup victory against Southampton standing out from his first year at the Club, but then his progress was delayed by injury and he struggled to make an impact as the Royals suffered relegation in 1997–98. The appointment of Tommy Burns helped reignite Caskey's time in Berkshire – the Scottish manager was trying to instil an attractive passing style of play into his new team and Caskey's clever range of skills fitted the bill perfectly. Having been largely left out by previous manager Terry Bullivant, Caskey now found himself as an automatic selection in Burns's XI and started to thrive as Burns attempted to evolve the team into a passing outfit. He missed just four games – all of which resulted in defeats – during the Club's first season at Madejski Stadium and ended up topping that season's appearance charts alongside fellow midfielder Phil Parkinson and goalkeeper Scott Howie.

That 1998–99 campaign also saw Caskey weigh in with a commendable tally of nine goals, an aspect of his game that had been somewhat expected from such a creative and attack-minded player but had been strangely lacking during his first few seasons in Berkshire – at one stage between 1996–98 he went an astonishing 75 League games for Reading without registering a single goal. But, if the previous season's goal tally of nine had been encouraging, Alan Pardew's appointment just after the beginning of the 1999–2000 season triggered nothing short of an explosion of goals from the midfielder. He started off by netting the only goal of Pardew's first game as manager (against Chesterfield at Madejski Stadium) and then simply could not stop scoring. Caskey ended the season with an amazing total of 23 goals – the fact that he converted nine penalties over the course of the campaign certainly did not harm his goalscoring potential, but it was still a remarkable achievement and deservedly earned Caskey the supporters' Player of the Year vote by some distance, along with a place in the

Division Two PFA team of the season.

Despite his obvious qualities, Caskey was a player who often split opinion. Never the most speedy or athletic of performers, he was frequently criticised by supporters who perceived him as being lazy and lacking mobility. Other fans preferred to concentrate on what he did with the ball rather than without it, and there could be no doubting the creativity he imparted on Pardew's fast-developing team. An excellent passer of the ball who created many goalscoring opportunities for his teammates, he was also a dead-ball specialist whose prowess from set pieces was never better demonstrated than during a 3–3 home draw with Bournemouth in May 2001, when he stepped off the subs' bench to curl home a free kick with his very first touch. But the very fact that Caskey was on the bench for that encounter with the Cherries was telling – Caskey's lack of athleticism meant that he was never able to wholly convince manager Pardew that he should start every game, and he lost his place in the side to Keith Jones when Pardew opted for a more combative approach towards the end of the 2000–01 season.

Caskey regained a place in the starting line up for the unforgettable play-off semi-final victory against Wigan but was an unused substitute in the cruel Final defeat to Walsall that followed, and that was that. Caskey was released at the end of the season, and his Reading career was over with a total of 45 goals in 232 appearances. It had in many ways been a frustrating period for both player and club; when he first

moved to Berkshire, the Royals were getting over the disappointment of the previous season's play-off final defeat to Bolton, and that period of adjustment was followed by the frustration of relegation to Division Two, which seriously tempered the excitement of moving to Madejski Stadium. The latter stages of Caskey's time at Reading featured far more wins than losses, with his own creative instincts playing a major role in that turnaround, but his final season still ended in the heartache of that play-off final loss to Walsall – promotion was not to follow until the end of the following season.

Caskey's post-Reading career was also something of a let-down. An unremarkable three-year spell with Notts County was followed by stints at Peterborough and Rushden before he moved into the amateur leagues with Nuneaton and Halesowen. As a result, he will probably be remembered as a player who failed to fulfil the potential that had been shown at the dawn of his career. But, for a brief period at the start of the Madejski Stadium era, Darren Caskey was an undeniably instrumental member of the Reading team, and his part in the progress of the Club during those early days at the new stadium cannot be questioned – even though the nagging feeling persists that he could have achieved so much more.

Going Green

As you have already seen in Chapter One, Madejski Stadium was not simply about the erection of a football stadium. It also sparked the regeneration of an area of town previously reduced to wasteland. The A33 access linked an area of bleak, low-grade agricultural land, lying within the flood plain of the river Kennet to the M4 and its corridor of high-powered hi-tech business. So a masterplan was devised by Foster & Partners (designers of the Hong Kong and Shanghai Bank and London's Stansted airport), and a vision – first conjured as the stadium was being built – to create a modern,

attractive and environmentally inspirational park for business was soon being realised. The long-term project is still continuing, but by its completion and with its offices fully occupied, 10,000 people are expected to work within the 180-acre office site.

Developed and managed by Prudential, the stylish architecture incorporated into the GreenPark infrastructure was married with a natural, landscaped, 'green' setting, cultivated around the man-made 11-acre Longwater Lake to charm big multinationals as well as smaller emerging local businesses into its office

space. Before long, some of the world's leading corporates such as Cisco Systems, Symantec and LogicaCMG were housed next door to Madejski Stadium, and the amenities at GreenPark grew as occupancy rose. Lime Square acts as the social and leisure hub of GreenPark, hosting Lsq2 – an award-winning bar and brasserie with open-air seating – the GreenPark Day Nursery, a kids' play zone called The Mad House, and Cannons Health & Fitness Club, which has a gym, a 20m pool and health and beauty studios. The complex also accommodates wholesalers Costco.

Access to the park became a huge benefit to businesses; the road structure took shape alongside a system of cross-town cyclepaths and footpaths. In an exciting future development, plans for a new railway station on the Reading–Basingstoke line have been granted planning permission. And the link with its neighbouring football club has only grown stronger – the lettering on the GreenPark mast turns blue when the Royals are playing at home. The park has also hosted the start of the Reading Half Marathon in recent years (while Madejski Stadium has staged the race's finish), with a smaller-scale 3K run titled The Green Park Challenge being launched in addition to the long-distance event.

The business park's environmentally friendly image was only furthered when an 85m wind turbine was erected in November 2005, towering over junction 11 of the M4 and casting an intriguing shadow with the turn of every blade. The 2mw Sir Norman Foster-designed turbine is one of the

largest land-based wind turbines in the UK, generating in excess of 3.5 million units of clean, renewable wind-generated electricity a year, supplying green energy straight into the local grid to the benefit of more than 1,500 homes and businesses in the area. It soon became an icon synonymous with GreenPark, Madejski Stadium and Reading FC.

Besides GreenPark, other out-of-town business outlets have profited from the area's growth, with B&Q, British Home Stores, Carpetright, Comet, McDonald's and Pizza Hut all currently owning stores on the former wasteland. Another peripheral commercial centre grew further down the road, while a brand-new housing estate has only recently been built – apartments and houses are fast being snapped up in Kennet Island. And it all began with Reading Football Club's relocation.

Chapter 3

Teething Troubles

Tommy Burns was unable to mould a team to challenge for promotion.

So the Royals had opened their new home in great style with a 3–0 victory over Luton Town and, inspired by their luxurious new surroundings, they embarked on a five-month unbeaten run to cruise to promotion...if only it had been that simple! In fact, Madejski Stadium's early fixtures often seemed to inspire the opposition players more than Reading's, and Tommy Burns's team were finding it tough going in Division Two, following their relegation at the end of the previous season.

The inspiration for that historic victory over Luton was newly signed Liberian forward Mass Sarr, who had run the Hatters' defence ragged with a performance of great promise. Sadly, that game proved to be the highlight of his Reading career and, weighed down by fitness problems, his form rapidly deteriorated to the extent that he was unable to command a place in the team. A number of other new

Jim McIntyre heads home Grant Brebner's cross to seal a 2-1 win over Stoke.

signings were similarly struggling to make an impact, and Burns made frequent sweeping changes to his team in a desperate attempt to find the winning formula.

The second fixture at Madejski Stadium was a League Cup tie when Peterborough United, managed by Barry Fry and containing ex-Reading boss Jimmy Quinn alongside future Premiership stars Matthew Etherington and Simon Davies, were dispatched 2–0 with strikes from Darren Caskey (penalty) and Grant Brebner. Burnley's Andy Payton then became the first opposition player to score at the Royals' new home in a 1–1 draw, and Colchester and Barnsley also claimed 1–1 draws before an exciting 2–1 victory over Stoke City on Saturday 3 October.

The scorer of the winning goal against the Potters was striker Jim McIntyre, one of the many fellow Scotsmen recruited by Burns. Also included in that group were midfield dynamo Brebner, striker Robert Fleck, defender Stuart Gray, winger Mark Reilly and goalkeeper Scott Howie. Burns had been a very busy man in the transfer market, capturing midfielder Jimmy Crawford and striker Paul Brayson from the reserve team of his former club Newcastle United, Dutchmen Peter Van Der Kwaak (goalkeeper) and Elroy Kromheer (defender), Manchester United starlet Chris Casper and veteran defender John Polston.

Of course, he had also inherited a large number of players to compete for places in the congested Reading

dressing room. Phil Parkinson, Darren Caskey, Linvoy Primus, Keith McPherson, Andy Bernal, Byron Glasgow and Ray Houghton were among those who succeeded in gaining a regular place under Burns, but there were also a number of casualties, with players such as Carl Asaba, James Lambert, Andy Legg, Gareth Davies, Jason Bowen and Martin Booty being deemed surplus to requirements, while former captain Barry Hunter, future captain Graeme Murty and midfielder Lee Hodges sat out the majority of the campaign with long-term injuries.

And that was not all. Not content with the plethora of players already at his disposal, Burns frequently dipped his toes into the loan transfer market to further add to his resources. Among those coming and going during the first season at Madejski Stadium were defender Neil Clement, striker Tony Thorpe, wingers Andy Wright and Mark McKeever, full back Andy Maybury and centre half Tony Barras.

If that all looks confusing on paper, it was just as unsettling on the pitch, and the Royals found it understandably difficult to find any fluency or consistency in their play. Trying to get the most out of his enormous selection pool, Burns took squad rotation to the extreme by fielding an astonishing 44 different players during the 1998–99 campaign. In fairness, many of those changes were enforced by wretched injury problems that kept physio Paul Turner one of the busiest people at the Club. Among those to be sidelined was Martin Williams, who had been converted from a winger into a central striker and responded impressively to lead the goalscoring charts with 11 strikes in the League before his season was ended by a cruciate knee ligament injury in a 1–0 home loss to Walsall in early February.

The inconsistency in team selection was matched by inconsistent performances on the field. September and October offered promise with four consecutive away wins at Walsall, Wycombe, Manchester City and Northampton, but the momentum was taken away by defeats against Macclesfield, Wigan (who became the first opposition team to win at Madejski Stadium) and Chesterfield.

One good piece of news for the Royals supporters during this difficult period was the return to favour of fan favourite Phil Parkinson. The all-action midfielder was left out of the team at the start of the season and was then asked to play an unfamiliar central-defensive role, before finally convincing Burns that he was worth a place in the centre of midfield. In an exclusive interview for this book, Parky has revealed just how close he came to leaving Reading. 'I wasn't even on the bench for the new stadium's opening game against Luton, which was a bit hard to take because I'd been at Reading for a number of years and really wanted to play in that first game. Tommy Burns made it clear that I could move on and I was very close to joining Wycombe. I went to see them play in a game, but my gut feeling was that it wasn't quite right, and I felt that I could turn things around at Reading and win back my place in the team – which eventually I did.'

But Parkinson's excellent form in midfield was one of the few bright points in a disappointing campaign. Recalling those difficult days, Parkinson believes that Burns needed time to adapt to his new role, saying, 'Tommy would be the first to admit that he didn't quite understand the level he was operating at. He was a top-class player with Celtic and Scotland and he had never been down in the Second Division. At that level what's important is to roll up your sleeves and grind results out. It's a bit of a dogfight, and it took Tommy a while to adjust from the Scottish Premier League and understand the kind of football and the players that were required to get out of the division.'

Escaping the division always looked an unlikely prospect during that 1998–99 season. While Burns's men were never really close to the drop zone and were occasionally capable of stringing together some impressive football, they lacked consistency and were unable to gain the momentum to sustain a serious challenge for

The scoreboard says it all at the end of a sorry afternoon.

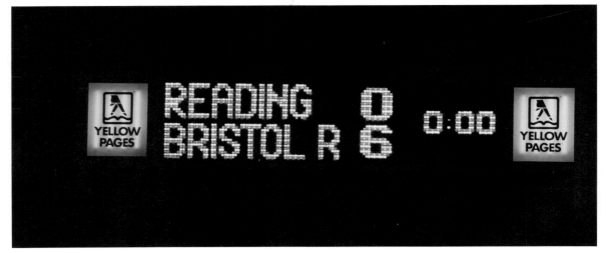

Kevin Keegan brings his title-winning Fulham to Madejski Stadium in April 1999.

promotion. There were fleeting moments of excitement – including a thrilling 3–3 home draw with Bournemouth on 7 November and a 4–0 thrashing of Wrexham in early January, when even Parkinson got onto the score sheet – but the season contained a sufficient number of bad days to prohibit a place in the top six.

Without doubt the lowest point came on 16 January 1999 at Madejski Stadium, at the end of an unusual sequence of five consecutive home games, when mid-table Bristol Rovers gained a 6–0 victory, which was made even more remarkable by the fact that the game was goalless at half time! The Reading central defensive pair of former club skipper Keith McPherson and Dutchman Elroy Kromheer certainly paid the price for the horror show – McPherson never started another game for the Royals and Kromheer was given just one more chance before being dropped for good. They had been terrorised by the Rovers strike force of Jason Roberts and Jamie

Terry Cooke curls home a free kick in Man City's 3-1 victory.

Cureton. Roberts netted the last two goals in the dying stages, but Cureton had already done the main damage by scoring the opening four goals in the space of just 21 minutes. In doing so, he became the first player to net a hat-trick at the Royals' new home, but as we will see in later chapters it was by no means the end of his goalscoring feats at Madejski Stadium.

Manager Burns responded to the thrashing by walking into the press room and murmuring, 'Where's the noose?', and midfielder Parkinson recalled, 'I remember it was Andy Gurney's debut after signing for us from Torquay, and what a day for your debut – especially as his first club had

been Bristol Rovers! As a team we were all over the place at the time, Curo scored four goals against us, and I really remember that afternoon – even though you should really wipe games like that out of your memory! That was possibly the lowest point of my time at Reading.'

Burns was able to elicit a decent response from his team after that humbling by Rovers. A last-minute penalty winner from loan striker Tony Thorpe against Preston, whose grievance at the result would be matched on many of their subsequent visits to Madejski Stadium, proved the starting point for a vastly improved run of form, with the highlight of a 4–0 victory at promotion candidates Stoke City. By the end of March, Burns's team prepared to welcome the giants of the division, Manchester City, on the back of a six-match unbeaten run and poised for the first time to make a serious assault on the play-off positions.

The visit of City was preceded by the transfer deadline day, and predictably boss Burns took the

Lee Hodges - one of many players dogged by injury during the Burns era.

opportunity to get his cheque book out again and sign five new players – winger Andy McLaren, midfielder Sean Evers, striker Keith Scott, full back Alan Maybury and defender Tony Barras – with the latter two arriving on loan. Three of them – Barras, McLaren and Maybury – were named in the starting line up against City, with Scott on the bench. But in front of Madejski Stadium's highest attendance so far, 20,055, Burns was left to rue his decision to ring the changes as City raced into a three-goal lead after an hour. Scott came on to scramble home a debut goal in injury time, but it was meagre consolation and marked the beginning of a poor run of form that ended the team's promotion push.

Looking back, the City game was a turning point for the worse, and midfielder Parkinson feels the changes to the team were unnecessary. 'Before the City game we'd just had the best run of results during Tommy's time at the Club.

We'd put together a few unbeaten games, and I remember him saying to me that he wasn't going to change things much when deadline day came – but then he signed five players! He also changed the team for that game against City, and I thought he shouldn't have done that because we'd just started on a good run. Sometimes when you sign players you feel almost obliged to play them, and I think that was the case on that afternoon. One of the signings was Alan Maybury, who got sent off on his debut, and probably it would have been better if Tommy had just left the team alone. But it's easy to say that with hindsight!'

The final home game delivered a convincing 2–0 win over Millwall with goals from Player of the Season Parkinson and Stuart Gray, but that was the only victory in the last nine games of a disappointing first campaign at Madejski Stadium. The team finished in 11th position with 61 points, 15 off the

1998–99 Division Two – in and around us:

		P	W	D	L	GD	Pts
9	Chesterfield	46	17	13	16	+2	64
10	Millwall	46	17	11	18	-7	62
11	**Reading**	**46**	**16**	**13**	**17**	**-9**	**61**
12	Luton Town	46	16	10	20	-9	58
13	Bristol Rovers	46	13	17	16	+9	56

Promoted: Fulham, Walsall, Manchester City
Relegated: Macclesfield Town, Lincoln City, Northampton Town, York City

FA Cup: Second round (v Barnsley)
League Cup: First round (v Stoke City)

Top scorer: Martin Williams (11)

Most appearances: Phil Parkinson (42), Scott Howie (42), Darren Caskey (42)

Martin Williams

play-off places, and Burns acknowledged, 'Although there is no getting away from the fact that this season has been very disappointing, it's my job to make sure we don't dwell on that and keep everybody in a positive frame of mind. Looking back at the season, I think we ultimately paid the price for not having a proven goalscorer. With Martin Williams and Jim McIntyre both missing three or four months through injury, at times we've been playing without a recognised strike force, and that is something we need to rectify over the summer period. We have learnt a lot of lessons this season, and I think the most important one is that need for a goalscorer.'

It was far from plain sailing off the pitch as well, with Reading supporters still coming to terms with their new home. The biggest problem, by far, was access to Madejski Stadium. After a lifetime of making the short stroll from the town centre to Elm Park, all of a sudden fans were confronted with the mission of finding their way to a far more remote site nearly three miles from the town centre. Crucially, the A33 dual carriageway linking the town and the stadium had not been completed – nor had any proper form of access road to the stadium from junction 11 of the M4. All traffic, whether coming from the town centre or the motorway, was forced down a poorly laid single lane road – and the inevitable tailbacks were the cause of much frustration. A transport group

was set up comprising Reading Borough Council, Reading Buses, Thames Valley Police and Reading Football Club, but in truth there was little they could do to improve the situation until the road infrastructure was completed.

Now, 10 years on, with the area immediately surrounding the stadium so well developed with a thriving business park and retail park, it is easy to forget just how unattached the stadium was in its infancy. This was, remember, the site of a former household waste site, and much of it had changed very little. Gradually, though, improvements were made and the eventual completion of the new dual carriageway relief road was, literally, a great relief. Once the retail park opened for business, it became clear that the stadium's construction would act as a huge shot in the arm for south Reading, and in the years that have followed the stadium's impact on the regeneration of the immediate vicinity has become unquestioned.

Once access problems were out of the way, a more pertinent concern for

supporters was the fate of their football team and, after a disappointing first season at their new home, the Club hoped for a great deal more in the 1999–2000 campaign. Chairman John Madejski, recently returned from a year in the Far East to set up the Malaysian Motor Trader, made his expectations plain with a forceful address in his pre-season programme notes, warning Burns, 'The ambition and desire for success here is as strong as it possibly could be, and we are not prepared to accept another season of mid-table comfort. Last season was historic and memorable for the fact that it was our first at the new stadium, and everybody enjoyed our "honeymoon" period in the new surroundings – but now it's time to get down to business. There's no point in us having these fantastic facilities if we're in the Second Division. We need to get this place full every week, and the level of support we achieved last season proved we would undoubtedly do that if we had a successful team.'

By his previously frenetic standards, Burns had a quiet summer in the

Ruud Gullit surveys his Newcastle United team during a July 1999 friendly.

transfer market. But there was one significant addition in the shape of former England under-21 international striker Nicky Forster, captured for a £650,000 fee from Birmingham City. Forster was a pacy striker who showed great promise during spells at Gillingham and Brentford, but had seen his stay at St Andrew's ruined by injury. He had been a 20-goals-a-season man earlier in his career, and it was hoped that he would provide the firepower that had been so clearly lacking the previous season. Burns also added further steel to his midfield with the signings of Neil Smith from Fulham and former Celtic teammate Peter Grant, but he also lost a talented young midfielder as the Club was forced to sack Byron Glasgow after the 20-year-old was found guilty of cannabis and cocaine use.

The pre-season friendly schedule concluded with an entertaining 2–2 draw with Ruud Gullit's Newcastle United in front of a healthy Madejski Stadium crowd, and there was a positive start to the Division Two

campaign when promotion hopefuls Bristol City were beaten 2–1 thanks to a dramatic diving header in the 85th minute by midfielder Jimmy Crawford – one of the few highlights of the former Newcastle trainee's brief spell at Madejski Stadium. Despite the opening day victory, the main talking point of the afternoon came with the dismissal of Robins defender Gerard Lavin, who reacted angrily to the award of a throw-in by smashing the ball into the lower rows of the East Stand, breaking a supporter's wrist and earning the wrath of the fans as well as referee Mr George Cain, who promptly produced a red card. Lavin was later fined £1,000 for common assault.

The victory against the Robins soon looked like a false dawn, as consecutive League defeats against three unfancied sides – Cambridge, Luton and Colchester – followed to leave Burns under serious pressure by the time Preston North End visited Madejski Stadium on 1 September 1999. North End raced into a two-goal half time lead, giving the manager's position a

decidedly precarious appearance, before a stirring second half comeback yielded a respectable point, thanks to goals from summer signing Neil Smith and burly striker Keith Scott. Once again disappointment soon followed with a feeble 3–1 defeat at Bournemouth and, despite a creditable 1–1 League Cup draw at top flight Bradford, Burns was feeling the pressure.

Writing his programme notes for a home fixture with Chesterfield, Burns admitted, 'The inevitable thing in football is that everything and everybody is judged on results, and with that being the case we have to be prepared to accept the criticism that is coming our way at this moment in time. But by the same token we have to look for the positives, and I believe there are a lot of encouraging signs. I'm human like everybody else and when you get criticised it hurts, but I've been in the game for long enough to know that somebody always has to take the blame and it's generally the manager. I also know how fickle the game of football is, and that if you pick up two or three good results everything can suddenly change.'

Indeed, everything did suddenly change – but not as Burns had hoped, and those programme notes were never published because Burns was sacked two days before the game. Chairman John Madejski never likes sacking managers, demonstrated by his record of just four dismissals in 18 years (Burns, Terry Bullivant, Mick

Bristol City's Gerard Lavin sees red after kicking the ball into the East Stand crowd.

Gooding/Jimmy Quinn and Ian Porterfield), so he was reticent to part with Burns. But the decision had to be made, and on Thursday 16 September he announced with regret, 'It was an extremely difficult decision to part company with Tommy, who has been dedicated and committed throughout his time at the Club, but the simple fact of the matter is that we currently find ourselves next to bottom of the Second Division, and that is an unacceptable situation. More importantly, the board felt that there would be no significant long-term improvement on that state of affairs under the management of Tommy Burns.'

John Gorman and Alan Pardew were tasked with turning around the team's fortunes.

Managing the Club through the transitional period of a new division and a new stadium was never going to be an easy task, and there was a great deal of sympathy for the Scotsman as he

struggled to forge a new team in new surroundings. Phil Parkinson recalled, 'The funny thing about Tommy is that, even though he had a bad time, he was a nice fella who was well liked by the players. He'd come down to a level that he'd never worked at before, and he didn't bring anyone with him who had the necessary experience to understand that level of football. So a lot of the signings he made weren't the right ones and, by the time he realised that, he'd got himself into a bit of a hole. Even though he later understood what he needed to do, by then it was too late because a lot of his signings weren't quite good enough.'

In Burns's place, Madejski and his board appointed Alan Pardew as caretaker manager, to be assisted by experienced former England coach John Gorman. Ex-Crystal Palace and Charlton midfielder Pardew was an ambitious and determined character who initially joined Reading as reserve team manager in the summer of 1997, when he was brought to Elm Park from Barnet by incoming boss Terry Bullivant. Pardew had one game as caretaker boss when Bullivant was dismissed towards the end of the 1997–98 campaign, overseeing a 2–0 defeat to Huddersfield before reverting

to his role with the second string when Burns was appointed. He was dedicated in his efforts to make a success of the reserve team during the first season at Madejski Stadium, but his role became redundant at the end of the season when Burns made the unusual decision to dispense with the reserve team.

Now, just a few weeks later, Pardew was back and determined to stake a claim for the job on a permanent basis. His second caretaker reign got off to a positive start with a 1–0 win against Chesterfield two days after his appointment. It was a drab affair, played in front of just 6,932 spectators and settled by a Darren Caskey strike, but a victory is a victory and Pardew was up and running. There was further encouragement three days later in the second leg of the League Cup second round tie against Bradford, who needed a penalty shoot-out to progress to the next round – the main memory from the evening being a stunning solo effort from striker Keith Scott, never normally noted for his nifty footwork, who jinked infield from the left wing

before curling a precise finish into the far corner of the net.

Back in the League, John Polston's only goal for Reading, lashed into the net deep into stoppage time, rescued a point against Oldham, and Pardew was able to boast a record of three games without defeat after his first week in the job. But he was promptly brought back to earth with a severe bump, suffering his first managerial defeat in humiliating circumstances with a 5–3 loss at local rivals Wycombe Wanderers. That wretched display prompted Pardew to make his first move in the transfer market, and he started at the back by signing a new goalkeeper, Phil Whitehead from West Bromwich Albion. Whitehead immediately gave a more assured look to the defence, but results continued to be mixed and the disappointment of a 2–1 local derby home defeat to Oxford United – a game that kicked off at the ridiculously early time of 11am on Sunday morning to cater for live television – was immediately followed by a harrowing 5–0 thrashing at Millwall when, as the saying goes, the Royals were lucky to get nil.

Despite some bad results, the board had seen enough talent, determination and ambition in their young caretaker manager to hand Pardew the post on a permanent basis, and Chairman John Madejski said, 'I am delighted to give Alan this opportunity. He and John Gorman have worked extremely hard since arriving here last month, and I have been impressed with them. They have

Darren Caskey gets Pardew's regime off to a winning start against Chesterfield.

Fans make their feelings known on 'Pants Day' in December 1999.

the respect of the players and they know exactly what we need to do to become successful. We know Alan well from his time here as reserve team manager, so we're already aware of the qualities he possesses and I had no hesitation giving him this responsibility, while John is a top-class coach who worked at the very highest level with the national squad. I am confident they will be able to bring success to the Club.'

In the long term it proved to be a very wise decision, but in the meantime these were dark days at Madejski Stadium. Pardew had to undertake a massive rebuilding project – the team was totally lacking in confidence, crowds were struggling to get past 6,000 and supporters were, to say the least, disillusioned. A number of them

stormed onto the pitch to voice their feelings after an insipid home draw with Scunthorpe, when Barry Hunter rescued a point with a last-minute header, and the next home game, against Wrexham on Saturday 18 December, was designated 'Pants Day' by supporters who wanted to deliver their message that 'Players Are Not Trying Sufficiently'. It was a light-hearted protest, containing the bizarre sight of East Stand fans waving (clean) pairs of underpants around their heads before throwing them onto the pitch, and strangely the atmosphere for the game against Wrexham was much improved, helping to contribute towards a stirring 2–2 draw and leading Pardew to comment, 'I hope that we can now use the Pants Day in a positive

manner, because there's absolutely nothing wrong with humour and crowd involvement at football matches, in fact it's something that's sadly often missing from today's game. My idea would be to continue the pants-waving, but it would be great for us if Reading fans can use it when we do something good or score a goal!'

There was a growing sense that a corner was being turned, and Pardew's team were certainly becoming less of an easy touch. Although the team was marooned on the fringes of the relegation zone and in the middle of a run of 13 games without victory, eight of those games were drawn. The humorous 'Pants Day' demonstration had somehow lifted the mood among the supporters, and after a 0–0 draw

with Cambridge on 15 January 2000 the Royals were unbeaten in six successive home games – OK, they were all draws, but it was a big improvement on the team's early-season form.

Looking back on that difficult period, Phil Parkinson recalls, 'When Pards first came in he was well liked by the lads. But it's easy enough to say that somebody is liked, the more important thing for a manager is to be respected, and we did also respect him because he was a good coach and very straight talking. It took a bit of time for his tenure to get up and running but I always thought it was a good appointment. He had to make a lot of changes and the difficult thing is trying to get short-term results while you're making long-term changes. But I always had that feeling inside me that it was about to take off and good times were around the corner. It was just the case of finding the right formula.'

That formula was taking shape and, if you are looking for a single specific

Goalscorers Phil Parkinson and Nicky Forster after a 2-0 win over Millwall.

turning point in the recent history of Reading Football Club, here is the date: Saturday 29 January 2000. Colchester United were the visitors to Madejski Stadium, and two goals from free-scoring midfielder Darren Caskey gave Reading their first victory in three months in front of just 7,304 spectators. Both goals were assisted by Nicky Forster, recently returned to the team following injury, and there was a highly impressive debut performance from marauding left back Matthew Robinson, signed from Portsmouth for a bargain

£100,000. Barry Hunter and Peter Grant were back in the starting line up, and the touchline was patrolled for the first time by a prowling 'Mad Dog', Martin Allen, who had been appointed Pardew's assistant manager following Gorman's sudden departure to join Glenn Hoddle at Southampton.

Another important piece of the jigsaw was put into place the following week with the £750,000 signing of striker Martin Butler from Cambridge

Martin Butler - a key Pardew signing - bursts into action.

Chairman and manager in consultation.

United. Finally Forster had an effective strike partner and Pardew's formula for success was in place: Pardew and Allen's high-energy and aggressive management style complemented by the more studied approach of recently appointed chief scout Maurice Evans and first team coach Nick Hammond; Forster and Butler's potent strike partnership; Caskey's goals and creativity from midfield; Parkinson and Grant's fierce tackling central backbone; Robinson and Andy Gurney's attacking approach from the full back positions; and a new-found exuberance from supporters who were spurred on by the East Stand 'Beard Band'.

It all added up to a 'new Reading', who followed up that victory over Colchester with an extremely impressive showing in a 2–2 away draw at champions-elect Preston, where Allen wound up the home team by making his players warm up in the same half of the pitch as North End, Butler grabbed a neat debut goal and Forster notched a memorable solo effort following a 50-yard burst.

The corner had been well and truly turned, and for the remainder of the season Pardew's team played like champions. The final 20 games of the season yielded 40 points (12 victories, 4 draws and 4 defeats) – a sequence of results that would have achieved automatic promotion if it had been maintained over the course of the full season. As it was, Reading's position at the end of January was so dire that the subsequent upturn could only take the

team into a comfortable mid-table position, but for the first time in a few years there was plenty to be optimistic about, and Pardew cautiously noted, 'In the last two weeks I have stressed publicly that we are now a team to fear, but I am not being fooled into thinking that the troubles of recent months are all behind us. There is still a big job in hand here, and all of the management team are focused on securing our status in this division, and then building as much momentum as possible for next season.'

There is no coincidence that around this time Madejski Stadium really started to feel like 'home' and the atmosphere improved dramatically. Of course, Elm Park was still missed, but supporters were starting to feel comfortable in their new surroundings. For reasons still unknown, the theme tune from TV's *Terry and June* had been adopted as an unofficial club anthem, hummed on the terraces every weekend, and the East Stand was starting to take on the role of the old South Bank at Elm Park, which had always given the Royals an unusual

position of housing the majority of the vociferous 'hardcore' supporters along the side of a ground rather than behind a goal. Crowds were also well up, surpassing 10,000 on a regular basis for the first time since the stadium's inception, and the general mood was one of growing momentum.

So which came first, good performances from the team or an improved atmosphere in the stands? Did the fans inspire the team to success, or were supporters given something to sing about by their team's improved performances? It is an age-old question, and the less than clear cut answer is 'probably a bit of both'. Supporters understood that Pardew was building a new team and they liked what they saw – although it took a while for consistent results to follow, there was an increased effervescence and determination about Pardew's teams, even in the early days. There was also a realisation among supporters that their afternoons would be more enjoyable, and the team would probably play better, if they threw themselves into matches with greater exuberance – hence the 'Beard Band',

'Pants Day', a giant new 'URZ' banner and a general upturn in terrace 'banter'.

Sensing the new mood, recently appointed coach Martin Allen played his part in further strengthening the bond between team and supporters. Allen was a 'man of the people' who became immediately popular with the fans due to his confrontational, passionate manner and his Reading roots – he was born in the town and his father Denis played nearly 400 games for the Club in the 1960s. Allen frequently spoke of his pride at working for his hometown club, repeatedly emphasised the importance of the supporters and regularly orchestrated unusual stunts to boost the atmosphere. Before home games the players were made to warm-up directly in front of the most vociferous East Stand supporters, and after away victories the team carried out celebratory Mexican waves in front of the rejoicing travelling fans (most memorably after a convincing 3–1 victory at Oxford). It was even leaked to the press that one morning Allen scrapped training and ordered the squad high into the East Stand, where they were encouraged to shout abuse at imaginary players on the pitch.

Between them, the management team and the supporters were creating a more positive, buoyant atmosphere to give confidence to the players, and this was reflected in a more self-assured, expansive style of play on the pitch, typified in an assured 2–0 victory over promotion-chasing Millwall on 12

February. Parkinson opened the scoring with a close-range finish after a well-timed burst into the box and Forster made sure of the points with another fine solo effort.

Bournemouth and Brentford were similarly beaten before Bristol Rovers became the fifth consecutive visitors to Madejski Stadium to leave empty handed, as goals from Forster and Caskey helped expunge memories of the previous season's 6–0 hammering by the same opponents, much to the disgust of livewire Pirates manager Ian Holloway, who was sent to the stands after a sequence of touchline altercations with a typically mischievous Allen, who somehow managed to get away scot-free with his part in the unpleasantries!

Despite the team's vastly improved performances, Pardew was refusing to rest on his laurels and continued the rebuilding of his squad. He made one particularly popular foray into the transfer market with the recruitment of former favourite Adrian Williams, a Reading-born central defender who had captained the Club with distinction in the mid-1990s before departing for

Adie Williams was a popular signing towards the end of the 1999-2000 season.

Wolverhampton Wanderers a year after the 1995 play-off final defeat to Bolton. Williams's playing opportunities at Molineux had been severely restricted by injuries, but after returning to Berkshire he immediately looked at home, even managing to score the only goal in a 1–0 victory over Brentford, and all parties were delighted when his loan move was in due course made permanent.

Another big player that Pardew was able to bring into the team was winger Graeme Murty, who had been signed by previous manager Tommy Burns for £750,000 from York City. Murty's first two years as a Royal were almost entirely wiped out by a series of injuries – he played just 13 League games in his first 18 months with the Club – but by March 2000 he was finally fit and anxious to show why he had been so highly rated at York. Further signings came before the transfer deadline in the form of diminutive but speedy winger Sammy Igoe for £100,000 from Portsmouth, and no-nonsense utility man Ricky Newman on a loan move from Millwall that was later made permanent. There was also a breakthrough into the squad for powerful young striker Darius Henderson, who had produced a series of impressive Academy performances to earn his first team chance.

So, in an impressively short space of time, Pardew's team was taking form. He had quickly identified the need for

improvement in a number of areas and had shrewdly added to his squad by signing players such as Phil Whitehead, Martin Butler, Matthew Robinson, Adrian Williams, Sammy Igoe and Ricky Newman. Naturally, Pardew's rebuilding effort also led to casualties, and among those to be shipped out were Andy Bernal, Scott Howie, Keith Scott, Andy McLaren, Stuart Gray, Jimmy Crawford, Paul Brayson, John Polston and Martin Williams. Some players from the Burns era did survive the cull, with the likes of Nicky Forster,

Graeme Murty, Darren Caskey, Barry Hunter and Phil Parkinson all going on to play important roles in the Club's ongoing future progress.

By the end of what had been at times a turbulent 1999–2000 season, Pardew's squad was looking in good shape, and it was easy to see the backbone of a team that could be successful for years to come. Crucially, virtually every signing the new manager made was a success and went on to cement a regular place in the team, something that unfortunately

Adie Williams celebrates his goal in a 1-0 win over Brentford.

1999–2000 Division Two – in and around us:

		P	W	D	L	GD	Pts
8	Notts County	46	18	11	17	+6	65
9	Bristol City	46	15	19	12	+2	64
10	**Reading**	**46**	**16**	**14**	**16**	**-6**	**62**
11	Wrexham	46	17	11	18	-9	62
12	Wycombe W.	46	16	13	17	+3	61

Promoted: Preston North End, Burnley, Gillingham
Relegated: Cardiff City, Blackpool, Scunthorpe United, Chesterfield Town

FA Cup: Third round (v Plymouth Argyle)
League Cup: Second round (v Bradford City)

Top scorer: Darren Caskey (17)

Most appearances: Darren Caskey (43), Andy Gurney (35), Scott Howie (35)

Darren Caskey

could not be said of his predecessor's forays into the transfer market. Pardew had reduced the squad to a much more manageable and competitive size, and he had also added significantly to the quality at his disposal while also greatly strengthening the bond between the players and the supporters – and all this was achieved without the need for a significant outlay in the transfer market. Not a bad effort for a young manager in his first job who had inherited a team in the relegation zone!

Reflecting on his first season in charge, Pardew commented, 'During my eight months at the Club I have radically changed the playing style and, although on the surface it looks to be a simple and more direct approach, the demands on the players have increased. Our results since the turn of year have only been matched by the likes of Preston, Burnley and Gillingham, and this is an indication of our prowess in this League. Although the season is now coming to an end, the heartbeat and spine of this side, I can assure you, will remain intact. Although

as a new manager I made mistakes, they are ingrained in my memory and I have learnt from them. That is the key factor in anybody's business, and I hope the players and all my staff adopt a similar attitude.'

Chairman John Madejski was also pleased with the progress that the team had made since Pardew's appointment, noting, 'There is no doubt that Alan deserves a lot of credit for the work he has done in the past eight months, and I would like to warmly congratulate him on the way he has got the team back on the right track. Alan has also surrounded himself with a formidable management team, and the contribution of Martin Allen, Maurice Evans and Nick Hammond cannot be underestimated. Of course, the players themselves can also take a great deal of credit for turning our season around, and if they continue to show the same levels of skill, determination and vigour from the opening whistle next season, I am sure we will enjoy a memorable year.'

The season concluded on a fitting note as a late penalty by Darren Caskey

earned a 1–0 home win over play-off bound Stoke City in front of 13,146 spectators at Madejski Stadium – the highest home attendance since the campaign's opening day, which felt like an awfully long time ago. Remarkably, it was Caskey's 23rd goal of the season, a mightily impressive effort (even though nine of them were penalties) and an all-time Football League record haul for a midfielder. The former Tottenham man had contributed to plenty more goals with assists, and his excellent passing ability was warmly appreciated by the Forster and Butler strike pairing. Unsurprisingly and fully deservedly, Caskey was the landslide winner of the fans' Player of the Season vote as the Royals finished the season in 10th place with 62 points, two-thirds of which came in the final 20 games.

It had been a season of contrasts, and it left Reading supporters eagerly anticipating the new season. Success, it was felt, lay just around the corner, and Madejski Stadium was ready to host it.

PHIL PARKINSON

Reading appearances: 391 (+34)
Reading goals: 24

During the dark days of Reading's early troubles at Madejski Stadium, one light shone brightly and consistently – skipper Phil Parkinson. The central midfielder was already a huge favourite with the fans, having joined from Bury in 1992 and producing nearly 300 no-nonsense, fully committed performances. Despite never being the most technically gifted performer, the man universally known as 'Parky' more than compensated for his deficiencies with an exceptionally strong mentality and a never-say-die approach that gained immense respect from the Elm Park terraces and teammates alike. The man simply exuded positive attitude and passion.

But by the time Madejski Stadium's doors opened, Parkinson appeared to be on the way out. Unfancied

by recently appointed manager Tommy Burns, who was keen to introduce more technical players to his team, he was initially played out of position in the centre of defence and then left out of the squad altogether for the stadium's first game. Burns was even prepared to let the midfielder join Wycombe Wanderers for a nominal fee, but Parkinson did not feel comfortable about the prospect and turned the Chairboys down to fight for his Royals career. How different would life be now if he had accepted the move to Buckinghamshire?

Fortunately the transfer never transpired and it did not take long for Burns to become convinced that Parkinson deserved a place in the team, back in his rightful central midfield role and reinstated as club captain. During the first season at Madejski Stadium, Burns experimented with a range of formations and a huge number of personnel as he tried in vain to find a winning formula, but Parkinson's presence in the midfield battleground quickly became a rare constant in a season of turmoil. He led the appearance charts with 42 starts from 46 League games, also adding a respectable five goals as he won the supporters' Player of the Season vote by a landslide – just as he had done at the end of the previous campaign.

One of the hallmark sights during those early days at Madejski Stadium was Parky's 'pre-match charge'; after leading the players out of the tunnel, he would break away from the group in a full-paced sprint towards the East Stand, arms and legs pumping, chest and cheeks puffing out in a defiant early demonstration of his commitment to the cause. It was a self-motivating ploy rather than a crowd-pleasing gimmick, but the sight never failed to gee up the hardcore Reading fans located in the East Stand – Parky is here and he's going to fight for us!

New manager Alan Pardew, previously the Club's reserve team chief, was well aware of those inspirational leadership qualities, and after being appointed to replace Burns in September 1999 he immediately made Parkinson a mainstay of the side. He captained the team throughout their quest to gain promotion from Division Two and, although Jamie Cureton will always be remembered as the match-winning hero, Parkinson played a central role in the goal that finally ensured promotion at Brentford in April 2002. Showing typical Parky-like desire, he rose high on the edge of the Brentford penalty area to deftly flick Adi Viveash's deep free kick goalwards, allowing Cureton to do the rest.

Parkinson's celebration when the final whistle sounded some 15 minutes later offered a neat encapsulation of his Reading career. Rather than joining his teammates by galloping gleefully towards the away fans as the party got underway, Parky took a few seconds to simply stand with his arms outstretched and his head turned skywards, emitting a passionate roar of relief. It meant too much for joyous levity to be enough. The first outpouring of intense emotion had to contain a more serious element. The laughing and joking could wait.

A few weeks later, there could have been no more fitting way for the Royals to mark promotion to Division One in 2002 than by celebrating Parkinson's testimonial, and the supporters once again showed their high regard for the midfielder, as a crowd of 20,000 amassed to watch a Reading XI take on an ex-England team. The evening allowed a reunion for former favourites such as Shaka Hislop, Michael Gilkes, Stuart Lovell and Jeff Hopkins. Central defender Hopkins had become one of Parkinson's closest friends before moving to Australia, and his unannounced appearance from 'down under' was the icing on the cake for Parky on his special evening.

Towards the end of his time at Reading it was no surprise to see Parkinson spending an increasing amount of time directing training sessions rather than taking part in them. His inspirational personality made him a likely prospect for a move into management, but everybody – including Parkinson himself – was slightly taken aback by the speed with which that career change arrived. In February 2003, Colchester United recognised the potential in the ambitious young coach and offered him the manager's post at Layer Road. Breaking the Reading bond was a difficult thing to do, but the opportunity to begin his managerial career was too good to resist and Parky was on his way.

There can be no doubt that Phil Parkinson is a true Reading FC legend and one of the men most responsible for making Madejski Stadium feel like home. As John Madejski neatly summarised upon his departure, 'He will be greatly missed, but he has given us some marvellous moments, and the memory of Parky lifting the Division Two promotion shield on his testimonial night at the end of last season is something we will never forget.'

More Than A Game:

An Oval Alternative

Rarely do the two shaped balls cross paths on the same pitch. In general, football fans do not appreciate the merits of a canny reverse pass on the blind side or a bruising ruck and maul, just as staunch rugby followers proudly sing the praises of their 'gentleman's game' while scoffing at the glitz and glamour of top flight football. But rugby plays an important part in the life of Madejski Stadium, hosting Richmond Rugby Club in its very first year.

Richmond had outgrown their Athletic Ground home, and owner Ashley Levett made the bold move to follow in Saracens' footsteps by decamping outside of the capital. Hoping to hold onto the club's stalwart supporters, they also aimed to form a new fanbase in Berkshire. But the reduced crowds and revenues meant Levett was continually personally financing the club, and despite halving the wage bill he placed the club into administration in March 1999, and the third-oldest rugby union club in the world soon ceased to exist.

Many then believed that Saracens' success at Watford's Vicarage Road was an exception rather than a model for other rugby clubs to follow, but Wasps found some success at QPR's Loftus Road, Bristol profited within Bristol Rovers' walls and, in June 2000, London Irish announced that

they would end their ground share with Harlequins to take up residence at Madejski Stadium. Confident they could attract a Thames Valley

audience, the Exiles swapped their London catchment area for Reading, while keeping their training and operational base in Sunbury-on-

Thames. 'We look forward to a long and mutually beneficial association,' the Royals' chief executive Nigel Howe declared.

The groundsmen had to prepare pitches for regular use throughout a busy season, and Madejski Stadium had to be staffed most weekends, as Irish encounters were scheduled in alongside Reading's. And both prospered. London Irish won their first piece of silverware in the same season Reading achieved automatic promotion; they beat Northampton Saints in the Powergen Cup Final in 2002. Attendances for the Exiles steadily grew, and every year the highlight arrived on or around St Patrick's Day, when all-day party events attracted record rugby crowds.

In 2007 22,648 people saw Irish play Wasps in the March extravaganza to create a new Premiership attendance record at a club ground, and the same fixture a year later saw London Irish break their own record with a Madejski Stadium sell out.

Earlier in 2008 London Irish's stay at Madejski Stadium had been happily extended until 2026. 'We've been here since 2000, we've built up a very good supporter base and been made incredibly welcome,' Exiles Chairman, John Conlan told BBC

Radio Berkshire as the news broke. 'It's a brilliant stadium – the best in rugby outside Twickenham and the best club stadium in Europe. When we first came here, it was the beginning of professional rugby and there was a doubt in everybody's mind that perhaps the professional game wouldn't survive in the UK. We now know that it will, and this deal reflects the longer-term future of professional rugby.'

Besides landlording London Irish, Madejski Stadium has staged many other oval-balled match-ups. It hosted both Tetley Bitter Cup semi-finals on the same April double-header afternoon in 2000; eventual winners Wasps beat Bristol, and Northampton defeated London Irish. There was also a Heineken Cup semi-final between

Northampton and Llanelli and two Parker Pen Challenge Cup Finals, which saw Wasps beat Bath in 2002 and Harlequins oust Montferrand by a single point in the dying seconds of 2004's showpiece. Plus Madejski Stadium opened its doors, for the only time to date, to rugby league in November 2000 — staging New Zealand's 84–10 demolition of the Cook Islands in the sport's World Cup. Only 3,982 watched the one-sided Group Two clash, but chants of 'Who Cooked all the pies' echoed through Madejski Stadium in support of the underdogs to provide a light-hearted and enjoyable atmosphere in a competition blighted by bad weather and empty stadia.

Chapter 4

Promotion Push

Reading's performances in the second half of the 1999–2000 season, which saw Alan Pardew's men lose just four of their last 20 League games, provoked great confidence among both players and supporters alike that the corner had been turned. Manager Pardew, who cut a self-assured figure even at the worst of times, prepared his team for the 2000–01 campaign with just one thing in mind – promotion. But those hopes took a serious blow in the closing pre-season friendly fixture, when striker Nicky Forster – an absolutely central figure to Pardew's plans – suffered a cruciate knee ligament injury in a challenge with Charlton Athletic defender Chris Powell and was ruled out for virtually the entire campaign. Pardew reacted quickly to the loss of his star striker by signing Port Vale striker Anthony Rougier, who made an encouraging debut in an otherwise disappointing opening-day 2–0 defeat at fellow promotion hopefuls Millwall, with both goals coming from Tim Cahill.

A floral tribute to Maurice Evans before the opening home fixture of the 2000–01 campaign.

Determination is etched on Phil Parkinson's face as he leads out the troops.

The opening home game of the campaign was preceded by sad news, with the passing of legendary Maurice Evans. Reading-born Evans had started out as a player at Elm Park back in the 1950s and later became a very successful manager of the Club before enjoying unsurpassed glory at Oxford. He had been brought back to Reading as chief scout by Pardew, who openly regarded the wise old head as a mentor. Evans passed away suddenly but peacefully at his home the day before Swindon visited Madejski Stadium, and a wreath of flowers was placed on the pitch before kick-off as a small token of respect. Evans would have wished for no greater tribute than a Reading victory, and the team obliged with a fairly comfortable 2–0 success, thanks to goals from Martin Butler and Darren Caskey, leading Pardew to comment:

> You can't possibly put a figure on the experience that Maurice gave to my staff and me since he returned. His role here under

New signing Anthony Rougier goes for goal as Swindon are defeated 2-0.

my management can be best described as quality control. Our conversations would normally start with me saying 'I like the look of so and so, what do you think?' If Maurice said 'No, he's not for me,' then that was the end of it. He not only served me as a scout but also guided me through some of the difficult situations that arise almost daily in this job.

The victory over local rivals Swindon lifted the mood following Evans's sad passing, and that feeling of optimism was further heightened two days later by an exciting move in the transfer market. In addition to capturing Rougier, Pardew had significantly strengthened his squad in the summer by completing the permanent signings of Adie Williams and Ricky Newman, who had spent the tail-end of the previous season on loan at Madejski Stadium, while also snapping up defender Adi Viveash and dogged midfielder Keith Jones on free transfers, as Paul Brayson and Linvoy Primus were the main summer departures.

Pardew's most significant move in the transfer market came on 21 August with a £250,000 swoop for Bristol Rovers frontman Jamie Cureton. This was the man, you will remember, who had notched four goals in a 6–0 victory for Rovers at Madejski Stadium 18 months previously, and the price tag was undoubtedly modest for somebody who had scored 53 goals in his last two seasons. Pardew was understandably pleased with his piece of business, commenting:

We set out goals and targets this year, and with the loss of Nicky Forster those goals and targets were going to be very difficult to achieve. The signing of Jamie Cureton means they are now feasible, and the players can appreciate that they are feasible, which is the most important thing when you set goals and targets. We all believe we can do it, and bringing in Jamie Cureton alongside Tony Rougier has made us even stronger than we were before Forster's unfortunate injury.

Jamie Cureton claims the matchball after the first Reading hat-trick at Madejski Stadium.

Celebrations as Anthony Rougier seals a thrilling 4-3 derby win.

If Reading fans needed any convincing of Cureton's capabilities – and that was hardly the case – proof was provided on his home debut against Stoke City at the end of the month. With just six minutes to play and 3–1 down, Pardew's men rescued a draw thanks to a Darren Caskey penalty and a typically predatory strike by Cureton deep inside injury time. Cureton then scored the only goal of the game at Port Vale before registering an excellent hat-trick – taking his club tally to six goals in as many games – to sink Brentford 4–0 at Madejski Stadium. By now the feeling was growing that Pardew had assembled a team capable of mounting a serious challenge for automatic promotion, and those hopes were further heightened with a 5–0 home thrashing of Oldham Athletic in the middle of the national petrol crisis in September 2000. The Royals supporters concocted one of the wittiest chants ever heard at Madejski Stadium, taunting the tiny group of visiting supporters with a chorus of 'What a waste of petrol!'

Further comprehensive home victories followed against Welsh duo Wrexham (4–1) and Swansea (5–1), with Cureton's strike partner Martin Butler issuing a reminder that he should not be forgotten, by netting five goals in those two games, including a connoisseur's hat-trick against the Swans – one with the left foot, one with the right and one with his head. A reality check was provided by a humbling 4–0 defeat at Bristol City, worsened by a serious knee injury to inspirational defender Adie Williams, before the visit of local rivals Oxford United for a game that proved to be one of the most bizarre and dramatic fixtures ever staged at Madejski Stadium.

It took place on 28 October 2000 in front of 16,022 spectators, and it rained and rained and rained. The opening half hour was unremarkable enough, as Reading moved into a 1–0 lead through a Caskey penalty. But then all hell broke loose. Oxford got back onto level terms when the Royals keeper Phil Whitehead slid out to collect a back pass from Ricky Newman. The wet conditions got the better of him though

and, as his long slide on the slick surface continued, he was forced to release the ball on the byline to prevent a corner. That allowed Oxford striker Derek Lilley, who had been hopefully jogging forward, to calmly collect the ball and walk it into an empty net for the equaliser. A real 'what happened next?' moment, and indeed it was not too long before the goal was replayed on the BBC's *Question of Sport* show.

In the second half, Reading retook the lead when Cureton slotted home from close range, but within a minute Oxford levelled again when Adi Viveash put through his own net from a Lilley cross. With playing conditions worsening in the thunderous rain, the visitors then took a shock 3–2 lead through Jon Richardson's header from a corner. By now the players were splashing around in huge puddles as the ball alternated between skidding fiercely and stopping dead with a soggy squelch, and Oxford put everything they had into defending their lead. Pardew's last resort was to introduce a man who could hardly be expected to adapt to the conditions, Trinidad & Tobago ace Anthony Rougier. In the words of the manager himself, it was 'time to unleash The Rouge on 'em'.

On his day, Rougier was a terrifically exciting and entertaining player. He was an awesome physical specimen and used his considerable power to lever opponents off the ball while simultaneously dazzling them with nifty footwork more commonly seen on the dance floor. He could be great to watch and a real handful for

As Martin Butler would attest, it rained a bit during the match with Oxford.

opposition defenders. But scoring goals was most certainly not among his strong points – in fact, since arriving from Port Vale two months previously, he was still waiting to break his Royals duck and had rarely looked like doing so, all of which made the events of the next 10 minutes even more remarkable. Firstly, with 78 minutes on the clock, he pounced on a loose ball inside the area to steer home an equaliser. Then, with just three minutes remaining, he was again in the right place at the right time – momentarily looking like the penalty-box predator that he clearly wasn't – to react quickest to a skidding cross from Lee Hodges and bundle the ball over the line, sending the Royals to the top of the League with a 4–3 victory!

After the mayhem at that derby victory, it was no surprise when Madejski Stadium's next fixture was an altogether more sedate affair, notable only for a brilliant long-range winning goal from Colchester's Gavin Johnson. But the goals were soon flowing again, with a 3–0 League victory over Cambridge and another Cureton hat-trick in a 4–1 pre-Christmas thrashing of Luton, although those wins were interspersed with the disappointment of an FA Cup second-round replay exit against York City.

2002 began in dramatic fashion, as a trademark Caskey free kick rescued an injury time point against Northampton, followed by an opportunity to avenge the opening day defeat to League-leading (and future champions) Millwall. The Lions were

managed by ex-Reading boss Mark McGhee, who was still roundly despised by many Royals supporters for the manner of his departure from the Elm Park hot seat more than six years previously. Unfortunately, one of those to still feel resentment towards McGhee was in charge of the pitchside microphone before the game and attempted to whip the crowd into a pre-match frenzy by urging fans to 'never let him forget' what had happened all those years ago. Needless to say, a new pitchside announcer was in place for the next game. The meeting with McGhee's Lions did not go exactly to plan either. The south Londoners raced into a 4–0 lead shortly after half time, and although goals from Sammy Igoe, Cureton and Caskey gave the

Jamie Cureton is all smiles after his goal defeats former club Bristol Rovers.

scoreline greater respectability, the Royals were well beaten.

Cureton got himself into trouble in the next home game. His former club, Bristol Rovers, were the visitors, and the striker was taunted mercilessly by Pirates supporters, who had spread scurrilous rumours about the nature of his departure from Rovers in the weeks leading up to the game. Cureton netted the only goal of the game in the first half, right in front of the visiting fans in the South Stand, and could not resist the opportunity to celebrate in front of the Rovers faithful by pulling his mouth wide apart in a strange grin. It was a rather odd facial gesture and not particularly offensive, but it still landed 'Curo' in a spot of bother, with a charge from the Football Association which angered Pardew. The Royals boss said:

In my opinion, after the abuse he had suffered in both encounters with Rovers, his reaction to scoring was somewhat understandable. The lies spread about Jamie, mainly through the new medium of the internet, were totally out of order, and the fact that he scored at their end was unfortunate. The frustration he had suffered over these lies came out in what could only have lasted 10 to 15 seconds, and I thought the referee and the media have shown little understanding of the full situation in their reaction to this brief display. The fact that he's now been charged by the FA is disappointing, and when the full facts are produced I hope a sensible decision is made.

Indeed, sense did eventually prevail as Cureton escaped punishment. The Reading bandwagon was rolling on though, and Pardew's side remained unbeaten throughout February 2001 to maintain their promotion challenge. March began with a huge home game against one of the Royals' biggest promotion rivals, Rotherham United, and the squad was bolstered by the capture of young midfielder James Harper from Arsenal, a signing that delighted his new manager, who said:

James Harper is a player whose progress I have followed for the last two years. I never expected him to become available, because I thought he would be a big player for Arsenal. When I found out he was available I had no hesitation – he has athleticism

James Harper wheels away in delight after netting on his debut against Rotherham.

and an arrogance on the pitch that a modern footballer must have. He's also highly ambitious, and that fits in well with me.

(Incidentally, at roughly the same time, another less-heralded arrival was a £25,000 signing from Leyton Orient. Taken on as 'one for the future' after a tidy trial game for the reserves, he would later become the first Reading player to play for England in more than a century…Nicky Shorey.)

Harper made an immediate impact, scoring the opening goal against Rotherham with a deflected strike from a corner, before Martin Butler made the game safe in the closing stages. That was followed by another important home win against fellow promotion candidates Wigan Athletic, which was televised live on Sky on a Friday evening. Wigan were defeated by a Jim McIntyre strike from an excellent Harper cross midway through the second half.

By the time Bristol City visited Madejski Stadium in the middle of March for another Friday night game, the Royals were unbeaten in 11 League games since the 3–4 home reverse to Millwall, and Pardew was keen to avenge the 4–0 loss against the Robins earlier in the season, saying:

The game at Ashton Gate in October probably represents my biggest disappointment this season. The contest was effectively over at half time, and it was one of the few occasions this year when we haven't performed to our usual standards. There remains a quarter of the season to go, crammed into a six-week period. We are in a great position

Time to celebrate another Jamie Cureton goal.

to achieve automatic promotion, and through all the ups and downs of this season we have stayed focused that we can do it.

In-form City dealt a serious blow to the Royals' promotion aspirations, running out 3–1 winners in front of 15,716 spectators, but the game was memorable for something that was a real rarity at the time and has become even more of a rarity since – a goal from Graeme Murty! The former York man scored the game's opening goal – and his first for Reading – after nine minutes, cutting inside from the right wing before arrowing a low drive into the corner from 25 yards. We would have to wait more than five years for another Murty goal, but that is another, very memorable, story.

There was a prompt recovery from that defeat to City when the short trip along the M4 resulted in a narrow 1–0 derby victory at Swindon, with Cureton on target again, followed by a 2–1 home win over Notts County, which provided a double boost – three valuable points and the return of Nicky Forster, who had missed the entire season to date with the cruciate ligament injury suffered during pre-season. Three potentially tricky away fixtures followed, with damaging 1–1 draws against Luton and Cambridge, followed by a dramatic 2–1 victory at Bournemouth, when all three goals came in the opening 10 minutes.

Back at Madejski Stadium, the Royals needed to keep winning when lowly Bury came to visit on 14 April. With automatic promotion still very much in the offing, a bumper crowd of 16,829 flocked to see the visitors take an early lead through Colin Cramb, only for little midfielder Sammy Igoe to level almost immediately with one of the most sweetly struck shots ever witnessed at the stadium – a 25-yard piledriver that simply flew past Bury keeper Paddy Kenny and into the net via the underside of the crossbar. Igoe had signed a year earlier from Portsmouth and remained an enigmatic player throughout his time at Madejski Stadium. His preferred position was through the centre of midfield, but Pardew preferred to employ his tricky ball skills and perceptive passing down the right hand side. He never truly established himself as a regular starter, but his scorcher against Bury set the team on their way to an important and

Sammy Igoe smashes home one of the Stadium's most spectacular goals.

eventually comprehensive win as goals from Cureton and Butler (2) made the final score 4–1.

A routine 2–0 derby victory at Oxford duly followed, leaving the Royals in contention to continue challenging Rotherham for the second automatic promotion spot with just three games remaining. Ronnie Moore's men were enjoying an unexpectedly durable season, defying all expectations that their form would slip. With a fortnight of the season remaining, Reading were three points ahead of Rotherham, but the Millers had a game in hand. Reading's next visitors were fourth-placed Walsall, and joy was in the air when Pardew's team raced into a two-goal lead through a brace from the prolific Cureton. But Walsall battled back, earning a draw with goals from Jorge Leitao and former Reading defender Tony Barras. The disappointment at the draw was heightened by news from the JJB Stadium, where Rotherham had gained a 2–0 victory over Wigan, leaving them just one point behind the Royals. They overturned that deficit with their game in hand the following Tuesday – a narrow 1–0 victory at Luton, leaving the Royals two points adrift with two games to go.

Victory at Colchester in the final away game was now imperative, and another goal from Cureton gave the 2,000 travelling fans hope that the promotion dream would be kept alive. But Colchester responded with goals from Barry Conlon and a controversial Aaron Skelton penalty, which shattered those hopes; Rotherham sealed the second automatic promotion spot with a last-minute 2–1 victory over Brentford. It was a serious blow for Pardew's men, who had been so focused on automatic promotion for so long – now they had to prepare for the play-offs.

First there was the closing League fixture of the campaign, and the visit of Bournemouth turned out to be a highly entertaining affair in front of a stadium record crowd of 20,589. A pulsating game took place after a pre-match salute from a pair of army helicopters, with Wade Elliott and Jermain Defoe firing the visitors into a two-goal lead before Player of the Season Butler pulled one back with his 26th of the season, only for Elliott to restore Bournemouth's two-goal cushion. With 18 minutes remaining, the Cherries still led by three goals to one and the Royals won a free kick on the edge of the box. Darren Caskey was introduced from the bench and promptly stepped up to curl a beautiful free kick into the top corner – Madejski Stadium's most immediate impact from a substitute. The home side pressed for an equaliser and finally got their reward with four minutes remaining when substitute Nicky Forster bagged his first goal since returning home from injury. A point was assured thanks to a brilliant goalline clearance from Graeme Murty inside injury time, and the play-offs awaited.

The semi-final pitted the third-placed Royals with sixth-placed Wigan Athletic, sending Pardew's men to the JJB Stadium for the first leg. The late show against Bournemouth had restored a sense of optimism following the disappointing failure to gain automatic promotion, and a healthy contingent of travelling fans were pleased to see their side gain a hard-fought 0–0 draw at the JJB. The return leg at Madejski Stadium on Wednesday 16 May 2001 was an eagerly anticipated sell out among Royals supporters, with the stadium record crowd of 22,034 only failing to reach capacity because Wigan did not take their full allocation. It was by far the biggest game staged at the stadium so far, and it certainly did not disappoint on an evening that earned a permanent place in Reading FC folklore.

The opening stages of a nervy game offered little indication of the drama that lay ahead. Neither team started particularly well, with a lack of goalmouth action until Kevin Nicholls drilled home a free kick to give the Latics a 26th-minute lead. Reading kept pushing and probing, but the equaliser would not come and the game seemed to be slipping away. Finally, as a last throw of the dice, Pardew introduced Forster from the substitutes' bench, deploying the pacy striker on the right wing with the hope of increasing the supply to front men Butler and Cureton. The plan worked a treat.

As the scoreboard clock ticked onto 85 minutes, Wigan won a corner. Reading cleared and broke forward. The ball came to Forster, who sped down the right wing, beat his man and fired over a low, firm cross. It deflected off a lunging defender and bounced out slowly towards the lurking Butler. Time seemed to stand still as the striker steadied himself to shoot, but he made no mistake and prodded home to equalise from close range.

Extra time loomed, but Forster had other ideas. With one minute remaining

Drama as Nicky Forster turns home a late winner in the play-off semi-final against Wigan.

Celebrations after the dramatic play-off semi-final victory against Wigan.

he set off on another full speed dribble, carrying the ball all the way into the penalty area before being felled by Arjan De Zeeuw's desperate lunge. Referee Laws pointed to the spot — penalty! The responsibility fell to Cureton, the division's top scorer with 30 goals that season, but Wigan keeper Roy Carroll was equal to his 12-yarder, diving to his left to push the ball away. Despair turned to immediate joy though, as the rebound fell out to Forster and the most super of super subs buried a low shot into the bottom left corner to make it 2–1. The restart was delayed by a pitch invasion, which was eventually cleared with the help of police horses, and the Royals supporters had to endure a Wigan corner before the final whistle blew to confirm Reading's victory and signal another pitch invasion. The players brandished a 'We're going to Cardiff!' banner as they embarked on a lap of honour, and the crowd rejoiced in Madejski Stadium's most dramatic game.

Those fans were soon back at Madejski Stadium queuing for tickets for the Final, to be played against Walsall at the Millennium Stadium in Cardiff. Around 35,000 supporters flooded down the M4 on Sunday 27 May, but they were to witness an unbearably painful experience as underdogs Walsall pulled off a shock victory in the most bizarre circumstances — with the Royals leading 2–1 in extra time thanks to goals from the potent Butler and Cureton, defender Barry Hunter smashed a clearance downfield from inside his own penalty area. Unbelievably, the ball took a freakish deflection off Anthony Rougier on the edge of his own box, looped high in the air and flew past Phil Whitehead in the Reading goal. Walsall were level, and a minute later they led when a still stunned Reading defence gave Darren Byfield space to shoot into the bottom corner. This time there was no way back, and Walsall were promoted. Skipper Parkinson reflected, 'We had

fancied our chances for automatic promotion, and even in the play-offs we were always confident that we would win it. When it went to extra time against Walsall I could only really see one winner, they looked really tired and we looked strong, but then a very strange goal cost us. It was horrible. The fans had been through it all before at Wembley six years earlier, and getting on the coach after that game was difficult.'

Undeterred, the ebullient Pardew immediately started planning for another promotion assault in the 2001–02 campaign. He released seven players including Darren Caskey, Jim McIntyre, Scott Howie and Lee Hodges. Physio Paul Turner also departed to be replaced by Jon Fearn. New playing arrivals were Andy Hughes from Notts County, Alex Smith from Port Vale and defender Adrian Whitbread, who made his loan move from Portsmouth permanent, while Ricky Newman and Parkinson were handed new contracts. Pardew was in a

2000–01 Division Two – in and around us:

		P	W	D	L	GD	Pts
1	Millwall	46	28	9	9	+51	93
2	Rotherham	46	27	10	9	+24	91
3	**Reading**	**46**	**25**	**11**	**10**	**+34**	**86**
4	Walsall	46	23	12	11	+29	81
5	Stoke City	46	21	14	11	+25	77

Promoted: Millwall, Rotherham, Walsall
Relegated: Oxford United, Swansea City, Luton Town, Bristol Rovers

FA Cup: Second round (v York City)
League Cup: First round (v Leyton Orient)

Top scorer: Jamie Cureton (26)

Most appearances: Phil Whitehead (46), Phil Parkinson (44), Martin Butler (42)

Jamie Cureton

18 August 2001 - Madejski Stadium's first game of the season gets underway.

determined and a typically positive frame of mind, stating:

> After a real transition, I believe we're now in our best-ever position to challenge for honours. It has been a long and sometimes painful road, especially for the Chairman, the board and the supporters, but there is at long last some stability here. The building blocks of success are individual improvement – this is a key element of my management. I won't tolerate a lack of ambition or a step backwards, and even with the disappointment of defeat at Cardiff, it must be onwards and upwards.

After an enjoyable pre-season friendly loss to Tottenham at Madejski Stadium, the season kicked off with a 2–0 win at Blackpool and a 1–0 home victory over Huddersfield, and there seemed to be no ill effects from the previous season's disappointment. The 'Adrian's Wall' defence of Viveash, Williams and Whitbread kept two more clean sheets in a sweltering goalless draw at QPR and a 2–0 win at Port Vale, and all seemed well. But then the hangover kicked in. September was an odd month, containing a home defeat by Cardiff, away losses at Stoke and Bournemouth and a drab 1–1 home draw with Bury. There were also high spots – an emotion-packed League Cup victory over top-flight West Ham and a 2–0 local derby victory over Wycombe Wanderers, which was notable for Darius Henderson's first League goal.

The Cup win over the Hammers was achieved in strange circumstances on Monday 11 September 2001. Earlier that day a terrorist attack had struck the World Trade Centre in New York, and the enormity of the tragic events was still sinking into the crowd of

Alex Smith signs on in July 2001.

21,173 as the game kicked off. It was an absorbing tie between two well-matched teams, who were unable to find their way past a pair of in-form goalkeepers, Phil Whitehead and ex-Royal Shaka Hislop. There had to be a winner, and eventually the game went to penalties which were settled when Scott Minto's effort was saved by Whitehead, and Adi Viveash slotted home the winner.

The next round pitted the Royals against the Premiership's other claret and blues, with an enjoyable trip to Aston Villa, where Pardew's men gave a spirited display before being ousted by a strike from Dion Dublin. By now, League form had become a real concern as the after-effects of the previous season's disappointment became all too apparent. After making such a bright start to the season, the Royals had slipped into a mid-table

Left back Matthew Robinson prepares to take a throw in against Cardiff.

position, and the nadir came on Saturday 13 October at Madejski Stadium, when local rivals Swindon strolled to a 3–1 victory, leaving the Royals fans to digest the unpleasant sight of Robins defender Neil Ruddock celebrating euphorically in front of the packed away end. Pardew was livid. 'It was clear from the outset today that we looked nervous, we had players who don't look anything like they did last season,' he lamented. 'That is a problem, and the only way it can be resolved is by me and my staff working harder on the training ground to turn it around, and that's what we're going to do. That performance today was unacceptable. That is not us, we're better than that, we're going to have to prove it, and we're going to have to prove it quickly.'

For the first time since taking over as manager, Pardew was under real pressure. His team had narrowly missed out on promotion the previous season and were expected to challenge again, but two months into the season they were marooned in 14th position, already eight points behind the top two. It was by far the most difficult spell that Pardew had faced in his brief managerial career, but salvation came with a nerve-jangling 4–3 victory at Notts County and a 1–0 triumph at Oldham three days later. As Parkinson recalled, those victories – especially the one at Meadow Lane – bought Pardew some time. 'That was a key game for Pards,' Parkinson later recalled. 'We'd had a bad run of results, just lost at home to Swindon and the pressure was really on. We went 4–1 up but they

came back to 4–3, and they had a penalty appeal in the last minute which the referee waved away. Pards and I have discussed that moment many times – if the penalty had been awarded and they'd scored, Pards might not have lasted another week in the job.'

The corner had not quite been turned though, and the next home game resulted in a 2–1 home defeat to Brentford, with future Royal Ivar Ingimarsson smashing home a spectacular goal for the Bees. Pardew took decisive and unexpected action, axing assistant Martin Allen and replacing him with youth team manager Kevin Dillon, a former Reading player. He also signed two loan players, midfielder Kevin Watson and winger John Salako, and replaced left back Matt Robinson with youngster Nicky

Martin Butler slots a penalty past Brentford - but the Bees won 2-1.

Midfield pair Kevin Watson and Andy Hughes celebrate victory against Bristol City.

Shorey, who had been impressing in the reserves. The moves paid immediate dividends, with the team gaining a 2–0 victory at Northampton and then winning their next four matches to earn Pardew the Division Two Manager of the Month award and take his team to within two points of the top of the table. That run of results included a 3–2 victory over Bristol City, when the opening goal was scored by another of Pardew's recent introductions into the team, John Mackie – a rugged central defender, who had been signed from non-League Sutton United and displayed all the traits of determination and hunger that are usually associated with late entrants into the game.

December started badly, with a 1–0 home loss to Chesterfield and two Cup exits – 1–4 at Barnet in the LDV Vans Trophy and 0–2 at York City in the FA Cup. But the team regained form around the busy Christmas period, starting with respectable draws against Wigan and Cardiff. A 2–0 victory at snowy Wrexham triggered another superb run of form, as the Royals started the new year with seven straight victories. Seven consecutive clean sheets were also racked up with the help of two loan keepers – Fulham's Marcus Hahnemann and Charlton's Ben Roberts – who had been drafted in during the absence of injured Phil Whitehead.

A long-term injury to Martin Butler during a home victory over Wrexham in November had forced Pardew to rethink his attacking approach, but Butler's absence allowed Nicky Forster to establish a regular starting place for the first time since his cruciate ligament injury at the start of the previous season. Forster played a bit-part towards the end of the 2000–01 campaign and in the early months of 2001–02 but re-found his very best form after Butler's injury. He scored nine goals in the space of eight games between Boxing Day and the end of January, including a spectacular solo effort in a 2–0 win at Wigan and a hat-trick to demolish Blackpool 3–0 at Madejski Stadium. During this period his strike partner was Anthony Rougier, with last season's 30-goal hero Jamie Cureton relegated to the bench and powerful youngster Darius Henderson offering another option.

With a solid defence of Graeme Murty, Nicky Shorey, John Mackie and Adie Williams, a strong central midfield pairing of Phil Parkinson and Andy

Nicky Shorey was integrated seamlessly into the team.

Hughes and creativity on the wings from John Salako and Sammy Igoe, there was a settled look to the powerful Reading line up. Having laboured through the earlier stages of the season, Reading were now not just winning games – they were winning convincingly. Victory at Huddersfield on 12 January sent the Royals to the top of the table, and by the end of the month the lead on second-placed Brighton was nine points.

Having survived his difficult autumn, Pardew's natural buoyancy had returned and the ever-confident manager told supporters 'My whole management style is based around positive thinking, positive actions and a positive way of playing. We can be proud of what is going on. Good times are few and far between in football.

John Salako is signed thanks to revenue raised by the Club's website.

We're sitting at the top of the League, we should enjoy it.' There was another boost when Salako's move from Charlton was made permanent. The former Crystal Palace and England winger had been in sparkling form since his arrival on loan in November, and his signing was clinched in unusual circumstances. These were the days of the 'dot com' boom, with huge sponsorship deals being shelled out to football clubs for a piece of the internet cake. With the Royals' website, under the auspices of website manager Craig Mortimer, performing well in terms of 'hits' from supporters, the Club was correspondingly handsomely rewarded by the Football League's internet partner, Premium TV, and the funds were used to buy Salako!

Aside from the minor blip of a 3–1 loss at in-form Brighton, the wins kept on coming through February, including an important triumph over fellow promotion candidates Stoke City, when a season-high crowd of 21,032 swarmed to Madejski Stadium, where they witnessed a typically predatory strike from Cureton secure the points. That was swiftly followed by a convincing 2–0 derby victory at Wycombe Wanderers, and when Pardew celebrated with an impromptu jig on the Adams Park pitch you knew what he was thinking – 'We're going up.' Most supporters shared those sentiments because promotion seemed an absolute certainty. With just 10 games remaining, the Royals were six points clear of second-placed Brighton and a whopping 10 points ahead of

Bristol City in third. It would take an almighty collapse for Pardew's men to be caught now. But...

After a come-from-behind 2–2 draw at Cambridge, Bournemouth travelled up from the south coast and were only prevented from returning with all three points by a last minute penalty miss by Wade Elliott to keep the score at 2–2. Brighton were the next visitors, and a nervy game in front of 22,009 spectators produced few chances, as both teams seemed more concerned about preventing goals than scoring them. For the second consecutive game there was an injury

time let-off for Reading when Gary Hart bundled home a loose ball, but goalkeeper Phil Whitehead was controversially adjudged by referee Mike Dean to have been fouled. Both teams were left reasonably content with a point from the goalless stalemate, but the Royals had now drawn three consecutive games and nerves were starting to creep in.

Those anxieties only intensified when Oldham sneaked a 2–2 draw from the next home game, a breathless encounter at Bristol City ended in a 3–3 tie and yet another draw came with a frustrating goalless home encounter with Northampton. With three games now remaining, the Royals had drawn six games out of seven and Brighton had taken over at the top of the table. In-form Brentford were in hot pursuit of the second automatic promotion place and were now just three points behind Alan Pardew's men, with a better goal difference. By a quirk of the fixture list, the two teams were due to play each other at Griffin Park on the final afternoon of the season; from a seemingly insurmountable position of strength just six weeks previously, fingernails were now being furiously chewed. The sequence of draws continued in another nervy game at Tranmere, where goals from wide men Anthony Rougier and John Salako rescued a point on a hot Sunday afternoon. Brentford had won their weekend fixture and were now just one point behind Reading. Pressure was building and the draws were taking their toll. Parkinson recalled:

It was incredible really. We kept on drawing and we just couldn't get over the finishing line. But I always remember when we went up with Mark McGhee a few years earlier we had something similar, so I was always confident that we'd make it. We were a long way clear but we just couldn't make that final surge. I think the expectation weighed heavily in the players' minds, and maybe a little bit of complacency set in – perhaps we thought that we'd already done it when we were so far ahead at the end of February. It was a funny period.

The final home game brought Peterborough United to Madejski Stadium, while Brentford had a west London derby against QPR. Supporters spent the week leading up to the game working out the permutations. The dream scenario would be a home win for both hoops – Reading and QPR – which would leave the Royals four points ahead of the Bees and celebrating automatic promotion. Desperately hoping for that situation to arise, a home sell-out crowd of 22,151 buzzed with anticipation as the game approached. Chairman John Madejski marched around the pitch and took his seat in the East Stand to show his solidarity with the supporters. The match ball was delivered by helicopter and opera singer Laurence Robinson belted out *Nessun Dorma*, while Martin Butler was named on the bench for the

The matchball for the final home game of the season was delivered by helicopter.

Celebrations after Nicky Forster scores against Peterborough - but promotion would have to wait a week.

first time since returning to fitness from injury.

Peterborough were in no mood to succumb and threatened to spoil the party after half an hour when Matthew Gill's harmless-looking long-range drive squirmed through the arms of an embarrassed Whitehead to give the visitors the lead. It stayed that way for an uncomfortably long time, before Nicky Forster intervened with two goals in an electric five-minute spell. That lead only lasted four minutes though, before Leon McKenzie got the Posh back on terms. With time running out, attention turned to Loftus Road and the goings-on between QPR and Brentford. The game there ended goalless, meaning that the Royals could not be promoted due to Brentford's superior goal difference, even if they found a winner against Peterborough. Perversely, in the final stages at Madejski Stadium, Pardew's main concern was making sure that his side did not concede a goal and lose the game; a point was sufficient to maintain the lead over Brentford going into the final week of the fixture. The whistle blew and the picture was clear – Reading were one point ahead of Brentford with one game remaining, which would be played between the two teams at Griffin Park, where the equation for the Royals was simple: avoid defeat = promotion, defeat = play-offs.

Demand for the 2,500 away tickets at Griffin Park was predictably high, and they had been promptly snapped up by season ticket holders weeks in advance. To allow more fans to watch the game, the Club had arranged for a giant screen to beam the live action back into Madejski Stadium, and those 4,000 tickets were quickly taken too. So on Saturday 20 April 2002 it was onto Brentford for the final fixture of the season to decide whether promotion would be assured or whether the torture of the play-offs would lie in wait.

Thousands of fans watch the drama at Brentford unfold on a big screen.

Throughout the week, Pardew's potential team selection was the subject of much speculation, and there was something of a surprise when Martin Butler was named in the starting line up for the first time since November after returning from injury. He played up front alongside Forster, with Andy Hughes taking a central midfield berth alongside Phil Parkinson at the expense of Kevin Watson. Sammy Igoe filled the right wing slot vacated by Hughes, with John Salako on the opposite flank. The Adrians – Williams and Viveash – formed a solid central defensive partnership ahead of Phil Whitehead, with Graeme Murty and Nicky Shorey occupying the full back positions.

Watson was on the bench alongside Jamie Cureton, goalkeeper Frank Talia, defender Leo Roget and striker Bas Savage, surprisingly preferred to Anthony Rougier.

The first half was predictably tight, with few chances at either end. Brentford, managed by Steve Coppell, just about enjoyed the majority of possession, but pacy wingers Stephen Hunt and Martin Rowlands were able to provide little service to the dangerous front pairing of Lloyd Owusu and Ben Burgess. Steve Sidwell was a good competitive match for Phil Parkinson in midfield, and the Royals were getting little change out of Bees defenders Darren Powell and Ivar

Ingimarsson. Midway through the opening period, Whitehead made a great save to tip over Burgess's header, and on the stroke of half time Murty made a brave clearance to thwart Owusu's dangerous cross.

So far, so good. But with five minutes of the second period played, Owusu broke down the left and pulled back a dangerous cross into the path of Rowlands, who made no mistake with a firm, low shot past Whitehead. Griffin Park was rocking, and the Royals were staring down the barrel of the play-offs. Pardew's team tried to respond but created little. Time was running out. Midway through the period, Pardew turned to Cureton – so prolific the

Pitch invasion with a difference as the Royals secure promotion…30 miles away!

New meaning to 'open top bus' as the newly-promoted Royals return to Madejski Stadium.

previous season but a much more marginal figure in the current campaign. He replaced Igoe, with Forster shifting out to the right wing and Cureton resuming his once-lethal partnership with Butler. It was the same formation and personnel that had dislodged Wigan from the previous season's play-offs. Would it have the same results?

The moment that has been solidly planted into Reading FC folklore came with 12 minutes remaining. Cureton took a skilful controlling touch, judging the weight perfectly, and it nestled in the corner of the net. Goal! The away terrace erupted and so did the East Stand back at Madejski Stadium, as thousands roared at the big screen. Promotion was within reach, and just over 10 minutes

later it was confirmed when referee Stretton blew his final whistle.

The celebrations at Griffin Park were long and joyful, and back at Madejski Stadium a good-natured pitch invasion took place as loyal Royals surrounded the big screen that had transmitted the historic pictures. For a while afterwards it seemed that the supporters did not know what to do — after all, the players were 30 miles away! But before long a big crowd starting to gather outside the players' entrance, awaiting the team coach's return. When the bus finally pulled up the hill from the A33, there was pandemonium. Having already started their celebrations with a few cans of lager during the journey, the players

tipsily forced the sunroof open and, one by one, climbed up from the seats and onto the roof of the bus. Gradually the crowed dispersed, although many supporters ended up drinking the night away in the Millennium Madejski Hotel, where they were invited by manager Pardew to join the players in their celebrations.

They were all back at Madejski Stadium on the top of another bus the following day, but this time the vehicle had actually been designed for that purpose — a celebratory open-top bus tour through Reading. The town centre was mobbed with celebrating fans, and around 15,000 showed up at the stadium to see the squad and management individually introduced

Manager and Chairman salute the fans at the post-promotion celebrations.

Nobody could suggest that Andy Hughes hadn't fully partaken in the celebrations!.

onto the pitch. It was party time, and the players were more than happy to let their hair down and soak it all up – in fact it seemed that some of them had been 'soaking it up' all night! Defenders John Mackie and Adrian Whitbread, who both ended the campaign injured, seemed to be particularly enjoying the celebrations and had to be practically dragged off the pitch after their lap of honour. Skipper Parkinson still recalls the weekend vividly, saying:

I'll never forget it. My wife and kids were back at Madejski Stadium watching the game on the big screen because they couldn't get tickets for Brentford. When Curo scored it was a brilliant feeling that I will remember for as long as I live. I remember doing an interview in the dressing room after the game and saying that the feeling was relief. Having been through so much, it was just relief that we'd got the Club back up there. I've got a picture in my living room with the lads on the roof of the bus, and we had a great time! It was a great set of lads and we all got on so well, which was central to the success – you need good players with big characters

Tribute to a Reading legend - Phil Parkinson enters the field for his testimonial.

and, to give Alan Pardew credit, a lot of the players he signed were good characters who did add to the team spirit.

There was still time for one more big event at Madejski Stadium before the season ended for good, and it was a fitting way to bring a triumphant campaign to a climax, as Parkinson celebrated his testimonial with a Reading versus ex-England XI fixture on Monday 13 May. More than 20,000 fans turned out to honour Parky, joined by a number of former Reading favourites including Shaka Hislop and Jeff Hopkins, who flew over from Australia especially for the evening. They lined up against an England legends team including John Barnes, Stuart Pearce, Dennis Wise and Chris

2001–02 Division Two – in and around us:

		P	W	D	L	GD	Pts
1	Brighton	46	25	15	6	+24	90
2	**Reading**	**46**	**23**	**15**	**8**	**+27**	**84**
3	Brentford	46	24	11	11	+34	83
4	Cardiff City	46	23	14	9	+25	83
5	Stoke City	46	23	11	12	+27	80

Promoted: Brighton & Hove Albion, Reading, Stoke City
Relegated: Cambridge United, Wrexham, Bury, Bournemouth

FA Cup: Second round (v York City)
League Cup: Third round (v Aston Villa)

Top scorer: Nicky Forster (18)

Most appearances: Graeme Murty (43), Nicky Forster (36), Andy Hughes (34)

Waddle, and the evening was rounded off when Parky managed to score. Admittedly, it was a softly awarded penalty and ex-England goalkeeper Tim Flowers did not seem to try particularly hard to save it.

After the game, the Club was presented with a silver salver from the Football League to mark the promotion, and the players received their individual runners'-up medals. It drew a neat line under a glorious season

and allowed everybody to head off on their holidays with the prospect of Division One football ahead. The Royals were going up!

A fitting end to Parky's evening - the promotion shield is paraded.

JAMIE CURETON

Reading appearances: 89 (+38)
Reading goals: 55

One of the greatest moments in Reading Football Club's recent history was provided by Jamie Cureton. The story is so familiar that it hardly needs telling again, but it is a story worth telling so why not relive it just one more time?

Seventy-eight minutes have been played at Griffin Park on the final day of the 2001–02 season. Second-placed Reading are taking on third-placed Brentford, with the Bees, managed by Steve Coppell (yes, that Steve Coppell) needing a victory to overtake their visitors and claim automatic promotion. Inspired by winger Stephen Hunt (yes, that Stephen Hunt), Brentford are leading 1–0 when Steve Sidwell (yes, that Steve Sidwell) is penalised for handball close to

the halfway line. Adi Viveash launches the set piece forward to the edge of the Brentford penalty area, where Phil Parkinson flicks it goalwards. The ball drops and Jamie Cureton is there. With the inside of his right boot, he softly controls the ball perfectly. With his second touch, he lifts a deftly cushioned volley over onrushing goalkeeper Paul Smith. The ball drops gently and bounces slowly towards the right-hand corner of the Brentford net. Bees defender Ivar Ingimarsson (yes, that Ivar Ingimarsson) scrambles desperately towards his own goal, trying to scoop the ball away, but his efforts are in vain and Cureton has scored the goal that seals promotion.

That was by no means the first time that Reading fans had celebrated a brilliant Cureton goal. By then, everyone was so used to his goalscoring antics that few eyebrows were raised when skipper Phil Parkinson noted, 'I honestly wouldn't want anyone else in that position, and I include the top, top players in that. You'd want Curo before Michael Owen, and I'm not exaggerating, he's that good.'

Cureton enjoyed playing at Madejski Stadium from his very first visit, when he sealed a place in history as the first player to score a hat-trick at the ground – albeit while playing for Bristol Rovers when they romped to a 6–0 victory in January 1999. So when Cureton was snapped up by Alan Pardew 18 months later it was a popular move, even more so when the pint-sized striker scored a last-minute equaliser on his home debut against Stoke City. Another hat-trick followed in his next Madejski Stadium outing, against Brentford, and for the

next two years the goals continued to flow freely. 'Curo' netted on 30 occasions during his first year as a Reading player, and another 16 followed as automatic promotion was clinched the following season – including that crucial strike at Griffin Park.

Promotion to Division One initially did nothing to reduce the striker's goalscoring ratio, as Curo bagged twice against Sheffield Wednesday to secure a come-from-behind victory in 2002–03's opening home fixture. But after netting six goals in the opening five games of the campaign he struggled to reproduce the consistency that had been shown in his first two seasons at the club, and in the summer of 2003 he declined a new contract in favour of a lucrative offer to join Busan Icons in South Korea.

Cureton ended his Reading career with a total of 55 goals in 127 games, but his impact is impossible to measure in statistics alone. Supporters always love a goalscorer; in Jamie Cureton, Reading fans had their first Madejski Stadium hero. Although he often offered little outside the penalty area, he had that impossible-to-teach instinct to be in the right place at the right time and the composure under pressure to make the most of his opportunities. Most of his goals were smartly taken predatory strikes, but he was certainly also capable of the spectacular, with his particular speciality being 'The Dipper' – long-range volleys that fizzed through the air before dipping under the crossbar at the last moment – Madejski Stadium goals against Burnley (August 2002) and Brighton (April 2003) offer prime examples of the art. Above all else,

Cureton will always be remembered for one goal. So let us relive it just one more time, in his own words:

After Adi Viveash played the free kick, I could see from the flight of the ball that it was going to be a straight fight between Parky and the Brentford defender, so I just took a chance and gambled that Parky would win it. When the ball dropped towards me, I'd already moved so I was in a bit of space because none of the defenders had followed me…I knew it would be difficult to shoot first time, so as the ball came to me I concentrated on getting a good touch on it. Fortunately I managed to do that, and that first touch set the whole chance up. The keeper came flying out and dived at my feet, but the ball had bounced and was in the air, so he made my mind up for me and the only thing I could do was try to lift it over him…Once I hit it, I knew it was going on target and my only worry was that a defender might be able to get back and clear it off the line, because I hadn't put too much pace on the ball. But as it drifted towards the corner I realised it was going in. I've tried to keep it fresh in my memory – I watch the video of the goal every now and then, and it brings back memories of the whole day and the celebrations afterwards. It's definitely something I'll always remember!

So will we Curo, so will we.

More Than A Game:

Staying at the Stadium

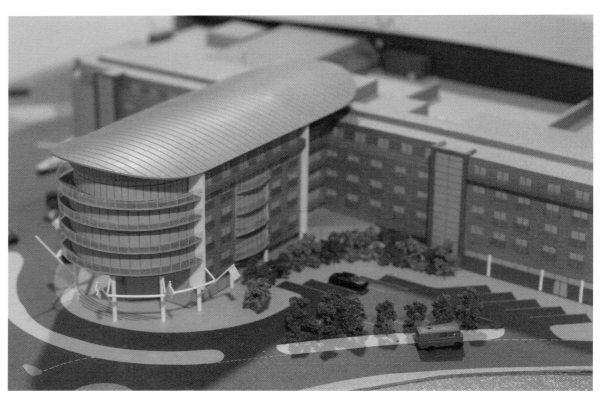

When the bold designs were being drawn up for Madejski Stadium's construction, part of the blueprint was to include hotel facilities within the infrastructure, primarily to complement the Royal Berkshire Conference Centre but also to satisfy an identified need for more rooms in Reading. 'We discovered there was a hotel bedroom famine in Reading,' stadium manager Ray Booth remarks, 'and it was difficult to sell conference space without bedrooms. So we pushed forward with the hotel which was

designed, specified and negotiated with the same contractor that built the stadium.'

The 140-roomed four-star deluxe Millennium Madejski Hotel opened its doors in 2000 and, situated just off the M4, the luxurious and chic facilities were soon swarming with businessmen and women during very busy working weeks. Those facilities included the Le Club Health & Fitness centre, which boasted a swimming pool, a fully fitted gym, a solarium and a whirlpool as well as a beauty treatment service. An à la carte fine dining restaurant named Cilantro served up seven-course meals for those looking to indulge, while Le Café offered a more informal dining experience throughout the day.

The beautifully designed Atrium Bar was also open to residents all week, and the Royals fans immediately warmed to it as a relaxed and stylish pre-match and post-match place to meet and socialise. 'People sometimes forget that we have a hard-working conference centre and a very busy commercial hotel here,'

comments Chairman John Madejski, who now happily resides in his penthouse suite at the peak of the hotel. 'You wouldn't think the two separate businesses are running together – a football club and a hotel – and we try to keep them separate from each other, which I think has worked well. An industrious international hotel of high repute has flourished since it opened.'

Besides the football, the hotel used nearby attractions as draws, including Legoland, Windsor Castle, Ascot and Newbury racecourses, as well as its proximity to Henley, Oxford, London and of course Reading, so before long the hotel was doing a roaring trade seven days a week. Such success warranted plans for a 60-room extension, which also added a further few ground-floor meeting rooms as well as an enhanced reception and entrance area. The hotel's general manager, Ruraigh Whitehead, said 'After opening in 2000, the hotel was an immediate success and almost by popular demand we are now growing to meet the ever-increasing requirements of Reading as a thriving business centre and leisure destination.'

Construction on the extension began before a 4–0 thrashing of Norwich in January 2006, and by the time the Royals had safely negotiated their first season in the top flight, the hotel's capacity had been successfully supplemented with a new five-storey arm. Le Café subsequently presented a new look in June 2008 and its gourmet partner Cilantro – which was awarded two AA Rosettes early into its existence – also began an exciting refurbishment.

Chapter 5

Premier Dreams

The magnificent memories of Griffin Park glory and the permanent party that ensued had to be sidelined come August 2002 and attentions were turned to a new and exciting challenge in an open and fiercely competitive division. Visions of climbing to the top of the English football pyramid had become a little less hazy with automatic promotion but, without making wholesale changes to such a successful squad, the Club knew that next gap was going to be the most difficult to bridge. The Royals' return to the second tier had ended a four-year absence from the division, but the previous season's thrilling accomplishments saw Reading start the 2002–03 campaign with a wave of new-found optimism as Madejski Stadium finally had the chance to host Division One football.

The pre-season friendly schedule kicked off with three low-key encounters against timid opposition during a week-long trip to southern Germany, but came to an enjoyable conclusion with two high-scoring clashes with Premiership

The scoreboard tells the tale of an entertaining pre-season friendly.

Fun and laughter as the squad take part in the annual photocall.

opposition at Madejski Stadium — a 3–4 defeat to Charlton Athletic and a 5–4 victory over West Ham United leaving boss Alan Pardew in a positive frame of mind: 'We need to tighten up at the back and we'll work on that this week. The most pleasing thing was we gave Charlton and West Ham problems with our movement and passing. To move them about and cut them open is a tribute to us.'

The much-anticipated opening League game provided a stern test with a trip to Derby County, freshly relegated from the Premiership and still boasting star names such as Fabrizio Ravanelli and Robert Lee among their line up. After a stalemate in the opening hour, the Rams eventually overpowered their nervous-looking opponents with goals from Lee, Ravanelli and Malcolm Christie.

Four days later Terry Yorath's Sheffield Wednesday were the visitors for Madejski Stadium's first Division One fixture, and Pardew's side gladly received a big confidence boost as they sealed a come-from-behind victory against the Owls; an excellent brace from the previous season's promotion hero, Jamie Cureton, securing three points. The encounter was watched by just 13,638 spectators, slightly dampening hopes that Madejski Stadium would immediately attract significantly higher average attendances in the new division, but victory was paramount and midfielder Andy Hughes paid tribute to Cureton, saying, 'Jamie may sometimes be one of the worst players on the halfway line, but in the 18 yard box he's

Loyal Royals greet Division One football to Madejski Stadium as Sheffield Wednesday visit.

Jamie Cureton celebrates his winner in the home opener against Wednesday.

immediate success, with Forster producing a brilliant hat-trick to defeat Ipswich Town 3–1 on Saturday 19 October 2002 at Madejski Stadium. Forster was understandably pleased with his efforts, but was also quick to point to the contribution of his teammates: 'I was delighted with the second goal. I got a good ball down the line from Adie Williams and saw the keeper shuffle across so I smashed it early, and luckily it went across him. I think it caught him by surprise – he probably didn't expect me to shoot from there.

'Rouge and John Salako were switching sides and causing them problems, and I think the system's working very well for us at the moment. Rouge's physical presence and strength on the ball is so good for the side. He's got the ability to turn on the ball and attack the defenders, he did that a number of times.'

Forster also revealed his relief to be rewarded with a place in attack rather than the right-wing spot he had occupied for the first few months of the campaign, saying, 'I haven't been outspoken about it, but I have been frustrated because I wanted to play up front. I had to sit and wait because we've got some very good strikers here, and hopefully I can stay in now but scoring goals by no means guarantees you'll keep your place in the side – it's about general play as well.'

Pardew's new formation was largely motivated by a desire to tighten up defensively by putting an extra man in

the best finisher I've ever played with. He's a pure finisher and his movement and 20 yard sprinting is something a lot of people would love to have. I don't know how he does it!'

The pre-season talk was dominated by musings over how Pardew would accommodate three strikers – Cureton, Martin Butler and Nicky Forster – into the same starting line up, with speculation that Forster would be asked to fill the right-wing berth. Initially that was the case and Cureton started well with six goals in the opening six games, including a brilliant long-range volley in a 3–0 home victory over Burnley which led Pardew to comment, 'We call it "The Dipper", because we see it in training so often. He lets it come down, he doesn't rush, and gets a clean strike on it. He's right on the top of his game.'

But after a disappointing run of results Pardew decided to adopt a more defensive 4–5–1 formation, with the explosively speedy Forster deployed as a lone frontman. The decision was an

Cureton and Butler celebrate another goal - but their strike partnership was soon dismantled.

midfield, but whatever the reasoning it worked a treat. The 4–5–1 shape particularly suited Forster, who revelled in his new role as a sole striker. Defenders just did not know how to handle him – drop deep and he would turn to run at you, stay close to Forster and the ball would be knocked over the top for him to sprint past you. This was best illustrated by a hapless display from Bradford City defender Robert Molenaar at Madejski Stadium on Tuesday 29 October. The 32-year-old Dutchman was given a torrid evening by Forster, who led the defender a merry dance, with Molenaar desperately chasing his shadow for much of the match. Despite creating countless chances, somehow Forster did not get himself onto the score sheet (Nicky Shorey did, sliding home his first professional goal to seal a 1–0 victory), but the striker's display that night was still one of the most eye-catching individual performances ever seen at the stadium.

Pardew was highly appreciative of his striker's efforts, commenting, 'I don't think anybody could have lived with Fozzy – he didn't score and he's frustrated about that, but he shouldn't lose confidence because he caused havoc. I think he could be the best player in this division. In the last three games he's run the opposition ragged, the system we're using suits him and although the goals didn't come for him, they will.'

By this time Pardew had also made changes in defence, recruiting 23-year-old centre half Matthew Upson on loan from Arsenal and making the permanent capture of free agent goalkeeper Marcus Hahnemann, who had last been with Fulham. Hahnemann was already a familiar face to the Madejski Stadium supporters following his successful loan spell the previous season, and the giant USA stopper wasted no time in deposing Phil Whitehead to claim the number-one jersey that would remain his for a number of years.

Upson, meanwhile, proved a massive success during his three-month

Matthew Upson was brilliant during his loan spell from Arsenal.

Nicky Forster scores the first of his hat-trick against Ipswich.

A rarity…Anthony Rougier celebrates a goal against Stoke City.

loan stint. After a shaky start which saw the Royals crash out of the League Cup with a 3–1 defeat at Cambridge (a certain D. Kitson etching his name onto the score sheet for the home team), Upson gradually gained match fitness and just got better and better. With Hahnemann in goal, Graeme Murty and Nicky Shorey in the full back positions, and Upson accompanied by Adie Williams in the centre, the Royals suddenly had a rock solid defence.

During a 12-game period between late September and early December, Reading conceded just four goals in total including a run of seven consecutive clean sheets to earn Pardew the Manager of the Month award for November – helped by a brilliant Hahnemann penalty save in a 1–0 victory over Watford. The last game of Upson's loan spell was an evenly contested goalless draw with League leaders

An emotional Matthew Upson shows his gratitude to Reading fans at the end of his loan spell.

Marcus Hahnemann makes a superb penalty save to deny Watford's Neil Cox in a 1-0 home win.

Nicky Shorey scores his first goal for Reading (with his right foot!) to down Bradford.

Portsmouth on Saturday 7 December, which saw the defender produce yet another excellent display for his 10th clean sheet in 15 Reading appearances.

Memorably, Upson was then afforded a rousing standing ovation as he embarked upon an emotional farewell lap of honour. Despite the brevity of his stay at Madejski Stadium, he had become a huge favourite with the Royals supporters and had nothing but good things to say about his loan spell. 'Coming to Reading was exactly what I needed. It has helped me no end. I am back physically to what I'm all about, and I'll take all this positive energy back to Arsenal with me. I'll be going there with an open mind and a positive attitude. I know that I am stronger and physically fitter.'

Upson's true impact was realised when he returned to Arsenal; the end of his loan spell leading to a dip in the team's form, despite a bizarre attempt by Pardew to create a fervent atmosphere inside Madejski Stadium. Whilst watching the American baseball play-offs on TV, the Royals boss noted how Anaheim Angels fans made their home stadium a fortress with the assistance of 'Thunderstix' – two plastic tubes that made one heck of a din when banged together. Pardew decided they were just what Reading fans needed (although they were to be renamed Rumblestix), and even recorded a video piece for the Club's website with his goalkeeper Hahnemann to demonstrate exactly how they should be used! They were introduced en masse for a home game with Sheffield United shortly before Christmas, but unfortunately Neil Warnock's men claimed a 2–0 victory courtesy of Jon Harley and Dean Windass...and 'Rumblestix' were rarely seen again!

After two away defeats, Reading fans were given some belated

Local boy Nathan Tyson – up against Millwall defender Glen Johnson – never quite became a first team regular.

Christmas cheer on 28 December with a 2–1 victory over Derby County, avenging the Pride Park defeat to the Rams on the opening day of the season. Nathan Tyson opened the scoring in the fifth minute – the homegrown winger's first (and only) goal for the Club – before Craig Burley equalised almost immediately. An entertaining game appeared to be heading for a 1–1 draw until injury time, when visiting keeper Lee Grant committed possibly the biggest goalkeeping howler ever seen at Madejski Stadium. Standing inside his six yard box to gather a high, looping ball, Grant inexplicably dropped it and Cureton – ever the predator – gleefully accepted the festive gift with a close range sweep into the net for a 2–1 victory.

The New Year started with a Madejski Stadium first – the first game to be postponed. The Royals were facing promotion-chasing Leicester City, but as a big crowd gathered the heavens opened and spewed out prolonged surges of heavy rain to create a number of large puddles on the pitch. Managers Alan Pardew and Micky Adams were keen to play, and referee Mark Warren decided to let the action start as scheduled. It was a decent enough first half, and the Royals created the better chances without being able to break the deadlock, but playing conditions worsened and the puddles began to exert a stronger influence. Considering the forecast for more rain and the danger to players' safety, it was no surprise at half time when Warren decided play would have to be halted – although both managers would have preferred to continue. 'The conditions

Keeper Marcus Hahnemann started a post-match ritual of throwing his shirt into the crowd.

Jamie Cureton and Nicky Shorey celebrate a last minute winner against Derby.

were tough and awkward for players but if a goal had been scored in the first half he might have let the game continue,' Pardew said. 'At half time he told me that he would give it 10 or 15 more minutes to see how it went. Then he knocked on the door and told me he had changed his mind and he was calling it off. That angered me.'

January was a fairly forgettable month for the Royals, containing three games in a fortnight against Walsall (one in the League and two in the FA Cup), but there was one particular note of interest with the signing from Arsenal of a young flame-haired midfielder…Steve Sidwell. The former Gunners' youth team captain would go on to play a huge role in the Club's eventual elevation to the Premiership, but he enjoyed a less than auspicious

start by missing a penalty on his debut as the Royals lost their re-arranged fixture with Leicester by three goals to one.

After that drab start to the year, a long journey to Burnley on Saturday 1 February was hardly anticipated with

A significant moment as Steve Sidwell signs on.

relish, but the trip to Turf Moor was to prove the start of a sensational run of form that surely sees February 2003 rank as one of the best months – in terms of the team's performances – in the history of the Club. Does that sound

Defender Steve Brown becomes Alan Pardew's latest signing.

Monday night live televised game, thanks to a late goal from John Salako. Then came a huge test – away games at Millwall and Sheffield United within the space of four days. The Lions were well and truly tamed by a classic counter-attacking goal – from a Millwall corner, James Harper cleared, finding loan winger Luke Chadwick who broke to release Andy Hughes, and his surging run and precise cross picked out Forster for a decisive finish. The Royals had gone the entire length of the pitch in just 12 seconds and with just eight touches of the ball. That goal typified Pardew's Reading at their best – fast, powerful, purposeful and penetrating. And their performance in the following game, a 3–1 victory at Sheffield United, was ranked by many supporters at the time as the greatest ever display by a Reading team. Warnock's Blades were in brilliant form, but they were destroyed by an outstanding Reading side who clinched the points with goals from Forster (two) and Hughes.

It was superb stuff, and an admiring Pardew said, 'We put on a really fabulous performance. Some of our movement and passing was beautiful, and I'm sure the travelling fans had to pinch themselves to believe it was Reading playing at times, especially in the last 20 minutes when we looked like we could overrun the Blades. When you end a game like that, it's easy to forget the start of the match, when we had terrible trouble trying to deal with Sheffield

like an exaggeration? Well here are the stats: played five, won five, scored 15, conceded four – and three of those games were away from Madejski Stadium!

It started with a stunning 5–2 victory over the Clarets, including two goals for recent signing Sidwell, before the month's least impressive display secured a 2–1 home win over Gillingham on a

Jamie Cureton and Leicester's Andy Impey splash about before a New Year's Day postponement.

John Salako salutes a late winner in the rain against Gillingham.

United's qualities. They really are a fine side and we had to be at our very best not to concede two early goals, because they were rampant in that period.'

Not everybody was happy though – the Bramall Lane media contingent were in a huff after Pardew refused to talk to the press after the game, although he later explained, 'There was no specific reason for that other than I wanted the performance to speak for itself. Whatever I could have said wouldn't have been able to do the performance justice. A lot of the time, too much emphasis is placed on what the managers say, instead of the performance, which is the most important thing.'

The month concluded with a first half dismantling of lowly Rotherham as goals from Forster, Hughes and Harper simply swept Ronnie Moore's team aside to set up a more than comfortable 3–0 victory. By now, we were forced to confront something quite startling – the suspicion had been growing all season, but that second month of the year had confirmed our thoughts – this Reading team were more than capable of claiming their second successive promotion and climbing into the Premiership! The top two automatic places were virtually out of reach with

Andy Hughes scores a cracker as Rotherham are thrashed.

Jamie Cureton through the North Stand net.

Leicester and Portsmouth completely dominating the division. But the four play-off places were well and truly up for grabs, and Reading looked on course to claim one of them.

There was still a long way to go, however, and February did contain one sad note with the departure of a true Reading legend, Phil Parkinson, who made the decision to begin his managerial career by accepting the vacant position at Colchester United. Parkinson was coming towards the end of his playing days, rarely featuring that season, and the signing of Sidwell made his return to the team even less likely. So when Colchester came knocking, it was hard to resist their offer.

Parkinson recalled, 'Pards called me one night and told me that he'd been approached by the Colchester Chairman who wanted to speak to me about the manager's job. So I went for an interview, but my heart wasn't set on leaving Reading – I just thought I might as well go and speak to them. Then I had a second interview, and on the train on the way back home I had a call telling me I'd got the job.

'It was a life-changing phone call, and I didn't have much time because the call came at 4.30pm on the Sunday and they wanted me to start the following day! I didn't get any time to contemplate it, and it was a big decision, but I felt that being offered a managerial job at a good club at my age was too good an opportunity to turn down. But I was at

Reading for 11 years, and it will always hold a special place in my heart.'

Moving on without Parkinson, March proffered a mixed bag of results – a 2–0 defeat at Wimbledon, a 1–0 victory at play-off chasing Norwich and a 1–0 loss at home to play-off chasing Wolves (an unpleasant omen for the end of the season). Then came the visit of Crystal Palace, when goals from Steve Brown and a last gasp James Harper effort sealed a 2–1 win. Brown had been signed at Christmas to plug the gap following

Upson's departure, and he had quickly forged a good understanding with Adie Williams to become a favourite with the Madejski Stadium crowd (even though he couldn't quite live up to Pardew's tag of 'the new Phil Parkinson'!) Brown was a wholehearted defender who made up for a lack of pace with an intelligent football brain, and he was also an excellent distributor from defence.

The up and down sequence of results continued with a 3–1 loss at Ipswich, a 1–0 victory at Bradford and a 2–1 home

John Mackie and James Harper celebrate the latter's late winner against Crystal Palace.

Loanee winger Luke Chadwick impressed towards the end of the 2002–03 season.

defeat to a Brighton side managed by Steve Coppell – whose next trip to Madejski Stadium later that year proved to be of an altogether different nature! The meeting with Brighton contained two memorable goals – one for all the right reasons, one for a piece of farce! The former was a brilliant 'dipper' from Jamie Cureton, a goal that fittingly turned out to be his last Reading goal at Madejski Stadium. The latter was Brighton's opener after a quarter of an hour, when Marcus Hahnemann was penalised for picking up an alleged back pass when Williams' challenge on Albion striker Bobby Zamora had simply cannoned off Graeme Murty and bobbled through to the keeper. As the Reading defence protested the decision, Zamora reacted quickly to square a short free kick to Paul Brooker, who tapped into an empty net.

After three defeats in four games, Reading's place in the play-offs was looking under threat and Pardew's team needed to bounce back. The inspiration for doing so – as was so often the case during that season – was Forster. Preston North End were the next visitors to Madejski Stadium, and those particular opponents always seemed to bring out the best in Forster, who had turned down a move to Deepdale in favour of joining Reading four years earlier. On this occasion the striker notched his second hat-trick of the season, including an archetypal Fozzy goal to get the ball

Adie Williams and Steve Brown formed an excellent defensive partnership.

rolling – racing onto a long ball from Graeme Murty to outpace the visiting defenders and fire home with aplomb.

So the Royals were back on track, and took a big step closer to securing a play-off berth three days later with the Good Friday visit of fellow promotion hopefuls Nottingham Forest to Madejski Stadium. It was a pulsating game, with Pardew's side exerting increasing amounts of pressure until the breakthrough was finally made 15 minutes from time when Murty's arrowed right-wing centre was

met with an unstoppable header by the onrushing Hughes. There was a palpable celebratory atmosphere amongst the 21,612 spectators after the game, and a certain sense that the play-offs were beckoning.

Spirits were high, the Royals were on a roll, and a delighted Pardew said, 'I've seen Premiership games not as good as that, with less quality and determination than was on show tonight. It was two fantastic teams, and a good advert for the division. With four games to go, we're in

Andy Hughes rises high to head a brilliant winner against Nottingham Forest.

a good position. We looked like ourselves, and we've still got two goals – get in the play-offs, and stay undefeated! The fans were terrific and this is what we want. We've got to give them the ammunition, and today they were fantastic. We filled the stadium up, and that made it more special. The more people come, the more everyone will enjoy it.'

Progress was briefly halted by Portsmouth in a 3–0 defeat against the champions-in-waiting at Fratton Park, but the Royals returned to Madejski Stadium the following weekend with the chance to clinch a place in the top six – with two games to spare. Grimsby Town were the opponents and the result was never in doubt after on loan winger Glen Little stroked home a second-minute shot. Hughes added another midway through the first half, and a late Mariners consolation did nothing to dampen the final whistle celebrations as Pardew's side made certain of their participation in the end of season play-offs.

The manager had no doubt over the root of his team's success, stating, 'It's because of the attitude of the players, the staff and the people who work at the Club. We've got a positive attitude on things, and that's why we've done so well. I don't want the fans to get too carried away. We've done fantastic and if the season ended today that would be fine. But we're in the play-offs, and there's no way we should be too disappointed if we get knocked out. We should have a party when we come back, but – and it's a big 'but' – we could achieve the ultimate dream, and you can rest assured that we'll give it a good go.'

Two League games remained, both away from home, and Pardew took the opportunity to rotate his squad – including substitute appearances for

Darius Henderson goes close but Wolves stand firm in the play-off semi-final second leg.

Darren Campbell and Peter Castle, who thereby became the Club's youngest ever first team player – in a 3–0 win at Watford. The regular season ended in a 1–0 defeat at Stoke, but all eyes were now firmly fixed on the play-offs – two games from Cardiff's Millennium Stadium and three games from the Premiership!

Pardew's team ended the campaign in fourth position, yielding 79 points from their 46 games. The season contained 12 away victories, as many as champions Portsmouth, and remarkably only four draws. Forster was top scorer with 16 League goals, followed by Cureton with nine, and full backs Graeme Murty and Nicky Shorey were leading appearance makers with 43 League starts apiece, while James Harper claimed the Player of the Season trophy after an exceptionally consistent campaign.

The division's fifth placed team was Wolverhampton Wanderers, so it was onto Molineux for the first leg of the play-off semi-final! Both League games between the clubs had ended with 1–0 victories for the away side, and at half time that scoreline seemed likely again as the Royals led with a 25th minute goal from Forster (who else?!). Reading started the second half well and looked the more likely team to add another goal, before, in the 61st minute, disaster struck. Forster, who had been enjoying another tremendous game, attempted to block a clearance from Wolves full-back Lee Naylor, landed awkwardly and lay flat out on the turf, clearly in agony. The Royals had lost their talisman to injury, and Wolves had been given a lifeline. They grabbed it with both hands, scoring twice in the final 15 minutes through a

deflected Shaun Newton strike and a free kick by Naylor, cementing a 2–1 first leg lead to take to Madejski Stadium.

Reading talked a good game, insisting that the tie was still very much alive. Pardew promised, 'Our stadium is going to be rocking on Wednesday night. I felt

Graeme Murty cuts a lonely figure as Wolves fans celebrate their team's victory.

Injured Nicky Forster joins a lap of honour after a desperately disappointing end to a superb season.

2002–03 Coca-Cola Championship – in and around us:

		P	W	D	L	GD	Pts
2	Leicester City	46	26	14	6	+33	92
3	Sheffield Utd	46	23	11	12	+20	80
4	**Reading**	**46**	**25**	**4**	**17**	**+15**	**79**
5	Wolves	46	20	16	10	+37	76
6	Notts Forest	46	20	14	12	+32	74

Promoted: Portsmouth, Leicester, Wolverhampton Wanderers
Relegated: Grimsby, Brighton & Hove Albion, Sheffield Wednesday

FA Cup: Third round (v Walsall)
League Cup: First round (v Cambridge United)

Top scorer: Nicky Forster (16)

Most appearances: Graeme Murty (43), Nicky Shorey (43), Andy Hughes (41)

Nicky Forster

we should have been 2–0 up and been really in the driving seat, but if someone said at the start of the day you'd lose by one goal I would have taken it because our place is going to be a different game.' Keeper Hahnemann added, 'We were under no illusions that we would win it easily and we knew when we scored, it'd be very difficult to keep that lead. 1–1 would've been better for us going into the second game, but 2–1 is alright and we know what we have to do at home.'

So the stage was set, and a place in the play-off final for promotion to the Premiership was at stake. It was Madejski Stadium's biggest game to date, and as promised by Pardew the sell-out crowd of 24,060 created a 'rocking' atmosphere. Without the injured Forster, the Royals boss called upon Jamie Cureton – who had rarely started in the closing weeks of the season – to produce more end of season heroics, and also handed a starting place to powerful young striker Darius Henderson.

Reading were on the front foot from the opening whistle, forcing Wolves onto the defensive as they held onto their slender aggregate lead. But the breakthrough would not come. Henderson had an effort cleared off the line, Cureton skied a decent opportunity over the bar, Little curled a shot just wide…and Wolves held firm. Reading's attacks grew increasingly desperate in the final stages, and their hearts were finally broken nine minutes from time when Wolves midfielder Alex Rae arrowed a fierce shot into the bottom corner. The Royals were beaten, the season was over, and Wolves went on to claim promotion with a play-off final victory over Sheffield United.

Despite the bitterly disappointing finale, it had been a marvellously exciting campaign as Pardew's team exceeded all expectations in their debut season in the division. So spirits were high during the summer break, with the Royals followers confident their team would go one better next time. Cureton departed, turning down the offer of a new contract to join Busan Icons in South Korea, and was replaced by Manchester City legend Shaun Goater. Adi Viveash, Sammy Igoe, Phil Whitehead and Anthony Rougier were also on the way out, with free scoring Bristol City winger Scott Murray joining for £650,000 and Jamaican international Omar Daley arriving on a season-long loan.

The 2003–04 season began with a trip to Ipswich Town in sweltering conditions on the UK's hottest recorded weekend. Temperatures at Portman Road rose as high as 37 degrees and Pardew was left fairly hot under the collar as an apparent dive from Pablo Counago earned a red card for Nicky Shorey with the Royals 1–0 ahead through Steve Sidwell, and then in injury time a definite dive by Jim Magilton after a challenge by Steve Brown resulted in a penalty which was converted by Tommy Miller to give the home side a scarcely deserved 1–1 draw.

Referee Brian Curson was not a popular man in the away team dressing room as aggrieved defender Brown noted, 'There was no iota of contact whatsoever. You just have to hope that

the officials get it right. Jim Magilton is quite within his rights to make the dive, and the referee has got to decide, and unfortunately this time it went against us.'

Pardew was even more incensed, raging, 'My players were magnificent today but they've encountered a ref who had a poor game. The assessor's report will be interesting to read and I hope I get a copy of it. Referees have a hard job, but they are judged and that's what I want to see. I want to see what that report says. I went over to the ref after the game and said "well played" because I wanted to get my players away from him. They were quite angry. I've also got a sore foot from kicking the wall.'

After a routine victory at Boston United in the League Cup, the home campaign began on a beautiful day on Saturday 16 August 2003, and the side delivered a performance as bright as the summer sunshine to claim a 3–0 victory over Nottingham Forest who, like Reading, had missed out in the

John Madejski delivers a passionate speech ahead of the home season opener against Nottingham Forest.

play-offs the previous season. One goal in particular was a gem – central midfielder Kevin Watson delivered a typically delicious throughball to release new signing Murray, who finished decisively. Afterwards Pardew crowed, 'Our kit man Ron Grant has been a Reading fan since time immemorial, and he just said to me that was as good a performance as he can remember. I'll go along with that, we were terrific today and the players deserve full credit.'

Former Rotherham skipper Watson was one of the chief catalysts for the display with his probing passing from the centre of the field. He became very popular with the Madejski Stadium faithful for his excellent distribution skills, but the presence in the squad of James Harper, Steve Sidwell and Andy Hughes meant that Watson struggled to command a place in the side and he made just 10 starts that season, eventually being allowed to leave to join Phil Parkinson at Colchester's Layer Road.

After away wins at Derby and Wimbledon, and a drab home draw with Rotherham, things were looking good. The Royals were unbeaten with 11 points from five games, leading many supporters and neutral observers to predict a successful promotion campaign. But a bombshell was about to be dropped.

West Ham United had just fired their manager Glenn Roeder, and

Shaun Goater scores on his home debut.

Pardew was being heavily linked with the vacant post. At first, few people took the rumours any more seriously than the usual tabloid gossip, but the speculation continued to mount until it reached the stage that the headlines were gaining serious credibility. Pardew was now in pole position to become the new manager of the Hammers. Finally, on Wednesday 10 September 2003, Pardew resigned with the intention of being appointed at Upton Park. The complication was that he was under contract, and the Royals Chairman John Madejski was in no mood to allow him to break it as he issued a statement that read, 'Alan Pardew has tendered his resignation, which the Reading board has not accepted. The team will be managed by Kevin Dillon, assisted by the current management team of Brian McDermott, Nick Hammond and Niall Clark, for the game at West Ham on Saturday.'

A protracted period of discussion and negotiation began – but there was also an important League game to prepare for three days later. The opponents? West Ham United! Pardew's assistant Kevin Dillon was named caretaker boss and led the team for the first time at Upton Park. He named an unchanged XI from Pardew's last game and saw his side

Alan Pardew chats to Rotherham boss Ronnie Moore before what turned out to be his last home game.

Kevin Dillon faces the press after being appointed caretaker manager following Pardew's departure.

unluckily lose 1–0 to a header from Christian Dailly. It was a busy period of fixtures and Dillon took charge of his first home game four days later with the visit of Cardiff City. On an emotional evening Steve Sidwell scored a thunderous late goal to seal a 2–1 victory, leading skipper Adie Williams to comment, 'This was a big result. The commitment, passion and flair were all there for us and I thought we deserved it in the end. We knew we had to raise ourselves and full credit to the boys because in the second half we did that.'

The next game saw a less happy outcome as visitors Coventry City came from behind to win by two goals to one, with the game being preceded by the confirmation of Pardew's departure after a compensation package was agreed with West Ham. As the search for his permanent successor continued, Dillon led the team to a morale-boosting 3–1 League Cup victory over Oxford United.

That was followed by two consecutive away League defeats at Sunderland and Norwich, who claimed

James Harper gets a pre-match cuddle from Kingsley before the home meeting with Cardiff.

Andy Hughes celebrates an equaliser against Bradford in the last game of the pre-Coppell era.

the points with a hugely fortuitous late goal when Paul McVeigh's long-range shot took an outrageous deflection off Adie Williams and looped into the net. On Saturday 4 October Bradford City visited Madejski Stadium, but as goals from Sidwell and Andy Hughes resulted in a scrappy 2–2 draw, the game itself was relegated to the background amidst increasing speculation over the identity of the Royals' new boss.

Many names were linked to the post, including Glenn Hoddle, George Graham, Ronnie Moore, Lou Macari, Steve Coppell, Tony Adams, Steve Cotterill, Iain Dowie, Peter Taylor, Bryan Robson, Gary Johnson, Lawrie Sanchez and Phil Parkinson.

In the wake of Pardew's departure, John Madejski had appointed former goalkeeper and Academy Director Nick Hammond as the Club's first-ever Director of Football, and Hammond certainly endured a baptism of fire in his new role as he was tasked with helping find the new manager. He commented, 'There have been a very large number of applications, which reflects the size of the Club and the fact that it's a very attractive club to be involved with. It's important that people realise the size of this football club now and the potential it has. We will follow exactly the correct procedures in terms of wishing to speak to people. We'll be absolutely clear in the way we do things, it will be done in the correct manner and certainly not made public. It would be wrong of us to talk about individuals.

'This is a major appointment for this football club, and it's very important that we take our time and come to the right decision. The new manager needs to be able to manage Reading Football Club in the Premiership, and there are a lot of qualities needed to do that. We have a very strong team of individuals who also build into the team process. Everyone has an important part to play, and a new manager must have an understanding of that. This club is geared for Premiership football, so the decision has to be very well thought out. We can't afford to rush into the decision, we have to look at all qualities needed and how he will fit in with the existing staff.'

Finally, on Thursday 9 October 2003, the waiting was over and the announcement was made…the new Reading manager was to be Steve Coppell.

NICKY FORSTER

Reading appearances: 179 (+35)
Reading goals: 67

Although he was one of the main catalysts for Reading's revival under Alan Pardew, striker Nicky Forster was in fact a rare success in the transfer market for Pardew's predecessor, Tommy Burns. The Scotsman splashed out £650,000 to bring 26-year-old Forster to Madejski Stadium from Birmingham City in June 1999. He had scored 11 goals in an injury plagued two-year spell at St Andrew's, having previously starred for Gillingham and Brentford.

The beginning of Forster's Reading career coincided with Burns's final few weeks in charge, and the striker made a slow start with just four goals in his first 24 games. His form was better than that return suggested though, and an acceleration of his goalscoring ratio was just around the corner.

The breakthrough was made against a team who had tried to sign Forster when he opted to join Reading – Preston North End – and it was perhaps no coincidence that the Lancashire club were often on the receiving end of his best performances. On 5 February 2000 the Royals emerged from a wretched run of form to take on League leaders North End at Deepdale, and earned a highly creditable 2–2 draw as Forster netted a truly memorable solo effort, racing from the halfway line and beating three defenders before firing an unstoppable drive past home keeper Tepi Moilanen. That impressive draw set Alan Pardew's team onto a brilliant run of results to climb away from the relegation zone and eventually finish in 10th position.

By this stage Forster was in outstanding form and Pardew clearly regarded him as a pivotal part of his team's 2000–01 promotion challenge. But with the campaign rapidly approaching, disaster struck when Forster's injury jinx returned as he suffered a cruciate ligament injury in a harmless looking challenge with Charlton's Chris Powell during a pre-season friendly – a blow that ruled him out of contention for the vast majority of the campaign and perhaps delayed the Royals' promotion by another season.

Jamie Cureton will be remembered as the 2001–02 promotion hero for his last-day clincher at Brentford, but Nicky Forster was in fact the team's top scorer that season with 18 goals. He was particularly impressive in January 2002 as he fired eight goals in a seven-game winning streak, including a hat-trick against Blackpool at Madejski Stadium and a superb solo effort in a 2–0 win at Wigan.

Although his early Reading games were played alongside Martin Butler in a strike force nicknamed 'FAB' (Forster And Butler), the former England under-21 international never really established an effective and settled partnership during his time at Madejski Stadium – failing to truly gel with Butler, Cureton, Shaun Goater, Dean Morgan, Les Ferdinand, Bas Savage, Lloyd Owusu or Dave Kitson – perhaps indicating that his marauding, high-tempo style of play was best suited to the freedom of the lone frontman role.

Operating in that position, Forster was simply sensational in the 2002–03 season, propelling the Royals into a play-off spot in their first season in Division One. He top scored with 17 goals, and, indeed, could well have taken his side all the way into the Premiership but for the cruel intervention of an ankle injury at the worst possible time – midway through the second half of a first leg play-off game at Wolves. Reading led 1-0, through a Forster goal, and looked very strong when their key man was injured, allowing Wanderers to fight back and win 3–1 on aggregate.

Bedevilled by a series of niggling injuries, Forster was never able to show his best form under the management of Steve Coppell – much to the frustration of a manager who had always been a big admirer of the striker from afar. Sadly, his Reading career fizzled out somewhat, although there were still a number of high spots such as a brilliant brace in a 2–0 win at Wigan and a long range goal of the season effort to secure Coppell's first away win at Sheffield United.

The 2004–05 season was particularly disappointing for the striker as he managed just seven goals in 27 League starts and at the end of the season he was allowed to join Ipswich Town, but his contribution to the rise of Reading FC had been immense. For lengthy periods he was the team's most dangerous attacker, and to a great extent the formation of Pardew's play-off team of 2002–03 was designed to bring out the best in the striker.

Despite all his considerable achievements as a Reading player, Forster will always be remembered at Madejski Stadium for one performance more than any other. In May 2001 the Royals faced Wigan Athletic in the Division Two play-off semi-finals. The first leg at the JJB Stadium was drawn 0–0, and the Latics led the second leg by one goal to nil with 10 minutes remaining. Forster was on the bench after recently recovering from that cruciate ligament injury, and his introduction as a sub in place of Sammy Igoe was Pardew's final throw of the dice.

Taking up an unfamiliar right-wing position, Fozzy appeared from the bench to produce possibly the most electrifying five minutes of football ever seen at Madejski Stadium. With 86 minutes on the clock he stormed down the wing and delivered an undefendable cross that dropped to Butler who fired home for a dramatic equaliser. Extra time loomed but Forster wasn't finished. Again he received the ball on the right flank and embarked upon a full pace, winding run that culminated in Arjan De Zeeuw's desperate lunge to concede a penalty. Jamie Cureton stepped up but saw his spot kick saved by Roy Carroll…only for the rebound to come out to Forster who smartly steered it over the line for the winner.

Just 10 minutes on the pitch, and Forster had created a goal, won a penalty and scored the winner to send the Royals to Cardiff! The 2002–03 season may have seen Forster at his peak, but that unforgettable evening was the defining moment of his Reading career.

More Than A Game:

The Finishing Line...

Having opted for the shorter-distance half marathon when first conceiving the idea of a running race around Reading, the town's first race started and finished at Reading University's Whiteknights Park on Sunday 13 March 1983. Three years later, the race moved to the South Reading Leisure Centre, before a new Thames-side starting and finishing line was created at Rivermead in 1990. By 2003 the race – open to fun runners and elite athletes – was attracting almost 10,000 annual runners, and Madejski Stadium's East Stand was chosen as the new end point for 2004's faster and flatter route.

In 2006 the course was tinkered with further, but Madejski Stadium remained as the finishing line as well as becoming the race's main site, with the starter's gun now sounding in the adjacent Green Park business estate. A kit marquee was erected, temporary toilets ordered in, massage tents and trade stands appeared and music blared out across the car park to create an atmosphere of excitement and anticipation. The hotel was used as a base for many of the athletes, and pasta parties were held in the conference centre before the starter's pistol was sounded. Once underway, the half marathon took runners north to the town centre, via a loop of the university campus, around Reading's centre, into west Reading and back south to the football ground. Huge crowds gathered to see loved ones struggle into the stadium and dip over the line with their last ounce of energy in front of a busy West Stand.

By 2008 almost 15,000 competitors took part in the event, which requires a huge amount of organisation: road closures, stewarding, water stations, parking provision and first aid are all

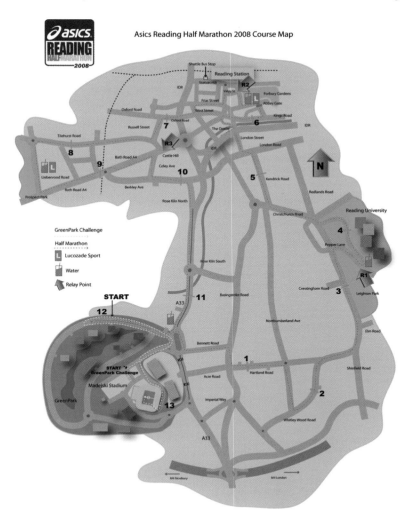

Asics Reading Half Marathon 2008 Course Map

vital in 'running' a successful marathon.

The current male course record is 61 minutes 19 seconds, ran by Patrick Makau in 2008. In the same year the female record was broken, with Liz Yelling completing in 69 minutes 35 seconds. Prize money has risen to £1,000 for the winners of both the men's and women's races, while all finishers receive a medal for completing the 13.1 mile course.

In footballing terms, Reading's season's end does not mean the finishing line for the stadium, with a variety of exhibition matches and local league finals extending Madejski's season. Twice the Soccer Six tournament has enticed an array of celebrities to Berkshire; 2004's crop included *Lock Stock and Two Smoking Barrels* actor Nick Moran, *The Royle Family* actor Ralf Little, *EastEnders* duo

James Alexandrou and Michael Greco (Martin and Beppe respectively), as well as pop stars Blazin' Squad, ex-Spandau Ballet vocalist Tony Hadley and Westlife heart-throb Brian McFadden. For some though, eyes were firmly fixed upon a six-a-side team of glamour models – a team that reappeared four years later to the crowd's delight. Despite the bank holiday rain in 2008, more fans swarmed into the stadium to see Tony Cottee help a team from *The Sun* lift the trophy, beating a Lee Sharpe-led side that included boyband McFly.

A higher-profile encounter was staged in May 2006. Reading had reached the top flight for the first time, and after prolonged celebrations, football fans had a World Cup to look forward to. And as a prelude to the Finals in Germany a 'legends' match was organised, pitting England against Germany. More than 21,000 tickets were sold for a spectacle broadcast live on Channel Five, who based themselves in a hospitality suite in the Upper West Stand. The match had everything. World Cup-winning skipper Lothar Matthaus had lost none of his class as he and Steffen Freund clashed with Ray Wilkins, John Barnes, Neil Webb and Chris Waddle in midfield. Paul Merson was on the score sheet for England and Matt Le Tissier set up Lee Sharpe for a

second, but Peter Reid's side lost 4–2 in a reverse of the 1966 World Cup Final scoreline. Aside from the footballing talent on show, there was also a comedic element to the encounter. Ex-boxer Nigel Benn was at fault for the first goal, unknowingly playing a number of Germans onside, while rugby stars Martin Offiah and Kieron Bracken would have much preferred to pick the ball up, but the story of the evening was Boris Johnson's cameo. The tottering Conservative MP and Lord Mayor-to-be

looked all at sea as soon as he stepped onto the pitch and, powering into some of Germany's footballing heroes with clumsy rugby tackles, his blond locks were soon tugged back onto the bench for everyone's safety but to the crowd's dismay.

Ex-Reading legends have also battled it out at showpieces, following two thrilling promotion campaigns in 2002 and 2006. More than 20,000 turned out for Phil Parkinson's testimonial in May 2002, and a very healthy crowd braved hangovers on May Day 2006, one day after Graeme Murty's late penalty had seen the Royals secure a record-breaking points haul.

Madejski Stadium has also hosted the annual Royals Cup six-a-side tournament which, ever since the stadium's birth, has consistently proved popular with local companies. Plus, more than 8,000 fans watched a mid-

season international friendly between Australia and Jamaica in September 2003, with the Royals' midfielder Omar Daley featuring for the Reggae Boyz but finishing up on the losing side after Harry Kewell's winner in a 2–1 Socceroos victory.

Chapter 6

A New Era

Steve Coppell was unveiled as the new Reading manager at a press conference deep inside the bowels of Madejski Stadium, where the man who appointed him, Chairman John Madejski, noted 'He is a vastly experienced manager who remains extremely ambitious and is determined to take us into the Premiership. We have taken our time to make sure we made the right decision, and we have also been determined to follow the correct procedures. I know the fans have been keen for news of our managerial appointment, and I would like to thank them for their patience.'

A reserved Steve Coppell is forced to pose for photos at Madejski Stadium.

'Experienced' was possibly the key word in that statement. Previous boss Pardew was a big personality and had exerted a strong influence throughout the club. His recent departure had been destabilising, and Coppell, with his broad range of managerial experience, calm outlook and consistent demeanour, was seen as just the man to get things back on track. But it was far more than a short-term 'ship-steadying' appointment – Coppell was also a fiercely ambitious man, something that is often hidden beneath his po-faced exterior, and easily convinced the Reading board that he would work extremely hard to take the Club forward. The former Crystal Palace, Manchester City, Brentford and Brighton manager had tasted top-flight management in the past, and he was hungry to do it again. The new Reading manager insisted:

A lot of managers will be envious of my position here – the potential of this club is massive. The team showed last season that they're a hell of a good team, and it certainly doesn't need a complete refit. The infrastructure is here for Reading to be a Premiership club, and this is an opportunity for me to try to pit my wits against the best and hopefully get into the Premiership. I just hope I can continue Alan Pardew's good work, put the players back on track and try to direct them further. I can't

guarantee success but I will be doing my utmost.

As you would expect, there was a positive reaction from the playing staff, with skipper Adie Williams presciently noting 'It's a good appointment. Steve Coppell's got a proven track record as a manager, and when you've been such a good player as he was, that warrants

Steve Coppell deep in thought.

respect. The appointment was dragging on for a while, but as Nick Hammond and the Chairman said, we wanted to get the right man and build for the future – in three or four years' time nobody will be worrying about an extra few days here or there.'

The appointment also brought about a promotion for academy manager Nick Hammond, who became

the Club's first director of football. It was to become a key development in the ongoing progress of the Club, and Madejski enthused 'During his eight years of association with Reading FC, Nick Hammond has been a most impressive member of the football management team, and has played a vital role in many different areas. He has an intimate knowledge of the workings of this football club and has been instrumental in building towards what we are today.'

Coppell's first game in charge was for a midweek visit of Gillingham, and

Reading fans were given an early indication of their new manager's temperament by his 'unveiling' to the crowd before the game. Rather than parading boisterously onto the pitch, waving a scarf above his head and enthusiastically gesturing to the fans, Coppell unfussily took his seat in the hidden depths of the directors' box and merely acknowledged the fans' applause with a slightly embarrassed wave and a gentle nod of the head. Steve Coppell, the master of understatement, was among us.

That first game resulted in a narrow

victory as Steve Sidwell's late goal secured a 2–1 win, and four days later there was an altogether more dramatic encounter for Coppell's second game against Preston North End. By now, North End were growing weary of their trips to Madejski Stadium – they always seemed to find new and entertaining ways to lose against Reading (Nicky Forster had scored a hat-trick in a 5–1 home win the previous season), and on this occasion they surpassed even their own high standards in one of the most eventful games ever to take place at Madejski Stadium.

Preston took the lead through in-form striker Ricardo Fuller, but towards the end of the opening period Forster was hauled down inside the penalty area by Marlon Broomes, who was shown his second yellow card. Shaun Goater stepped up to the penalty spot only to see Jonathan Gould make an excellent diving save, but the linesman ruled a retake after noticing Gould moved too early. Goater slotted home at the second asking, prompting apoplectic visiting boss Craig Brown to receive his own red card after furious protestations. Undeterred, Preston's 10 men took the lead in the second half through Graham Alexander's penalty, and as Goater had a goal disallowed for handball and Scott Murray twice hit the woodwork, it looked like being the Lancastrians' day. But with just five minutes remaining, defender John Mackie defiantly headed home a set

Fozzy is the hero with the winner against North End.

piece to make it 2–2 before Forster steered home a dramatic winner deep inside the five minutes of added time. Welcome to Reading, Mr Coppell!

An altogether more forgettable encounter provided Coppell with his first defeat as a trio of home games came to an end, with Walsall's Vinny Samways cleverly curling a quickly taken free kick past Marcus Hahnemann to give the Saddlers a 3–1 win. The new manager quickly reacted by making his first signing for the club, recruiting Ivar Ingimarsson from Wolves for £100,000. The Icelandic international made an immediate impression by helping the team to a 2–1 victory at Sheffield United.

The Royals' home form remained strong, with consecutive victories against Wigan, Millwall and Watford keeping the promotion challenge firmly on track, and in early December there was an enjoyable diversion with a Carling Cup fourth-round tie against Premiership high-flyers Chelsea. The London club, then managed by Claudio Ranieri, had recently been acquired by extremely wealthy Russian businessman Roman Abramovich, and a stadium record crowd of 24,107 flocked to Madejski to see the Royals hold firm for an hour before Frank Lampard and Hernan Crespo combined to set up Jimmy Floyd Hasselbaink for the only goal of the game. It was the first time that one of the top clubs had

Mackie, Murray, Forster and Goater celebrate a dramatic win over Preston at the end of Coppell's first week in charge.

ever visited Madejski Stadium, and Coppell's side acquitted themselves admirably in an entertaining encounter. Nobody present could have foreseen the explosive nature of the next meeting between the sides, but that is for another chapter.

Back in the League, a dreadful Christmas of three consecutive 3–0 defeats (against Stoke, Crystal Palace and Wimbledon) provided an unmerry festive season, and Coppell bolstered his strike force with the capture of relatively unknown striker Dave Kitson for an initial £150,000 from Cambridge United. 'Dave is a promising young player from the lower Leagues who can give us a bit more variety up front,' suggested the typically downbeat manager. 'And I hope he can fulfil his potential with this great opportunity.'

Another Christmas arrival was striker Lloyd Owusu who, like Ingimarsson, had played under Coppell at Brentford. There was no coincidence that the Royals boss had opted to bring two new big and powerful strikers to the club, because he had decided to abandon the four-five-one formation that had served previous manager Alan Pardew so well. When he first arrived in Berkshire, Coppell initially opted to stick with the set-up favoured by his predecessor, which featured Nicky Forster as the lone frontman, but that system went against all his attacking instincts – get the ball wide and get the crosses in – and now, three months into his tenure, he committed to reshaping

Sidwell and Murty embrace after victory.

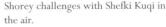

Shorey challenges with Shefki Kuqi in the air.

the team into his traditionally preferred four-four-two approach.

The 2004 new year brought Owusu's first goal for the club in a 1–1 draw with Ipswich, before Preston bucked their 'entertaining defeats' trend by winning a third-round FA Cup replay by two goals to one. The end of January arrived with a Shaun Goater brace in a 3–1 home victory against Derby, leaving the Royals handily placed just outside a very congested top six. An embarrassing 5–1 thrashing at Rotherham followed, leaving Coppell to plea for a greater level of consistency from his players:

The helter-skelter nature of our season continues and it quite often defies logic. From week to week our performances vary enormously and our results reflect this. I have tried to plot a steady course – not getting carried away when we win and not reacting to some of the sensational headlines when we lose. I have concentrated on the ability to react positively to a defeat and this is something we have been able to do regularly. From here it is obvious to say that for us to achieve anything we must become more consistent.

To illustrate his point, the Royals then continued their variable form by drawing with Burnley (2–2), defeating Sheffield United (2–1) and losing at Preston (2–1), meaning that the final two months and dozen games of the campaign were entered with the Royals in eighth place on 52 points, just one behind fifth-placed West Ham United. The division was looking increasingly hard to predict, with the exception of Wimbledon who were marooned at the bottom, and consecutive draws against Crystal Palace and Stoke City – when substitute goalkeeper Jamie Young made a miraculous tip-over save from a corner to preserve parity – gave few clues as to the outcome of Reading's season.

By now there was one date looming ever larger in the diary of every Reading fan – Saturday 3 April 2004, the visit of fellow promotion chasers West Ham United with their new manager Alan Pardew. The Royals warmed up well for that encounter, with consecutive away wins at Cardiff and Coventry City. The victory at

John Salako on the ball against the Blades.

Owusu's delight after scoring his first for the Club.

Sidwell and Hughes battle it out against Sheffield United.

Ninian Park saw maiden goals for Ivar Ingimarsson, Dave Kitson and Dean Morgan, a striker or winger who combined brilliance and inconsistency in equal measure, while the hero at Highfield Road was goalkeeper Jamie Ashdown, whose penalty save

The returning Alan Pardew deep in thought as his Hammers are upended.

reassured Reading fans that the goalkeeper's jersey was in safe hands during Marcus Hahnemann's injury absence.

And so onto Pardew's return. The former boss was sure to receive a frosty reception from the Reading fans who felt let down by the nature of his departure to West Ham six months previously and, although the typically conciliatory Coppell tried to calm the atmosphere by commenting 'May I remind you that Alan Pardew isn't playing. We have 11 fellas in blue-and-white shirts who are playing and they need your support,' the hordes of loyal Royals inside Madejski Stadium paid little heed to their new manager's

words. The atmosphere was electric, and Pardew had to withstand more than his fair share of verbal taunting as he took his place in the visiting team dugout. By the end of the day though, Reading fans were focusing their attention on a new hero – Dave Kitson.

The towering striker had made a quietly impressive start to his Madejski Stadium career, settling into his new surroundings gently by slamming home goal after goal for the reserves. His well-taken goal at Cardiff two weeks previously suggested there was more to come, and now he was ready to make his mark – big time! The game was 35 minutes old, with Reading well on top, when Graeme Murty angled a low ball towards Hammers' penalty area from the halfway line. Veteran defender Andy Melville thought there was no danger

Kitson shields the ball from Christian Dailly.

Murty flies in against Norwich.

Ingimarsson and Hughes chase a race-away Kitson.

and prepared to usher the ball behind for a goal kick, but he had completely misread the situation and allowed Kitson to steal in behind him, stretch out a leg and stab a shot past helpless keeper Stephen Bywater. Kitson was not finished yet, and he made the points safe early in the second half in emphatic style, smashing home an unstoppable volley after James Harper's free kick was half-cleared. After the game Kitson insisted 'The Alan Pardew situation had nothing to do with me whatsoever, I couldn't care less about it. That didn't motivate me. We know how important today was in terms of getting into the play-offs. We were fantastic all over the pitch and thoroughly deserved to win.'

That convincing performance sent Reading into joint-fourth place in an exciting play-off race that saw six teams separated by just one point, but frustratingly – and typically of the Royals' season – it was followed by three games without a win, as Coppell's men lost 2–1 at Bradford, 1–0 at home to promotion-chasing Norwich and drew

Dean Morgan squeezes through West Ham challenges.

1–1 at home with Crewe. That sequence of results put a huge dent in promotion aspirations, but Shaun Goater's only goal at Millwall kept the dream alive as the final two games approached.

The closing home game saw the visit of already-promoted West Bromwich Albion, and Coppell urged one last

Kitson lashes goalwards against West Ham.

effort as he asserted with unusual confidence 'I personally think we will reach the play-offs if we win our remaining two games.' Graeme Murty was awarded the Player of the Year award for the second time in three years before kick-off, and the supporters of both sides generated a fabulous atmosphere as they enjoyed the occasion with 'theme' days – Albion supporters donned horns for their 'Viking day' in honour of their Player of the Season, Thomas Gaardsoe, while

Sidwell heads for the fans after scoring a stunner against West Brom.

Kitson and Sidwell are joined by John Salako and Bas Savage for 'Ginger Day'.

home fans turned out in ginger wigs as they saluted two of the squad's key members, Steve Sidwell and Dave Kitson (although that display of affection was somewhat toned down when Kitson noted that he did not necessarily approve!).

The game itself was a tense, relatively chanceless affair. The Royals knew they had to win to sustain their play-off ambitions but those dreams were fading, as Russell Hoult was given a comfortable afternoon in the visitors' goal…until two minutes from time, when the in-form Sidwell received possession in midfield, surged forward and, with options on either side, decided to shoot from fully 25 yards. His low shot skidded dangerously along the turf and, with Hoult rooted to the spot, zipped into the bottom right-hand corner. It was a memorable moment and kept the Royals' season alive, ensuring they would enter the final game of the season with an outside chance of making the play-offs.

An outside chance it was; to finish in the top six, Reading would have to win and hope that Ipswich lost, while both Sheffield United and Wigan gained no more than a point. It was a tall order and perhaps that lack of genuine belief

A beaming Coppell shakes match-winner Sidwell's hand.

accounted for a real damp squib of a performance in the final game of the campaign against Watford at Vicarage Road. Coppell's team created next to nothing in a game they had to win, and in the end a rising star from the Hornets' youth ranks, Ashley Young, settled the game in his side's favour. It would have mattered little because Ipswich got the point they needed to wrap up the final play-off spot, and the Royals had finished Steve Coppell's first season in charge in ninth position, leaving the manager disappointed with his team's limp effort in that final game. He said 'I don't think there's one outfield player that can come out of the game with credit – Jamie Ashdown made some terrific saves but other than that everyone was below par. It's sad that the last game should be one like this, and the memory will be of this performance rather than when we beat West Brom last week.'

Coppell acted quickly to strengthen his team for the following season, signing Glen Little on a free transfer from Burnley, while fellow winger Paul Brooker saw his loan from Leicester made permanent. On the way out were John Salako, Steve Brown and Kevin Watson, who had all more than played their part in the club's progression, along with Jamie Ashdown, who solved Coppell's goalkeeping conundrum by accepting an offer to join Portsmouth.

Paul Brooker dodges balloons on a mazy run.

2003–04 Coca-Cola Championship – in and around us:

		P	W	D	L	GD	Pts
7	Wigan Ath	46	18	17	11	+15	71
8	Sheffield Utd	46	20	11	15	+9	71
9	**Reading**	**46**	**20**	**10**	**16**	**-2**	**70**
10	Millwall	46	18	15	13	+7	69
11	Stoke City	46	18	12	16	+3	66

Promoted: Norwich City, West Bromwich Albion, Crystal Palace
Relegated: Walsall, Bradford City, Wimbledon

FA Cup: Third round (v Preston North End)
League Cup: Fourth round (v Chelsea)

Top scorer: Shaun Goater (12)

Most appearances: Steve Sidwell (43), Andy Hughes (42), Graeme Murty (37)

Shaun Goater

Coppell in pensive mood.

During the course of his first season at the club, the new Royals boss had already allowed Scott Murray, Nathan Tyson, Darius Henderson and John Mackie to leave, and it was becoming apparent that Coppell was now reshaping the team into his preferred mould, which would be very different from the outfit created by his predecessor, Pardew. Joining Little and Brooker through the 'in' door were central-defender Ibrahima Sonko from Brentford and highly regarded American international wide man Bobby Convey. It was notable that three of the four players signed during the summer were wingers – Coppell was building a team that would be based around width, balance and crosses. There was also an addition to the coaching staff, with the recruitment of former Wimbledon 'Crazy Gang' founder Wally Downes, who would focus on defensive coaching duties.

Preparations for the 2004–05 season got underway in Sweden, where a duo of weak opponents were comfortably beaten and were rounded off with a 4–1 home defeat to Manchester City. Chairman John Madejski was optimistic about the season that lay ahead, commenting 'It is a measure of our progress in recent

Darius Henderson applauds the loyal Royals.

Kitson celebrates scoring Reading's opening goal of the campaign.

years that many people regarded last season's ninth-placed finish, just three points away from the play-off places, as a disappointment. We have very high hopes, and everybody is confident we can mount another strong challenge in the coming months.'

The opening day brought Coppell's former club, Brighton & Hove Albion, to Madejski Stadium after their promotion at the end of the previous season. On a blistering hot summer's day there was an equally blistering start to the campaign when Maheta Molango opened the scoring with the fastest goal scored at Madejski Stadium; he bagged for the visitors after just 10 seconds. But thrillingly, Dave Kitson equalised a minute later. Coppell's side ran out 3–2 winners after goals from James Harper and Nicky Forster, and the season was up and running. A narrow 1–0 defeat at

Alan Pardew's West Ham United was followed by the now customary victory at Sheffield United, courtesy of James Harper's excellent curler, and a 1–0 home win over Rotherham as Kitson netted from the spot to make it three wins from the opening four games.

After dispensing with Oxford in the League Cup, progress was slowed by a controversial 1–0 reverse at Millwall, when the Royals were furious to be denied apparently straightforward penalty decisions on no less than three occasions. The 100 percent home record was maintained with another 1–0 scoreline to Sunderland, this time thanks to Forster's early strike. Skipper Adie Williams was happy with his team's progress: 'It was a great result for us. We had to dig deep and I felt we could have passed the ball better. But we defended well as a unit and

thankfully kept a clean sheet for our third consecutive home victory. If we have aspirations of promotion, it's important that we keep our home record intact for as long as possible.'

That perfect home record was indeed prolonged for a little longer, as Preston and Gillingham were both beaten by three goals to one. The victory over North End was memorable for a brace from their nemesis, Forster, who often seemed to reserve his best performances for the team he had rejected in order to join Reading back in 1999. Coppell was torn between enthusing about his striker's display and lauding the team as a whole, commenting 'People have singled out individual parts of the team for praise recently but I always say that you defend from the front and attack from the back. You can't isolate single areas; if one

Kitson and Forster fast form a lethal pairing.

Shaun Goater controls a bouncing ball.

part of the team is doing well then it must be because everyone is working hard. It's a team effort from everybody.'

Then came 'Watford week' – firstly, a young Hornets outfit gained a comprehensive League Cup victory at Madejski Stadium, but the Royals more than compensated for that loss when they travelled to Vicarage Road for a League rematch four days later on 25 September. Steve Sidwell headed home the only goal of the game to secure the second away win of the season but more importantly to send his team to the summit of English football's second tier for the first time in the Club's history. An emotional captain, Williams, admitted 'I'm speechless really; we had a little huddle at the end because whatever happens we're top of the League. It's Reading Football Club's highest position ever. The lads on the pitch, in the stand and at home should be proud, as well as all the staff and everyone connected to the Club.'

Top spot was sustained with a good point at Ipswich who, despite Shefki Kuqi's 10th-minute opener, dropped their first Portman Road points of the season when Dave Kitson raced onto

Ibrahima Sonko calmly clears.

Owusu soaks up the adulation.

Nicky Forster's throughball and pushed the ball wide of Kelvin Davis on 26 minutes. Days later another point was secured at home against a dour Burnley outfit; the goalless stalemate saw Steve Coppell's side drop their first Madejski Stadium points of the campaign and relinquish their place at the pinnacle of the division.

A 25-yard Nicky Shorey free kick flew past Ed De Goey and separated the sides when the Royals travelled to Stoke at the start of October, and then more than 22,000 piled into Madejski Stadium for the visit of Leeds United. Reading were caught cold early on, as United took the lead in the opening minute – a speculative cross from the right wing was deflected high into the box, where Simon Walton firmly

Lloyd Owusu is mobbed after scoring.

headed the ball inside Marcus Hahnemann's top-right corner. Steadily the hosts grasped control, and parity was restored on the stroke of half time when Dave Kitson nodded Shorey's floating free kick goalwards. Neil Sullivan could only swat his save against the left upright, and substitute Lloyd

Owusu – on for the injured Shaun Goater – was in the right place at the right time to follow up and bundle the ball over the line from close range. 'I think it went in off my knee,' Owusu revealed after the match. 'I poached it. It was a Lloyd Owusu six-yard job!' Reading pressed hard for a winner, but

Dean Morgan uses his pace.

Owusu wheels away after turning home the equaliser against Wigan.

it was Marcus Hahnemann who sealed the point, with an impressive injury-time save from Brian Deane's experienced forehead.

A seven-game unbeaten streak was extended to eight when the Royals welcomed Dario Gradi's Crewe to Madejski Stadium and recorded their biggest victory of the season. An archetypal Steve Sidwell run ended with a typically unstoppable low drive on 21 minutes and, soon after, Kitson bullied his way past Steve Foster in the box to scrappily double the advantage. The third goal was one to behold and came just before half time – defending a Crewe free kick, the Royals' back line produced a tactic known to many as the Sunday-League charge, whereby they all race forward to catch countless clueless frontmen offside. It was timed to

perfection and, having calmly collected the cross, Marcus Hahnemann placed a stunning kick into Andy Hughes' stride down the left flank. Defence had been turned swiftly into counter-attack and, picking out Owusu's barnstorming run into the box, Hughes crossed for the flying frontman to power a diving header high inside the left post. Two minutes after the interval, Ivar Ingimarsson nodded home a fourth, and Reading coasted to three more points.

Owusu grabbed his third goal in as many games, with the opener at Coventry, but Sidwell's clumsy challenge on Stern John minutes later allowed the Sky Blues to level from the spot and clinch a 3–2 win, with second half goals from Andy Morrell and Eddie Johnson.

Skipper Adie Williams had, at the age of 33, been told no decision on a

new contract could be guaranteed before his current deal ran dry in the summer and, as a result, the centre back's name was being circulated. A hamstring injury had already seen the influential captain make way for up-and-coming Senegalese defender Ibrahima Sonko but, with Williams fit again, Coppell had to explain his captain's omission from the squad for the trip to Highfield Road. 'The last time I spoke to Adie was on Thursday night and he said he's agreed everything with Coventry's manager Peter Reid and he was coming here on Friday to have a medical. I intimated that it would be best if he didn't play against us, and that's the last I've heard. Nothing has gone through yet but I believe it will.'

Coventry boss Reid backed that rumour after their win, telling the post-match press 'We've had a chat with him and we're hoping we get his signature. Adie is an organiser and has got vast experience.' And so, just shy of his 400th appearance for the club, Adie Williams left Reading to join the Sky Blues. 'I wish the gaffer all the best and I hope he takes the team into the Premiership,' Williams declared. 'The biggest wrench will be leaving the lads – I could name the whole team but I've become particularly close to Fozzy and Hughesy in the last couple of years, and it will be difficult not to be training with them every day.'

A stirring second half fightback saw Dave Kitson score an injury-time equaliser at Plymouth, and less than a month after securing a 1–0 win at Stoke, the Royals repeated the scoreline at home over the same opposition – Kitson notching the only goal. Cardiff were beaten by Kitson's fifth goal in five – his 12th of the season – scored in the 39th minute, rounding Tony Warner to make it 2–0 after Dean Morgan had squeezed the first inside the near post. Graham Kavanagh was later dismissed for an ugly challenge on Sidwell, and Cameron Jerome's late consolation was not enough to prevent the Royals securing another victory.

A 1–0 defeat at Nottingham Forest suggested that away form was continuing to wane, but the team remained unbeaten at Madejski Stadium, which had begun to welcome bigger crowds each week as the team maintained a lofty League position. A crowd of 22,114 watched Coppell's men hold League leaders Wigan to a

Kingsley races to join in the bundle.

1–1 draw, with Lloyd Owusu making light of Dave Kitson's injury-enforced absence by powering home a 42nd minute equaliser. The demand for the Royals merchandise had grown so much that the club temporarily opened a branch of the Megastore in the town centre, giving Reading a presence in the town that Madejski Stadium, for all its benefits, simply could not offer.

December began with a trip to Molineux, where Wolves were far too strong – Glenn Hoddle's side coasting to a 4–1 win after Colin Cameron had broken the deadlock on the half-hour mark. 'We had a window of opportunity at 2–1 but we gave away two sloppy goals; it was criminal,' a furious Coppell commented. 'We frittered it away with careless errors. I'm a man of few words but most of them begin with f and s at the moment! The only word I can use for our away form is 'embarrassing'. Losing so many games away from home is a pattern we can't accept.'

An injury to skipper Graeme Murty in the defeat at Wolves meant Steve Sidwell was handed the armband for a trip to Leicester, replacing Steve

Hetzke in the history books by becoming Reading's youngest-ever captain. His leadership broke the hoodoo, as Siddy strode onto Glen Little's 68th-minute cut-back to drive an unstoppable 20-yard effort into the top right-hand corner for a brilliant first, before Ivar Ingimarsson glanced a second home to end the dismal sequence of away results.

Back at Madejski, QPR arrived for an early kick-off and the final game before Christmas. Rangers boasted a famous ex-Royal among their squad, and much was made of Jamie Cureton's return to the Stadium he had graced while wearing a different blue-and-white hooped shirt, but his reunion was soured by a bizarre red card. 'The ball was played to me, Siddy called for it and I thought that it was one of my own players, so I let it run,' Cureton explained after the match. 'I looked up and it's Siddy stood there, so for a few seconds I lost my head.' Lashing out with a kick and an arm, the Rangers striker was rightly sent off, and Nicky Shorey's gloriously inch-perfect free kick separated the sides at full time.

Sonko races away to celebrate his first Reading goal on Boxing Day.

Live on Sky, Boxing Day was brilliant. Kicking-off at 11am, the Royals kept their third consecutive clean sheet and fired three past Watford keeper Paul Jones to continue their unbeaten Madejski Stadium record into the new year. Rumours that Adie Williams' departure and Graeme Murty's injury troubles meant Steve Coppell would be searching for defensive cover spurred Ibrahima Sonko into scoring his first for the Club, a towering header to open the scoring after just three minutes. Nicky Forster scampered down the left to supply a cut-back into Sidwell's path for 2–0 and the third

came from Owusu's near-post header on 87 minutes.

Four pages of the matchday programme had been dedicated to printing the names of the near 10,000 season-ticket holders who had broken

Reading's record tally that season, and the resounding victory over the Hornets undoubtedly prompted a vast additional number to snap up the half-season tickets that were on offer for the remainder of the campaign. However,

A jubilant Sidwell is grabbed by Hughes and Kitson.

Nicky Forster rues a missed chance.

2004 ended disappointingly — a humbling 3–0 defeat on a bleak afternoon in Preston was followed by the drabbest of goalless affairs in torrential rain and howling winds at Gillingham on New Year's Day. 'We're not a Jekyll and Hyde team but the results would make it seem that way,' Coppell commented. 'It's not a crisis but there's a question mark in our mind and that can be detrimental long term. We have to respond.' The next fixture brought the season's first defeat at Madejski Stadium, with first half superiority counting for nothing when Derby County stole a 1–0 win courtesy of Tommy Smith's slotted winner on the stroke of half time.

With the talismanic Kitson sidelined through knee ligament damage, Forster a little out of touch and Goater out of favour, Reading were struggling for goals.

To address the issue, Coppell swooped to sign a major star who was looking for one last shot at glory. 'I've played against Reading in pre-season friendlies in the past and always knew it was a developing club,' Les Ferdinand told the Club's official website after signing for the Royals. 'They've come close to making it into the Premiership and they're in that position again now. Hopefully I can come here and give the boost that the team needs to take us all the way.'

On debut, the ex-England striker helped his new side secure an FA Cup replay at Swansea, although it was centre back Ivar Ingimarsson who provided the 88th-minute equaliser, thanks to a quite spectacular right-footed half-volley. A hamstring strain ruled 'Sir Les' out of another goalless encounter with Burnley at Turf Moor, before skipper Murty returned and

Forster bounced off the bench to score the extra time winner in the third-round replay at Vetch Field.

With Kitson and confidence both sadly lacking, Reading had not troubled the scorers for more than 450 minutes of Championship football, when high-flying Ipswich seemed to steal the points with an 89th-minute strike from Darren Bent – Murty was calamitously caught in possession on the edge of his area and Darren Currie rolled a clever pass in to the pacy striker, who gave reams of Royals fans a reason to head for the exits with a cool finish. James Harper picked the ball from the back of the net and raced to the centre circle, refusing to give up on a cause that looked lost. And, almost immediately from the restart, Glen Little chipped a right-sided cross in to Ivar Ingimarsson, who slammed a dramatic half-volley

A delirious Ivar Ingimarsson celebrates a dramatic leveller against Ipswich.

past Kelvin Davis to secure a point in a thrilling finale.

'That finish was all part of the master plan to keep the fans on the edge of their seats!' Coppell joked. 'It would have been cruel to decide the match on a mistake by my captain, Graeme Murty, but I think he's going to donate his bonus to Ivar for getting that late equaliser!' Murts himself was a relieved man, smiling 'I have to say a massive thank you to Ivar for getting me out of jail. I got myself in all sorts of trouble trying to hook the ball over my

head, but it was too close to me and when I saw it go in I was so down. I was praying we could get back into it – it would have been a travesty if we had lost. The way we came back was testament to the character of this team. We've got a lot of leaders out on the pitch.'

Cup football returned in the form of Leicester City's visit to Madejski Stadium, and Ferdinand played his part in a sublime one-two that allowed Forster to fire the Royals into a 10th-minute lead. Sir Les proceeded to miss

an absolute sitter and the game changed. 'It was a cardinal sin; I thought it was in before it actually was. I took my eye off it, it was unprofessional of me, I should have made sure it was in the back of the net,' the striker admitted. Buoyed by that incredible miss, Gareth Williams levelled scrappily on the half-hour mark, and the Royals midfielder Ricky Newman saw red for two yellow cards before Jordan Stewart's left-wing cross was placed past Marcus Hahnemann by James Scowcroft in injury time. On this occasion there was no time to respond

Sir Les nonchalantly salutes the crowd after scoring against Coventry.

and the Foxes crept through to the fifth round.

The following weekend, hosts Reading could not find a way through Plymouth despite dominating, Nicky Forster coming closest with a whipped volley that cannoned off the Pilgrims' crossbar. But with the newly signed Martin Keown – another high-profile Coppell capture – making his debut from the substitutes' bench, the Royals kept a clean sheet to earn a goalless point. David Healy and Rob Hulse then swept Reading aside at Elland Road and, although Ferdinand opened his Reading account with the first against Coventry back at Madejski Stadium in mid-February, Gary McSheffrey and Stern John struck second half goals to gift Adie Williams a winning return to Reading. Reading's promotion push was seriously losing momentum, and the answerless boss remarked:

Eight games ago we were in a great position, now we're probably the worst team in the division. I'm bemused to understand or explain how the team that got us up there is now finding it so difficult to play any kind of composed football. For that second half I can only apologise to the supporters, that's all I can do. If anyone is to be blamed then blame me, I pick the team, it's my fault. I'm not trying to be a martyr, I just want my players to be able to go out there and play. For a reason I can't understand, the players are not expressing themselves the way I know they can. Right now we have no flow.

Hope was provided in Kitson's return to fitness, and after signing a new contract the striker earned a point with an equaliser at Crewe. But two drab goalless affairs followed – at home to Leicester on a snowy Madejski Stadium pitch and at QPR a week later. Reading's post-Christmas winless run had been extended to a season-wilting 11 games, with only seven points claimed from a possible 33. Somehow clinging to sixth spot, Reading welcomed Alan Pardew's seventh-placed West Ham side back to Madejski Stadium for another fiery encounter.

Cometh the hour, cometh the man, and Kitson fired a brilliant hat-trick to end the slide with a memorable 3–1 home win over the Hammers – just as he had scored both goals in the previous season's encounter. Thirteen minutes in, Nicky Shorey's free kick was headed home by Kitson at the far post. Fourteen minutes later he had his second, again a header from a flicked-on Shorey set piece. Any ideas West Ham had of mounting a second half comeback were thwarted when Kitson completed his treble before the hour mark – pouncing on a parried Dean Morgan strike to smash a right-footed effort past Stephen Bywater. Teddy Sheringham grabbed a consolation, but Kitson was again the hero against the Hammers as promotion hopes were reignited and optimism returned to Berkshire.

'This win gives me a nice warm feeling,' admitted a much happier Coppell. 'I had tried to deny it but it was a little bit special for a lot of people today. This result is pointless unless we can push on though. We can enjoy the moment and realise that our hard work paid off in this match, but we travel to Rotherham in midweek and we have to prove we're not just big game players. Rotherham will be hostile, the dressing rooms are always freezing and it's a test the players have to overcome.' They didn't. Away from the glitz of a near-full Madejski Stadium, a total of 3,804 fans filled Millmoor to watch the Royals twice strike the woodwork but devastatingly fall foul to a last-minute winner from Paul Warne for the rock-bottom Millers.

A gutted Coppell had warned against it, but defeat had put his side on the back foot once again: 'The fact we beat West Ham and then lost tonight shows we are a flash in the pan with a soft underbelly. We have proved that. This really hurts me and the players; it's a massive, massive disappointment. We don't deserve to be sixth and the fact we still are is no consolation. Good teams don't lose so much.'

Contract wranglings had contributed to Nicky Forster's omission from recent starting line-ups, but the striker returned to bundle a controversial winner over the line with his hand, only five minutes after replacing Dean Morgan, in a meeting with Brighton at the Withdean. Lloyd Owusu's stiff neck had allowed for Forster's inclusion in the squad, and that goal was to keep the strike star at Madejski Stadium at least until the season's end. He hit the post against Neil Warnock's Sheffield United the following weekend, but despite excellent efforts from Andy Hughes and Steve Sidwell – who had been voted the best player outside of the Premiership in a FourFourTwo magazine poll – the Blades for once avoided a Reading defeat

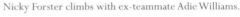

Nicky Forster climbs with ex-teammate Adie Williams.

Forster edges out Chris Morgan to fire at goal.

Teammates surround Fozzy after another fantastic strike.

to inflict the fourth goalless draw upon Madejski Stadium's season.

Reading were still in fifth position though, and a stunning comeback secured a 2–1 home victory over Millwall in midweek. Coppell had signed a new one-year contract before kick-off against the Lions, but for much of the match Daniele Dichio's sublime chip separated the sides. Not until Ingimarsson found Kitson in the middle did Reading draw level with a calmly side-footed 73rd-minute equaliser, and the volume rose as Madejski Stadium sensed three points were up for grabs. Reading reacted and substitute Paul Brooker skimmed down the left, crossed into Forster's path and his sweetly timed header sent the home crowd wild. More importantly it gave the Royals belief – the hosts had not come from behind to win since the opening day victory against Brighton, but with confidence returning Reading managed to repeat that feat thanks to

some inspired substitutions and a late Kitson brace at League leaders Sunderland the following weekend.

The penultimate Madejski Stadium encounter pitted Reading against Nottingham Forest, and a chaotic couple of minutes led to a slender victory that would mean a play-off berth was within sight, with only three games remaining. In the 71st minute of a goal-free encounter, Andy Melville's header back was undercooked and Paul Gerrard had to scamper to the very edge of his area to come and collect it. Les Ferdinand was closing in, so with no time to pick it up within the confines of his penalty box, Gerrard clumsily stumbled out of his area and scrambled the ball away while handling it. Referee Steve Tanner produced an inevitable red card, and substitute keeper Colin Doyle could do little to prevent James Harper stabbing home a loose ball that fell to him from a half-cleared Ferdinand knock down. Three

wins from the closing games would keep the promotion dream alive. But, as it turned out, three defeats seriously spoilt a season that had held so much promise.

First, Peter Thorne sprung the Royals' offside trap to put Cardiff in the lead at Ninian Park, and Cameron Jerome added another. Elsewhere, a late equaliser from Brighton saw West Ham held but Reading dropped to seventh – level on points and goal difference with Alan Pardew's men but behind on goals scored. An interesting side issue to the run-in was Sidwell's attempt to avoid any more yellow cards as he teetered two short of 15 bookings, therefore running the risk of a three-game ban and missing the play-offs. Les Ferdinand's retirement decision was also of interest to Reading fans, who had grown to appreciate his natural talents in between niggling knocks.

Madejski Stadium anticipated one last hurrah from their men, when Glenn Hoddle led 16-game unbeaten Wolves to Berkshire, and Forster scored the last home goal of the season and his last for Reading – a well-struck cushioned volley sailing over Michael Oakes to give the hosts an eighth-minute advantage. Nerves grew and Wolves pressed hard for an equaliser, which arrived eight minutes into the second half. Lee Naylor's corner kick was bundled past Marcus Hahnemann by Leon Clarke, and Martin Keown could do nothing to prevent it crossing the line for 1–1. Wanderers were now on top, and most home fans would have settled for a point. But six minutes from time, even that was

A melee ensues against Leeds.

denied by a wonderful winner from Rohan Ricketts. Sonko was positioned up front as Reading desperately searched for something to take into the last day, and Ferdinand's parting shot almost provided it – his powerful last-gasp strike unfortunately flying straight at Oakes.

Still level on points and goal difference with sixth-placed West Ham, Reading's destiny was not in their own hands and travelling to automatic promotion hopefuls Wigan on the final day was no easy task. 'It's as difficult as they come,' Player of the Season Dave Kitson admitted. 'They need to win to go up and we need to win to get into the play-offs. It's exciting. The way we've played particularly at the start of the season suggests we're certainly a play-off side. But it's all down to one game, one Cup Final and we need to win it.'

In truth, the feeling was that Reading had surrendered a fantastic position in that 11-game post-Christmas slump, and Reading never

looked like upstaging Paul Jewell's Latics to spoil a promotion party that was in full swing by the time Steve Sidwell nodded home an injury time consolation. Lee McCulloch, Jason Roberts and Nathan Ellington had already found paths through Reading's defence to seal their automatic passage into the top flight and force Reading players, staff and fans to witness sickening but deserved Latics celebrations at the JJB.

'I always say you end up where you deserve to,' Coppell philosophised. 'It never looked like it was going to happen today and that's the sad part. Our dressing room is bitterly disappointed. On Boxing Day we were in a great position, then we had a long run without a win and did well to get back into the equation with some good results. Three games ago we had the same points tally as we do now though – and that's the killer blow.' Amid joyous scenes of promoted glee, James Harper applauded the travelling fans at the far end of the JJB scene:

It's horrible, oh my god. Look at all these celebrations going on around us. Last season we went to Watford and missed out on the last day but at least they weren't going for anything. To see their crowd run on the pitch and celebrating is heartbreaking. We'll be feeling low for weeks after this. It all seems like such a waste now, we were top of the League at one stage and we were in the top six for a long time. Missing out now is rubbish. But it won't happen again like this next time, trust me.

The blip had lingered too long and ultimately cost the Royals a shot at promotion to the promised land, but final-day disappointment was magnified by jealousy as Reading watched Wigan's players celebrate achieving something they had yearned for. That experience would be key in spurring the Royals on to an astonishing 2005–06 campaign and an historic rise to prominence.

2004–05 Coca-Cola Championship – in and around us:

		P	W	D	L	GD	Pts
5	Preston NE	46	21	12	13	+9	75
6	West Ham Utd	46	21	10	15	+10	73
7	**Reading**	**46**	**19**	**13**	**14**	**+7**	**70**
8	Sheffield Utd	46	18	13	15	+1	67
9	Wolves	46	15	21	10	+13	66

Promoted: Sunderland, Wigan Athletic, West Ham United
Relegated: Rotherham, Nottingham Forest, Gillingham

FA Cup: Fourth round (v Leicester City)
League Cup: Second round (v Watford)

Top scorer: Dave Kitson (19)

Most appearances: Marcus Hahnemann (46), Nicky Shorey (44), Steve Sidwell (44)

Dave Kitson

ADIE WILLIAMS

Reading appearances: 388 (+8)
Reading goals: 23

Even if he had never played at Madejski Stadium, Adrian Williams would have been regarded as a significant player in the history of Reading Football Club. The local youngster progressed through the youth ranks and made his debut at the age of just 17 in October 1988. He became a regular over the course of the next few seasons, showing an impressive versatility that allowed him to set a bizarre record by wearing every shirt number from one to 11 (he had a brief spell in goal as substitute to replace the injured Steve Francis at Chester in 1991). Eventually he settled on the centre half position and played a key role as Mark McGhee's team stormed to the Division Two title in 1993–94 before reaching the following season's Division One play-off final. By that

time he had been adorned with club skipper status, and he had memorably scored the second goal of the Wembley Final against Bolton that ended in a heartbreaking 4–3 defeat in extra time.

The following summer of 1996 the Wales international (through his father) was signed by Wolverhampton Wanderers for £750,000, and a local hero's Reading career had come to an end. Or so we thought. Adie retained close ties with both the Club and the area, and it was no great surprise when, out of favour at Wolves after recovering from serious injury problems, he was re-signed on loan by Alan Pardew towards the end of the 1999–2000 season. By now the club had rehoused itself at Madejski Stadium, but Williams instantly felt at home and scored the only goal of the game to defeat Brentford in only his fifth game back.

The transfer was duly made permanent, but the following season Williams was struck by the injury problems that had dogged his stay at Molineux, and he managed just seven first team appearances as the team lost out in the play-off final to Walsall. He was back to fitness for the 2001–02 campaign though, and played a major role in the team's march to automatic promotion – especially with a series of dominant performances during a run of seven consecutive clean sheets midway through the season. Back in Division One and desperate for another shot at promotion to the top flight, Adie succeeded close friend Phil Parkinson as club captain but suffered more play-off agony at the end of 2002–03, seeing his team suffer a narrow semi-final defeat to his former club, Wolves.

On reflection, the surprisingly high number of defensive partners that played alongside Adie during his second spell at the club demonstrates the consistency of his presence throughout the side's ongoing development under Alan Pardew and then Steve Coppell. He partnered Barry Hunter and Linvoy Primus during the latter stages of the 1999–2000 season, before they both departed to be replaced by a combination of two more Adrians – Viveash and Whitbread. They were soon supplemented by John Mackie then Matthew Upson on loan and then Steve Brown. Finally, following Pardew's departure and Coppell's arrival, Adie was joined in the heart of the defence by the new manager's first signing, Ivar Ingimarsson. That's a total of eight partners for Williams, who remained a reliable constant throughout that occasionally turbulent period.

Adie was certainly regarded as 'one of us' by loyal Royals, who no doubt appreciated the fact that his presence in the squad provided a tangible link between the all-new Madejski Stadium and the Elm Park era. But his popularity with supporters was based on far more than mere longevity. He wore his heart on his sleeve and had bucketloads of the passion that supporters love to see. Despite setting that unusual record of playing in every position, he was first and foremost a defender in the old-fashioned sense of the word – ball might pass, man might pass, but never both together. That is not to suggest he was dirty – far from it – but he was a fully committed and wholehearted defender who would clear the ball first and ask questions later. His thumped clearances over the South Bank roof were legendary and he occasionally seemed determined to

set the record for the first man to kick a ball out of Madejski Stadium, too. He was also a clever player who used all the tricks in the trade to get under the skin of opposing strikers. When asked if he could be filmed by a 'player cam' throughout the duration of one match for the Club's website, he politely declined because he preferred not to have all his antics exposed in such close-up detail.

As his career tally of 23 Reading goals demonstrates, Williams also presented a significant attacking threat from set pieces – and, although the vast majority of his goals were standard issue centre half headers, he did record one beautifully dinked left-footed chip to beat Paddy Kenny in a memorable victory at Sheffield United in February 2003. By coincidence his last Reading goal also came at Bramall Lane, and although his routine header from a corner in October 2003 was somewhat overshadowed by Nicky Forster's 30-yard Goal of the Season in the same game, it still forms a minor footnote in Reading FC history as the opening goal in Steve Coppell's first away win as manager.

Williams finally lost his place in the team to Ibrahima Sonko in the autumn of 2004 and, deciding that he did not want his playing career to meander to a halt by sitting on the bench, he joined Coventry in pursuit of first team football. The final stop of his career was Swindon Town, where he was also given the opportunity to begin his coaching career. At heart he remains a Reading man through and through. He still keeps a season ticket at Madejski Stadium, and it would be no great surprise if he returns to the Royals in a coaching capacity at some point in the future.

England Expects...

Young England followers flock to Madejski Stadium.

Madejski Stadium's calibre as a modern, attractive, accessible and accommodating footballing venue was soon identified by the Football Association, and Reading were approached when the authorities were seeking out a home for a scheduled England under-21 clash with Luxembourg in September 1999. For the first time it brought together a gaggle of FA co-ordinators with the stadium's staff organisers, and the evening went swimmingly. More than 18,000 watched Steven Gerrard score on his under-21 debut in a 5–0 thumping of the international minnows.

Come August 2001 David Platt began his reign as England under-21 boss, with a majestic 4–0 win over the Dutch in front of 19,467 at Madejski Stadium. In an all-Premiership starting XI, seven of the line up would go on to represent the senior England side with differing levels of success – John Terry and Gareth Barry have captained the Three Lions since, while David Dunn and Francis Jeffers only managed 45

David Platt occupies the dugout.

England manager Sven stands alongside national boss-to-be Steve McClaren.

minutes against Portugal and Australia respectively. Dirk Kuyt was one of the famous names providing the opposition, while a very young Arjen Robben came off the bench to strike the crossbar and alert many to his fledgling talents. Darius Vassell wowed the Berkshire crowd with a booming 25-yard left-footed piledriver that fizzed into the top-right corner to break the deadlock, but his second half replacement, Jermain Defoe, bagged a brace to steal the show. Malcolm Christie added his name to the score sheet too, and England had stumbled across a potentially lucky venue. The watching Sven Goran Eriksson, sat in the stands, must have been pleased with what he saw.

Little more than a year later in October 2002 England's youngsters returned for a competitive under-21 European Championship qualifier with Macedonia, and a similarly convincing victory was secured courtesy of a Jeffers hat-trick. 'It's a good venue,' manager David Platt said before kick-off. 'The crowd for the friendly against Holland last year was an exceptional one and the players like that – playing with an atmosphere that they're used to at their clubs. I wouldn't be going back so soon if I didn't think it was a very good venue for us. It's a new ground, it's got good access for the supporters and I think that showed with the turnout last year.'

Chairman John Madejski hosted Sven once again and also met World

Chairman John Madejski meets Sven Goran Eriksson and Luis Felipe Scolari.

England's women battle hard against Nigeria.

Michael Owen is closely guarded in the box.

Aaron Lennon on the run.

Cup-winning manager Luis Felipe Scolari, while Michael Carrick, Jermaine Jenas, Joe Cole and Shaun Wright-Phillips all played a part on the pitch. It was Arsenal's 'fox in the box' Jeffers who impressed though. Neither the lack of quality provided by the opposition nor a swirling autumnal wind prevented 15,538 people from turning up for a 3–1 win.

It was not long before Reading players were featuring in England shirts at their home ground. On 6 February 2003 Nathan Tyson treated a record crowd – 16,820 – in an under-20 international with two goals, including a match-winning brace on debut – a stunning left-footed wonder strike that sparked gleeful celebrations around his home ground. 'It was absolutely fabulous,' a beaming Tyson commented. 'I scored two goals, won us the game and I'm just very pleased. It was a great debut for me and a great night for the fans as well. I don't know how I got here, now I just want more international games!'

Tyson pumped up on home turf.

Nathan Tyson rises to the occasion.

Lita dons the England shirt in front of his home fans.

England's women also staged a friendly at Madejski Stadium – losing 3–0 to Nigeria in front of more than 4,000 supporters in April 2004. Then the under-21s returned to Madejski Stadium to face Norway in February 2006, with Reading streaking clear at the top of the Championship thanks in part to strike sensation Leroy Lita. Featured by the FA in the matchday programme, Lita was named on the bench, but he strode out onto his home turf as a half time replacement for James Milner, receiving a great reception from the healthy but freezing cold home crowd. Peter Taylor's men recorded a comfortable 3–1 win, with two goals from David Bentley and a third from Peter Whittingham.

Sadly, Nicky Shorey's England B bow came one year too late to feature in the World Cup warm-up for Sven Goran Eriksson's B line up that May. Ahead of such a major competition, this Madejski-based event was one of the highest profile games staged at the stadium. Bizarrely, England lost to the 10 men of Belarus and the venue relinquished its 100 percent record, but with so many big-named internationals on show, the match served as an ideal opportunity to see some of the stars that Reading would come up against in their upcoming inaugural top-flight season. Michael Owen, Sol Campbell and Ashley Cole proved they were fit for the trip to Germany, surprise pick Theo Walcott debuted to a rapturous reception, Aaron Lennon electrified the 22,032-strong crowd with some world-class runs but Robert Green's World Cup dream ended with a ruptured groin that dramatically led to the Belarussian's equaliser.

Local lad Theo Walcott warms up for his surprise trip to the World Cup.

Chapter 7

Title Glory

It is strange to recall that the greatest season of success ever witnessed at Reading Football Club began with a dispiriting Madejski Stadium anti-climax, with defeat coming courtesy of a last-gasp Plymouth Argyle winner. At that time, few would have believed that the Royals' record for the rest of the season would remain virtually unblemished – but it did and Reading made history.

'The realistic ambition is a play-off place. Anything less than that will be judged as failure,' was Steve Coppell's honest opinion in pre-season. 'I have to face that fact. Everybody has to progress. I have to become a better manager. I'm the one who's got to drive the ship, and given an even break in the weather I think we'll be ok. We all have to have that desire to improve. If you're standing still you're losing ground. I've done a lot of years and a lot of games but I'm still desperate to

Leroy Lita, Reading's first £1 million man, on his debut.

Kevin Doyle soon became the signing of the season.

Shane Long would make his impact.

Brynjar Gunnarsson became a key cog in Reading's machine.

Livewire Irishman Stephen Hunt was a great addition.

compete at the highest level. I want to be as good a manager as I can be.'

The seeds Steve Coppell's scouting network had planted so carefully were about to bear fruit. Many months and a great deal of mileage had been invested in unearthing previously undiscovered talent that would catapult Reading over what was consistently dubbed the biggest gap to bridge in the footballing pyramid and, in a few successful summer weeks, key characters joined the Royals' ranks.

John Madejski was asked to write a seven-figure transfer cheque for the first time when Leroy Lita became the Club's record £1 million signing, switching from Bristol City in July. The speedy strike star's arrival somewhat overshadowed the earlier capture of two young unknown Irishmen, both of

whom were to make their names in emphatic style at Reading; Kevin Doyle and Shane Long had barely begun their football careers when Steve Coppell snatched the duo from Cork City for next to nothing in June. The fees were minimal but the true value of their signings and those of Stephen Hunt (Brentford), Brynjar Gunnarsson (Watford), John Oster (Burnley) and Chris Makin (Leicester) would be realised as a memorable season unfolded.

There were also a few departures – Shaun Goater ended his contract, Nicky Forster made the move to Ipswich and Andy Hughes also left for East Anglia (Norwich) a day before the rest of the squad travelled to Sweden for another Scandinavian pre-season schedule. Ricky Newman and Paul Brooker joined Lloyd Owusu in a move to Brentford, and the old guard who had signed for a six-month impact also exited – Martin Keown joining Leicester and Les Ferdinand quietly hanging up his prestigious playing boots.

A shuffled squad reassembled and returned to action in the form of three friendly trips to non-League teams. Dave Kitson bagged a first half hat-trick at Staines, and Kevin Doyle was in the goals when scoring his first two Reading strikes at Didcot. Roman Motyczak, a readingfc.co.uk competition winner, also got a run out as an 81st-minute substitute for Dean Morgan at Loop Meadow, stealing the show somewhat with a light-hearted cameo in the navy blue away strip. Defeat at Farnborough preceded the squad's outbound journey to Sweden,

where three victories against lowly opposition prepared Reading for a final curtain-raiser against Tottenham Hotspur upon their return. Jermain Defoe and Mido refused to allow Marcus Hahnemann a happy return from Gold Cup success, which he earned with Bruce Arena's United States side, with Spurs winning 2–0 but Reading promising much for the season ahead.

Critically, the new faces settled quickly. Long and Doyle were repeatedly described as 'low maintenance' – the pair seamlessly blending into their new surroundings on and off the pitch – while Lita opened his account with a hat-trick in the 6–0 thrashing of Swedish minnows Eneryda, before netting two more days later at Holmalunds. 'I was brought here to score goals and hopefully I can

start as I mean to go on,' the England under-21 international said before Plymouth tripped to Berkshire to open another Championship campaign. And he did, but Reading didn't. Graeme Murty collected a quick free kick from Bobby Convey and whipped the ball to the new striker, who nodded past Romain Larrieu from six yards – but that only levelled matters; Micky Evans had stunned the home support by touching home Rufus Brevett's low cross to give Bobby Williamson's side a first half lead. And despite Reading's desire to start the season on the front foot, Paul Wotton's mishit drive fell perfectly into Nick Chadwick's path, and the substitute scrambled the ball past Marcus Hahnemann to pilfer all three opening afternoon points.

'It was promising without being convincing, and at the end it was

Celebrations after Lita opens his Royals account with Reading's first goal of the season.

massively disappointing. To come away having lost, you feel more pressure,' the Royals boss reflected at full time. 'The desire is certainly there but we've got to maintain the discipline and tightness we had last year while also trying to score more goals.' Lita meanwhile revealed 'They came here for a draw and their players said afterwards that it's criminal they've come away with three points. They can't believe it, they're delighted! Winning on Tuesday at Brighton is the only way to put it right.'

Tricky wing star Glen Little had set up a number of goals in his first season as a Royal, but he had not found the back of the net until a pre-season trip to Farnborough ended the long-running 'drought' jibe. His swirling free kick heralded the opener at the Withdean days later, and Kitson added a second to start a streak that would soon become the talk of the town. Basking in his new-found goalscoring form, Little promptly doubled his account with the third – a header – at Preston. A stunning Lita double secured a confident 3–0 victory against an outfit Coppell rightly tipped to be 'up at the sharp end' come the end of the campaign. Belief was back and suddenly Reading were brimming with confidence; confidence that was showcased when Reading returned to Madejski Stadium to simply sweep Millwall aside.

In the same way Glen Little had taken time to open his Royals account,

his left-sided wing colleague also chose to break his Reading duck early in the 2005–06 campaign. Only six minutes in, an inswinging corner was calmly cleared and Lita won the scraps with an aerial challenge on the edge of his own box, flicking the ball into Bobby Convey's path. The US international sped off the shoulder of the first Millwall man and skipped neatly around a desperate lunge from another to race into an unguarded half and

gracefully sidefoot wide of Andy Marshall to give Steve Coppell's side the lead. The midfielder's composure was something to behold, and in stark contrast to the excited high-pitched tones yelled down the microphone by a local radio commentator, only dogs could hear BBC Berkshire's Tim Dellor come the end of the nippy Philadelphian's virtuoso goal!

And in Little's mould, Convey's first opened the floodgates – his second

arrived just 19 minutes later when a left-footed free kick squirmed its way through the Millwall wall and past defender Mark Phillips on the line. Phillips had just strapped Marshall's gloves to his palms after the Lions keeper, trying to atone for a poor clearance, had been rightly dismissed for parrying Lita's snapshot outside his area. Phillips was to see two more fly past him before the break, as Reading ran riot – James Harper's tame but well-placed header found the top-left corner, and ex-Royal Sammy Igoe handballed inside his box to allow Kitson to convert from the spot. Phillips happily handed the goalkeeping duties to the more agile Adrian Serioux in the second half, but the dreadlocked substitute could not prevent Steve

Sidwell adding a fifth with a stooped header. Five goals to nil and Reading were top of the League.

Bizarrely, that five-goal stroll was to prove less significant in the long term than the following home game, when hard-to-beat Burnley were the visitors to Berkshire. Lita had improvised to flick Kitson's scrambled reverse pass high into the net for a seventh-minute opener, but in a matter of moments three key players picked up a trio of injuries that would have dethroned the threadbare Royals squad in previous campaigns. Kitson landed awkwardly to jar his ankle, Nicky Shorey suffered a recurrence of a knee problem and then Sidwell hobbled painfully away from a stretch into a challenge. Kitson could not run

it off, Shorey only lasted until half time and, although Sidwell limped on to the end, he would not return to first team action for two crucial months. Burly Burnley notched an equaliser through Ade Akinbiyi before the break to make matters worse, but cometh the hour cometh the men. Kevin Doyle was Kitson's replacement, and the unknown Irishman scored his first for the club by nodding home Convey's inswinger from a short corner to present his new side with the bank holiday Monday win. Chris Makin stepped flawlessly into Shorey's shoes and Brynjar Gunnarsson was to write his own headlines as Sidwell's understudy, and suddenly Coppell's squad boasted a new-found strength in depth.

Doyle wheels away having scored his first professional goal – the winner against Burnley.

Remaining unbeaten on the road with points at Watford and Coventry, Madejski Stadium rocked when recently relegated Crystal Palace arrived to challenge for spoils on a pulsating Tuesday night in September. For sheer drama, many lauded the victory as one of the greatest games ever seen at the stadium. Its impact on Reading's season was undeniable. Doyle sparked it all off; allowed to turn 40 yards out, he scampered away from an early challenge and, as the Eagles' back four backed away, the Irishman coolly cut inside onto his left foot and arrowed an excellent low drive beyond the baggy grey tracksuit bottoms of Gabor Kiraly in the Palace goal. Andy Johnson's pace took him past Makin to equalise only minutes later, and soon after the interval Clinton Morrison stabbed home Darren Ward's knockdown and somehow Palace were leading. But an attacking encounter was only going to get even better.

Leroy Lita had already announced his arrival at Reading with some spectacular goals but none as outrageous as his 68th-minute equaliser – the £1 million man patiently waited for Emmerson Boyce's skied header to fall at the far post, timed his leap and sweetly scissored a stunning overhead shot past Kiraly for 2–2! 'Goals mean so much to strikers and how can you stop spontaneity? Do you want me to run on and tell him to keep his shirt on?' Steve Coppell commented after the match, following Lita's pumped-up celebration that saw him cautioned for passionately whipping off his shirt and circling the blue-and-white hoops above his head as he bulleted towards the bench in joy. 'When the crowd's erupting like that, it's human instinct,' the boss continued. 'It's fashionable and trendy now to do that kind of thing. I scored some goals as a player and I think, if it had been put in my mind's eye, I probably would have taken my shirt off too. I had the body to show for it then as well!'

The goal-hungry strike star soon had his jubilation tempered. Lita snatched possession of the ball and, with it, penalty-taking rights after Boyce had clumsily tripped Doyle in the box, but Kiraly palmed the in-form

Lita stuns Palace with an audacious overhead equaliser to remember.

with John Oster's cross to scramble a far-post header over the line for the only goal of a much less eventful encounter. More importantly the towering twosome had formed a rock-solid pairing at the heart of Reading's defence – one that proceeded to keep clean sheets against newly demoted Norwich and Southampton before the visit of high-flying Sheffield United on the opening day of October. If Doyle had starred in Kitson's absence, another unsung hero flourished in the limelight to deny a furious Neil Warnock the points – Brynjar Gunnarsson opened the scoring with a well-taken finish from Little's corner in the second minute of the top-of-the-table clash. Steve Kabba soon nodded home an equaliser, and with the score locked at 1–1 two

frontman's spot kick clear…only for referee Mr Curson to demand a retake after ruling the Hungarian had edged too far off his line. Glen Little was awarded the second bite at the cherry but again, this time legitimately, Kiraly saved. Amid chaotic scenes, a livid Iain Dowie was sent to the stands for his penalty protests – his gesticulations further fuelling the feverish Madejski Stadium atmosphere. It would have been wrong for such an eventful contest to end in a point apiece, so it was apt when Ibrahima Sonko kindly placed a powerful forehead on Little's 87th-minute inswinging free kick, celebrating by leaping into Wally Downes' waiting arms on the touchline. 'The performance was not inspired by anything other than two

good teams, the occasion, a lovely evening and two very vociferous sets of fans,' a down-to-earth Coppell said.

Sonko's central-defensive partner was the goal hero against Crewe four days later. Ivar Ingimarsson connected

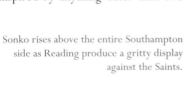

Sonko rises above the entire Southampton side as Reading produce a gritty display against the Saints.

Doyle challenges for the ball against the Blades.

strange refereeing decisions evened themselves out. Paddy Kenny only received yellow when he was rushed into fielding an under-hit header and handled outside his area. But in the second half Keith Gillespie was aghast at being denied a penalty when he tripped over James Harper's late challenge. Salt in Warnock's wound arrived in the form of big Icelander Gunnarsson, who strode into the area to glance on-loan Lens midfielder Sekou Baradji's inswinging free kick low inside the far post to cap a thrilling finish.

'We haven't practised that specific set piece but I got a bit of space and managed to get on the end of it,' Gunnarsson recalled. 'It was very

tough, both physically and mentally. We were under pressure and had to deal with it, but towards the end they looked a bit tired and we got back into the game. At the moment we are very confident – the last six games have been a very tough period and we haven't lost a game. And we will have an even stronger squad when the injured players come back.'

Although the impending international break was well received by the players, the fans just wanted to see the momentum Reading had gathered continue. After the break Nicky Forster returned to Madejski Stadium in Ipswich colours, telling the matchday programme 'I received lots of good luck letters from Reading fans when I joined Ipswich, and that was very nice. Players come and go in this game, and

Last gasp heroics from Gunnarsson crucially defeat and deflate Sheffield United.

Convey joins Doyle in celebrating a win over Ipswich.

I suppose for someone to stay at one club for six years is quite a long time these days. I thoroughly enjoyed my time with Reading and got on well with the fans. I gave my all for Reading and I hope there is a mutual appreciation from the supporters.' He was welcomed, but there was no room for sentimentality as his club were soundly trounced. Richard Naylor scored past his own goalkeeper and Doyle powered the meddlesome Little's sumptuous cross home for a second soon after the break, but in truth it could have been many more, as Reading tore Ipswich apart. From back to front, the Royals oozed conviction – Doyle and Lita both

struck the woodwork at one end and Ibrahima Sonko epitomised the Royals' defiance at the other by courageously blocking a fearsome Adam Proudlock volley with his head. In slow-motion replays, the block looked more impressive and chants of 'Sonko is

Superman' began to ring around Madejski Stadium's stands for the first time. Such a dominant display, broadcast to a wider audience courtesy of Sky's Sunday afternoon cameras, started murmurings about potential promotion.

Kingsley soaks it all up.

A point at Hull, and Kitson's spot kick winner at Stoke meant Reading needed to avoid defeat when Leeds visited Madejski Stadium at the end of October to equal their best-ever unbeaten run in a 134-year-long history; a 17-game Division Four streak without defeat was the one they were hoping to match. Shorey and Kitson were back – the latter in time to cover for Lita's ankle knock – and Sidwell returned to the bench, so Coppell's injury hindrances were lessening and had been minimal while in effect. Gunnarsson signed off his stint as Siddy's deputy with the opening goal of the game against Leeds, racing in to collect a low corner, take a touch and drive low inside the near post for a simple but stunning finish on the hour. Substitute David Healy stole a leveller

after pouncing on a heavy touch from Ingimarsson and profiting from a wicked deflection off the Icelander, but the Royals record was matched and then broken with a comfortable 2–0 Madejski Stadium win over Sheffield Wednesday three days later. Bigger records were to be smashed as the season unfurled.

Without boasting arrogance, winning was becoming par for the course for Steve Coppell's unstoppable outfit. Hull threatened briefly to steal a point from their trip to Berkshire, only for Reading to characteristically slide into another gear and fire two in two minutes – the second was a stunning counter-attack started and tidily finished by Little. Kingsley promptly received his first clattering as Little's windmill arms spiralled into the

mascot in front of a jubilant North Stand. Days later, Reading topped the table after another imperious performance sealed a 3–0 win at Ipswich. Steve Coppell, of course, remained the calming influence. 'You tell me that we're top, but I wasn't aware of that,' he informed the press. 'All we are trying to do is win games. We haven't been chasing anyone, it's not part of our psyche to try to chase or get away from anyone. Just stick the next game in front of us and we'll try to win it. People may think I'm putting a dampener on things, but it really means nothing to me at this stage of the season.' Then came one of the lines that would become a Coppell favourite in post-match analyses: 'We don't want the highlight of our season to be in November.' The down-to-earth boss

Skipper and strike star embrace.

Kitson salutes the crowd after another comprehensive win over Brighton.

would reiterate that way of thinking for months to come, even though Reading began to race away with the division in a manner that very few had ever done before.

The squad's strength had been evident in a Carling Cup campaign that saw a shuffled pack claim victories over Swansea City (in extra time), Luton Town and then promotion rivals Sheffield United – Kitson bagging a brace to upset Neil Warnock further. Those wins earned Reading a plum fourth-round tie at Arsenal. For the first time since the opening day loss to Plymouth, Reading tasted defeat, but the players had savoured a taste of top-flight football and had played a part in Highbury's farewell season. After Little's special 25-yard lob at Plymouth had given Reading some revenge over their opening day conquerors, the Royals returned to Madejski Stadium to dispose of Luton. 'Anybody who's got money on them can cash their chips in,' Hatters boss Mike Newell boldly claimed. On the flipside, Coppell was still praying the post-Christmas slump that ruined their previous season would not repeat itself.

As the festive season approached, half-season tickets began to sell in droves as an area of England somewhat starved of top-class football sensed the

Shane Long comes to the party with a last gasp equaliser at Derby.

Premier League might become a real possibility. Nobody wanted to miss out and as a frantic festive period got underway, crowds quickly built to regularly reach something approaching capacity for the first time in the stadium's history. Reading responded emphatically. Kitson struck a second half hat-trick as five were fired past a luckless Brighton, who started the rot with an own-goal before being reduced to 10 men and conceding a penalty six minutes after the break. 'The Reading people need to have a look at themselves,' a bitter Mark McGhee snapped. 'They sat there quiet for an hour and didn't get behind their team other than giving me some stick.' Despite finding themselves 17 points clear of third-placed Watford, Coppell again deadened the furore:

We don't mention the 'P' word. I never look at the table – but I'm aware of the gap because everyone keeps telling me! I don't want to look at the table because it can affect the way you do things. You end up tailoring what you do depending on the opposition, and we can't do that. I read the reports in the newspapers and look at the team line-ups, who's played where and done what, but I never look at the table. When I took Palace up I used to study the tables, so this is a fresh invention!

Consecutive 2–0 wins at Millwall and then Wolves on Boxing Day preceded a 2–0 home win over Leicester. Doyle was proving a revelation, netting his 10th of the season against the Foxes, and he was joined by former Cork colleague Shane Long for his debut late in the game. Long then scored a last-gasp equaliser as a substitute on New Year's Eve at Derby to dramatically keep Reading's unbeaten run going into 2006 and up to an early January meeting with Cardiff. For the third, and not the last, occasion in the season Reading scored five. In front of a 22,668 home crowd, Coppell's stars turned on the style – another Kitson brace adding to headed efforts from Sidwell (twice) and Sonko as the Bluebirds became the latest side to be dismantled by an unstoppable Royals team.

It was magnificent to watch the confidence flow throughout the side. 'It's unbelievable, 28 games unbeaten!'

Convey and ex-Royal Andy Hughes track the ball in another Royals rout.

Kitson remarked after scoring twice in the next win, a 2–0 success over Adie Williams' Coventry. 'The longer it goes, the less we want to relinquish it. I've forgotten what being beaten feels like…it's incredible. Every time we go forward I think we can score. Bobby Convey said to me the other day that he goes out and waits for us to score, because he knows it's going to happen. That's the attitude through the whole team. We just keep doing the right things, and we know eventually it will drop in the right place.'

Former Royal Williams himself was impressed, noting 'They're at the top of the League and they have a swagger about them.' The swagger was evident in Leroy Lita's celebrations after he shocked West Brom with a brilliant hat-trick, knocking the two-goals-up Premier League outfit out of the FA Cup in a feverish midweek replay. His second goal rivalled Little's sublime chip at Plymouth and even his own overhead spectacular against Crystal Palace in the Goal of the Season stakes, as the frontman swept a powerful 25-yard shot

into the top-left corner of stunned Chris Kirkland's goal to help set up a fourth round encounter with Birmingham.

Despite eventually bowing out of the Cup after a tight replay at St Andrew's, the Royals had more than matched two sets of Premier League opponents, and Steve Coppell's side seemed unbeatable in the League. Lita had returned from ankle problems in time to cover for a hamstrung Kitson and score in a 4–0 thrashing of Andy Hughes' hapless Norwich side, and four more were dealt up in a win at Crewe before a dogged Southampton visited Madejski Stadium on a Friday night. The evening atmosphere was electric – fans understandably anticipated a football exhibition, and they took to their seats fully expecting victory. The 11 men on the pitch did not disappoint; Little embarrassed Nathan Dyer by mugging him of possession at left back and drilling a low cross to Lita, who finished at the far post, and then Doyle capitalised on some ponderous defending to fizz a 20-yard effort inside the near post for a second before the

break. Lion-hearted Sonko had turned down a trip to Egypt for Senegal's African Nations Cup campaign, and he shrugged off a knee injury to battle through the full game and keep another clean sheet as Sky Sports' cameras again showcased Reading's prowess.

There was no love lost on Valentine's Day when a missed Kitson penalty in the final minutes meant Reading had to settle for a feisty point at second-placed Sheffield United, and an astonishing 33-game unbeaten run finally ended in a 3–2 defeat at Luton three days later – the one and only League loss Reading would suffer on the road all season. Sven Goran Eriksson had announced his England end would arrive after the summer's World Cup campaign, and Steve Coppell's name was loosely linked with the vacant role. His focus was on one thing and one thing alone: 'We've got another very important game next week,' he remarked. 'Tonight's defeat is just a game in isolation. It's got nothing to do with the end of a run. We lost a game tonight and it hurts. Does it hurt any more because it's been a long time? No, it just hurts. A footballer thrives on winning games and when they get beaten it's a kick in the groin.'

Preston North End were enjoying a 22-game unbeaten League run themselves but Reading's vow to bounce back from defeat brought the Lilywhites' streak to an abrupt halt. Steve Sidwell scored just six minutes in, but Callum Davidson somehow squeezed a free kick inside the left upright to level only moments later.

Lita delights in his opener against Saints.

Dave Kitson had to retire hurt after a hefty collision with visiting keeper Carlo Nash, but his replacement bagged the winner – Leroy Lita latching onto Doyle's through ball to stroke a well-placed effort home before the break. Two miserly defences held firm for the second half and, as second-placed Sheffield United were beaten elsewhere, the Royals were back on track, 12 points clear at the top. 'There were some very hurt players after the defeat last week and we were disappointed that it took eight days until another game came around. We just wanted to get back on the pitch and put right what had gone wrong,' Coppell stated. 'We showed a lot of character and determination today. Losing Kits was a massive blow, but then you've got someone like Leroy coming on who slots one away from such a tight angle. No one could catch him when he ran off celebrating – he's so quick.'

Lita's impact had not gone unnoticed elsewhere. The striker had been selected for England's under-21 team and earned praise from boss Peter Taylor after playing his part in a 3–1 win over Norway in an international held at Madejski Stadium. But his impressive season was to come to an early end at Burnley in March when, shaping to shoot, his standing ankle gave way underneath him and snapped. Bobby Convey's stunning 10th-minute top-corner strike set up another comfortable 3–0 win at Turf Moor, and although the win in Lancashire had mathematically guaranteed Reading at least a play-off place, Lita's loss was going to be considerable. His absence was all too evident in a goalless home draw with Watford the following weekend but, coupled with a point when Wolves visited in mid-March, Reading were edging closer to the top flight with every game.

Victory at Leicester on Saturday 25 March would seal Premier League football at Reading for the first time ever, regardless of results elsewhere. 'It's a little bit of a pity that the first game we can do it is away from home,' a greedy Doyle admitted. 'It would be nicer to do it at our place. But we won't argue too much! For the last couple of months we've been told we're only a couple of wins away, but now we mathematically know we only need three more points. Hopefully we'll do it as soon as possible – maybe if we win our next two games we can get the title at home to Derby! I don't know the exact maths for that though.' He did

know the maths and Reading timed it to perfection. The Irishman's 85th-minute equaliser at the Walker's Stadium was immaterial in the grand scheme of things; Leeds had been held to a goalless draw at Stoke and Watford were beaten by Millwall, so after a few eerie moments in an emptying Walker's Stadium the news broke – Reading, 20 points clear of third place, were promoted. History had been made.

Due to the London Irish St Patrick's Day fixture and contractual issues, the game could not be beamed back to Madejski Stadium and, without taking anything for granted, fans were told before the match that the players would not be returning to Madejski Stadium regardless of the result in Leicester. So, although the party began in and around a vibrant Reading town centre, the main celebrations were patiently and somewhat aptly saved for an unforgettable title-winning afternoon one week later.

The scene was set and another memorable afternoon added an historic chapter to Reading's fairytale season. Terry Westley's struggling Derby side arrived with intent but departed almost unnoticed. There never seemed any doubt that Reading would win, even though the Rams held firm for almost an hour. Then the stadium witnessed arguably its most devastating half an hour of attacking football, starting when James Harper pounced upon Kitson's return backheel to end Derby's resistance and send the home fans wild with a 12-yard stab that gave Reading the lead. Those listening to score updates on their personal radios had reason to report that this might be the title-winning day; Josip Skoko's goal had awarded Stoke an early lead against Sheffield United, meaning a win would be enough for the Royals to clinch top spot.

Six minutes later, Little released Convey down the right and Doyle obliged by heading the American's inch-perfect cross past Lee Camp for a second goal. The game was won when Coppell introduced Stephen Hunt and John Oster – more for sentimental reasons you felt, as everyone begged to savour some of the atmosphere – but both came to the party in style, with Oster placing home Hunt's low cross with his first touch of the game. Just when you did not think it possible, it got better. The third substitute, Shane Long, wasted no time in adding his name to the score sheet, connecting with Graeme Murty's excellent cross to thump a powerful header into the back of the net for four. That afternoon, Coppell was blessed with the 'midas touch' – everything he touched turned to gold. And when Long demonstrated that fact with his fine finish, a grinning Coppell strode purposefully towards the pitch to celebrate with an understated but undeniable (and now almost indescribable) finger click. It was a moment of spontaneous emotion only previously seen from Coppell in a joyous leap at Wembley, sparked by Ian

The title is sealed with a 5–0 thrashing of Derby.

Wright's goal that helped his Crystal Palace side clinch an FA Cup replay against Manchester United 16 years earlier. You got the impression this 4–0 lead was somehow rivalling that famous feat. The revelry had started in the stands – Reading and Rams fans alike all pushing a Mexican wave from corner to corner of Madejski Stadium – and a fifth goal (Long's second) capped it off. Danny Webber had pulled one back for the Blades at the Britannia, but United could not do any more to delay the inevitable – Reading were Football League champions!

Polite tannoy requests asking fans to stay off the pitch at full time were, predictably, ignored. Everyone poured

Champagne corks pop on the directors' box balcony.

onto the pitch, mobbing what players they could before a barrier of fluorescent stewards' bibs shepherded the stragglers down the tunnel and into the sanctuary of the home dressing room. It soon became apparent that clearing the pitch of the entire

attendance would be impossible, so the idea of a lap of honour was abandoned and players and coaches were all chivvied up three flights of stairs to join the Chairman in the directors' box seats. As the squad assembled on the balcony, John Madejski admitted:

I'm jolly pleased we're at Madejski Stadium rather than Elm Park because I don't know how we'd have coped there! This is so good, I can't tell you. It feels absolutely exhilarating, fantastic…a dream come true. We've achieved what we set out to do and it's come courtesy of a lot of hard work by a lot of people. And now we've got our reward. This is the fulfilment of a dream – it's what we set out to do 16 years ago. To get the Championship in style with a 5–0 victory is just absolutely sublime. It's almost surreal. The whole place is totally electric, and the occasion is numbing.

A jubilant Coppell commented:

I can't put it into words, it means everything to me and to everyone here. You graft away in football and often get nothing, so this reward goes way beyond anything. It really is very, very special. Once we broke the deadlock we played some terrific football, I know the supporters and the players both enjoyed it. It was a carnival atmosphere and that was fitting. 'Champions' is a special word. It implies and means a lot. From the chairman, who has given so much, to Shane Long, who came on and scored two goals, these moments will live with them for the rest of their lives. It was just such a buzz. You can't match that feeling, that

Coppell is doused in bubbly.

Hahnemann is a hero to Hunter and Austin.

The skipper applauds the swamped Madejski Stadium pitch.

mutual enjoyment, admiration, respect and exhilaration. It was fabulous!

Champagne was taken off ice and sprayed into those who were craning their necks in the Lower West Stand, but one bottle was saved to douse Steve Coppell, with Kevin Doyle doing the honours. Steve Sidwell danced about wearing Kingsley's head, crutch-less Leroy Lita caught some rogue underwear that was hurled his way from an unknown admirer below and Murty gave something back to the fans – his boots were carefully lowered to their intended target among the throng of camera-wielders below. 'I don't know how to put this feeling into words, it's beyond words…pure emotion,' the skipper said, leaning over the balcony

with thousands of swarming fans, waving flags and banners, providing an awesome backdrop to his Reading World interview. 'Everybody at the club – the players, staff, manager and the Chairman – they all deserve this. It has been a long, hard road but we're there now. The manager challenged us to turn it on. We did, and we got the result. The gaffer will probably challenge us again next week, but what are we going to do to top this?'

Murty had a point. Amazingly five games remained and a record points total was still in Reading's sights. But Murty had another plan on how to provide a fitting end to such a miraculous season. 'They might put me up front for these final few games, I'd like to see that! I'm on penalties, free kicks…bet on me, I am going to score before this season is out!' Few punters would have advised it but

with the season's story so far…it was surely worth a gamble.

Five more goals at Cardiff, points at Leeds and Sheffield Wednesday and a comfortable home victory over Stoke only reiterated Reading's total dominance in the division, and victory against QPR on the final day would seal a record-breaking 106 points tally. 'This is what the lads really want,' James Harper revealed. 'We've not talked about it as such but we want the record and we're going for it.' A town centre and Madejski Stadium promotion celebration had been intricately planned for bank holiday Monday, and the fans' appetites had been whet, but Sunday afternoon's task was to win against Rangers and clinch the 104th, 105th and 106th points to sign off in style.

The players were given a military guard of honour as they rose from the tunnel to an anthem the team had chosen to run out to – Neil Diamond's *Sweet Caroline* was a tune the side had adopted on a recent jaunt to Spain, and smiles appeared on the proud parade of players as it rang around the stadium. As they formed their final huddle of the campaign, the full house of fans 'raised the hoops' by lifting square blue-and-white plastic sheets (placed on every seat by supporters' trust STAR) to create one of the most magnificent Madejski Stadium sights. The entire stadium, barring portions of a sparse and disgruntled QPR following support, was hooped! The game itself, for once, played second fiddle for much of the afternoon. An archetypal Royals breakaway saw Convey race into Rangers' half and cross to Oster at the far post. He stabbed it back to Kitson, who calmly gave the hosts the lead before the brass band at the break.

Until Paul Furlong bundled a 72nd-minute equaliser past Marcus Hahnemann, it seemed as though Reading were going to coast to an uneventful win. But Reading upped it a gear and produced that 'something special' everyone was hoping for. With just six minutes remaining, Nicky Shorey's left-sided cross struck Richard Langley's arm, and referee Darren Drysdale pointed to the spot. There was no fight for penalty supremacy – skipper Murts had the ball and was not going to relinquish it. With a grand total of no goals in five years, the right back's scoring record left a lot to be desired, and as the only outfield regular without a goal from the 98 already

Murty keeps his cool to score a fairytale winner.

netted, all gazes were fixed on the skipper and his spot kick. It took an age as referee Drysdale separated an arguing Kevin Doyle and Danny Shittu, but Murty ran up unaffected by the delay to pound his penalty wide of Jake Cole's desperate dive for 2–1.

It was an unforgettably emotional and joyful moment for any Reading fan. Murty's celebration was something to behold too, as he led the charge in catching Kingsley and the entire Royals squad followed up to pile on top after tackling the lion to the ground. Murts admitted:

I knew there was going to be a penalty in the last home game. I had to pull rank on a few of the lads to make sure I took it! There was a bit of a delay, but no problem, I was just chilling out. I waited for Kevin Doyle and Danny Shittu to put their handbags down and get out of the way, got my head right, settled down…and then whacked it as hard as I could. I

couldn't have written the script better. It's in the realms of fantasy. It's a cliché, but you play football for days like today, lifting the trophy and getting a medal in front of your home crowd.

'Murts had a long time to think about it and we were joking on the sidelines that he was hyperventilating, so for him to keep his cool was impressive,' Coppell laughed after the final victory was secured. 'Actually, I don't think he did keep his cool, he just blasted it as hard as he could! But it was a great finish, and fitting in many ways. The League table is a sweet read!'

Any spare space on walls was cleared for more picture-perfect Madejski Stadium moments; a stage was fast erected, medals were ceremonially hung around each of the players' necks and the coveted Coca-Cola Championship trophy was delivered. Goal-hero Murty held the silverware aloft to start the celebrations and soon champagne corks were popping once more. 'Normally in football you're glad

Kingsley is mobbed and the whole record-breaking team pile on.

when the season comes to an end, but we wanted this one to go on and on,' the manager concluded.

The players' families joined the on-pitch revelry to parade their boyfriends, husbands, sons and dads around the pitch in a slow, indulgent lap of honour. Fans lapped up every moment and it did not end there. An internal party began proceedings, and celebrations overflowed into another town centre celebration that night. Then the following day — conveniently a bank holiday Monday — with a few nursing sore heads, two green open-top buses informed thousands of onlookers of its next stop: the Premiership. Players hung over the railings as the bus parade wound its way around the streets of

Reading, with a sea of blue and white beneath them. This success eclipsed any achievement Reading Football Club had mustered since its formation in 1871, and Reading's public were happy to help the squad realise that by spilling out onto the streets with flags, balloons and banners representing an outpouring of appreciation. The tour of the town finally came to a halt at Madejski Stadium, of course, where a 'legends' match had entertained a full house patiently waiting for the buses' arrival.

The trophy is lifted and Reading have made history.

The Chairman revels in a dream come true.

Sidwell cradles his youngster on a lap of honour.

The parade pulled up outside the players' entrance, and each individual involved in the first team's success was roared onto the pitch one by one as the trophy presentation was gleefully re-enacted. Another dazed stroll around the stadium saw fans applaud everyone and everything. The supporters did not want to leave, it was too much fun. After some of the players had tried to beat the keeper, Chairman John

Madejski Stadium 'raises the hoops' in honour of their heroes.

Murty kisses his title-winning medal.

The boss smiles after collecting his medal.

The bus weaves its way through hordes of town centre supporters.

Madejski was egged on into taking an impromptu penalty against Marcus Hahnemann. He missed, twice, but no one cared. Steve Coppell rolled back the years to take up the challenge too, his knee holding up well as he coolly slotted a spot kick past the stopper and wheeled away in celebration.

A man who had spent 10 months playing down Reading's promotion prospects, soaking up any pressure and deflecting as much attention away from his level-headed but whole-hearted squad of players, was finally now allowing himself to enjoy it. 'Reading Football Club – Champions...and don't you forget it!' he wryly beamed into the Reading World camera. Nobody who witnessed it will ever forget a season to cherish.

Lita lifts the trophy aloft.

2005–06 Coca-Cola Championship – in and around us:

		P	W	D	L	GD	Pts
1	Reading	46	31	13	2	+67	106
2	Sheffield Utd	46	26	12	8	+30	90
3	Watford	46	22	15	9	+24	81
4	Preston NE	46	20	20	6	+29	80
5	Leeds United	46	21	15	10	+19	78

Promoted: Reading, Sheffield United, Watford
Relegated: Brighton, Millwall, Crewe Alexandra

FA Cup: Fourth round (v Birmingham City)
League Cup: Fourth round (v Arsenal)

Top scorer: Dave Kitson (18)

Most appearances: Ivar Ingimarsson (46), Ibrahima Sonko (46), Marcus Hahnemann (45)

Ivar Ingimarsson

GRAEME MURTY

Reading appearances: 324 (+14)
Reading goals: 2

Graeme Murty's first few months as a Reading player offered few clues that he would become a true legend of the Club.

The young, exciting right-winger was snapped up from York City by manager Tommy Burns for a sizeable fee of £750,000 in the summer of 1998, just as the Club made the move from Elm Park to Madejski Stadium, and expectations were high that he would make an instant impact. Those hopes were dashed when he was ruled out of the start of the season through a string of injuries – and that was to remain the constant theme of his first two seasons as a Royal.

Murty had to wait until six months into the 1998–99 season before he was fit enough to make his debut in a 3–0 defeat at Burnley, but just six weeks later, after a series of highly promising displays, the injury curse struck again when he was cruelly scythed down by a terrible challenge from Luton Town's Paul McLaren. The ankle injury sustained at Kenilworth Road kept him out of action for another seven months, by which time Burns had been replaced by Alan Pardew, and the new manager was quick to spot Murty's potential in a more defensive right back position, where he promptly formed an effective flank pairing with diminutive midfielder Sammy Igoe.

Murty's propensity to suffer injuries at the drop of a hat was a source of great amusement to his teammates, especially during the final stages of the 2000–01 campaign when a minor training ground incident resulted in the embarrassed Yorkshireman being treated by an air ambulance that happened to be in the area. Anyone else, they reasoned, would have brushed it off with a few rubs of the magic sponge, but for Murts they had to call in a helicopter! Nobody was more frustrated with the 'injury-prone' tag than the player himself and, happily, Murty was finally able to put his fitness problems behind him and become one of the most consistent and consistently available members of the squad. That was certainly the case in the 2001–02 promotion campaign, when he started 43 out of 46 League games and was named the Player of the Season by the fans as Pardew's team finished second in Division Two. He remained just as consistent during the transitional period of Steve Coppell's early days in charge, winning the Player of the Year vote again in 2003–04, and the Middlesbrough-born full back was named as club skipper when Adie Williams departed the following season.

Then came the joyous nine months that will probably define Graeme Murty's Reading career for many, many years to come – the record-breaking

MEN WHO MADE THE MADEJSKI

Championship-winning 2005–06 campaign. Week after week, Coppell's men simply swept aside their helpless opposition in a breathtaking display of consistent excellence. Murty was proving to be an inspirational leader and conducted the celebrations at Madejski Stadium on a glorious spring day as the title was clinched with a 5–0 demolition of Derby (his superb cross for Shane Long's bullet header being one of the season's many enduring highlights). But just one thing was missing – a goal. Amazingly, Murts had only scored once throughout his Reading career – a sweetly struck long-range effort against Bristol City in April 2001, and as the 2005–06 season reached its heavenly climax the pressure mounted. With the title already in the bag, 'Will Murts score?' seemed to be the question on the lips of every Reading fan. He was urged to shoot every time he got the ball in the opposition half, was nominated as the official penalty-taker, and was even jokingly offered the chance to play up front by his amused manager Steve Coppell. But still the goal would not

come, leaving Murts as the only outfield regular not to score a single goal over the course of the season.

With just six minutes of the campaign remaining, the duck was still unbroken as the Royals found themselves tied at 1-1 with Queen's Park Rangers, knowing that a victory would break the Football League's all time record points haul. Then it happened – Nicky Shorey's cross into the penalty area struck the arm of Richard Langley, and referee Darren Drysdale pointed immediately to the spot. There was never any doubt that Graeme Murty would be the penalty-taker, but the skipper was forced to wait while Kevin Doyle and Rangers defender Danny Shittu engaged in a spot of handbags at dawn. Finally, order was restored and Murty stepped up…to power an unstoppable drive high past visiting keeper Jake Cole.

That penalty, and the scenes of celebration that ensued as Murts chased down the frantically fleeing mascot Kingsley, will live with every Reading fan forever – it was simply a fairytale,

too-good-to-be-true ending to a dream-like season, and 10 minutes later the proud skipper owned the honour of lifting the Football League trophy as the Royals leapt into the Premier League for the very first time as record-breaking Champions. He remained captain as the Club set the Premier League alight in their first season and played the role of Reading FC ambassador to perfection. An excellent interviewee, he was regularly in demand from the national media to share his views on the Reading phenomena, and he played a full part in the Club's ever-growing community activities alongside his wife Karen, who co-founded the 'Royal Families' fundraising group. And if that was not enough, he was a proud father to his first daughter Freya and became a regular fixture in Scotland squads as Walter Smith and then Alex McLeish's side battled for a shock Euro 2008 Finals qualification. Life could not get better.

Sadly, the story does not end there, and after two years of unparalleled success Murty and his teammates were brought back down to earth with a bump by relegation at the end of the 2007–08 season. But he remained an impressively dignified representative of the Club, earning even more respect from supporters by appearing live on a local radio phone-in the morning after relegation had been confirmed. During that emotional studio appearance Murts, who had recently been awarded a testimonial to mark his decade at the Club, stated his determination to captain the team back into the Premier League – if the first 10 years of his Reading career are anything to go by, only a fool would bet against it.

More Than A Game:

Madejski Melodies

Crowds flock to 'TheCall' concert.

At midday on Saturday 13 July 2002 Reading's home opened its doors to more than 16,000 Christian music-lovers for religious concert 'TheCall'. For the first time a stage was constructed in the South Stand and a central walkway laid over the off-season grass, which was mostly left uncovered for followers to stand or sit upon. Broadcast live on Sky's God channel, TheCall proved a great success and as the gig-goers dispersed through the gates after the music had wound down at 9pm, there was a confidence in Madejski Stadium's ability to present further crowd-pulling events in the future.

In June 2004 the stadium was chosen to replace a rainy Rivermead —

Summer XS festivals saw a host of heartthrobs entertain the masses.

the previous year's venue — in hosting 2Ten FM's Summer XS pop festival. The sun shone literally and metaphorically on a glorious Sunday afternoon event, which welcomed another new audience to the stadium; screaming teenage girls dominated the demographic as heartthrobs Blue performed five of their chart-toppers. One member of the boyband, Antony, was draped in the England flag, as Sven's men were facing a crucial Euro 2004 opener against France later that evening (a game they were to lead in but lose 2–1), and when Take That star Mark Owen triggered a Mexican wave at the end of his set, pop-lovers were whipped into a football frenzy and reminded that they were partying in a football stadium. Girls Aloud, McFly, and Busted continued to entertain thousands into the night.

Proving such a success, the same stage was erected in front of the North Stand the following year, when Rachel Stevens, Charlotte Church, Mel C,

Chesney Hawkes and Blazin' Squad headlined, and more than 9,000 young fans piled in to support 2005's summer spectacle. But a much bigger and more impressive event had taken place at Madejski Stadium only 10 days earlier — Elton John had announced that he would perform the first leg of his Peachtree Road Tour at Madejski Stadium. A much more elaborate stage

Flea rocks the Mad Stad.

was gradually rigged up in front of the South Stand, and the pitch was completely covered so rows of chairs could help accommodate a sell-out crowd.

Stadium staff heard the globally renowned star soundcheck with *Can You Feel The Love Tonight* during the afternoon, and happy fans streamed out of the stands after a hugely successful concert, suggesting more major events were to come. 'It was an absolutely brilliant night,' Chairman John Madejski remarked after merrily bopping away to Elton's classics with guests Cilla Black and Sir Cliff Richard. 'I had a wonderful, wonderful time. The weather was beautiful and Elton was tremendous. I thought it was universally accepted as a great success, and I haven't spoken to any detractors. After how terrific the night was, I can only encourage more big stars to perform at the stadium in the future.'

A vast amount of planning had gone into staging the event, but with only one call of complaint received and the whole stadium and surrounding area cleared within 45 minutes of the concert's end, any anticipated hiccups simply had not materialised.

Attempts to bring the legendary Luciano Pavarotti to Madejski Stadium were twice thwarted by the tenor's ill-health, but demand for more was satisfied by the booking of one of the biggest rock bands in the world – The Red Hot Chili Peppers rocked Reading in July 2006. Stage, sound and lighting had been set up, with the pitch again protected by a temporary floor boarding. Every one of the 28,000 tickets had been sold and eager fans began queuing outside the stadium at 9am, almost eight hours before the gates were due to open. 'Welcome good people of Readingshire!' singer Anthony Kiedis quipped at the start, before performing *Under The Bridge*, *Give It Away* and *By The Way* for the thrilled crowd, which included some of the Royals first team – Glen Little, Graeme Murty, Nicky Shorey and Steve Sidwell all brought their partners to enjoy the show, while Chairman Madejski was again in attendance. Madejski Stadium was helping Reading attract some of the biggest stars in the music world.

Red Hot Chili Peppers attract thousands to Madejski Stadium in 2006.

Chapter 8

Into the Big Time

More than 1,000 fans queued up to have their pictures taken with the Championship trophy in early June, but before Reading's Premier League preparations could truly begin, a number of curtain call events were staged at Madejski Stadium. With Germany readying itself for a World Cup Finals tournament, an exhibition rematch of the 1966 Final was held at the country's newest top-flight football venue, with ex-German legends matching up against a host of famous English names. More than 21,000 spectators saw Peter Lohmeyer and Bruno Labbadia give the Germans the lead, but Paul Merson and Lee Sharpe pulled an England side, led by Peter Reid and ably assisted by Paul Gascoigne, back to 2–2. Germany eventually completed a reverse of the 1966 scoreline but not before Boris Johnson MP had entertained the crowd with some unorthodox rugby-style tackles on his opposition.

Reading Football Club 2006–07 – Premier League!

Then more serious stuff as Sven Goran Eriksson led an England B side to take on Belarus in Berkshire, allowing Madejski Stadium to host the first B international since a 4–1 win over Russia eight years previously. Even with the thrilling talents of Michael Carrick, Jermaine Jenas, Joe Cole, Aaron Lennon, Theo Walcott and skipper Michael Owen on show, England lost 2–1 to the 10-man Belorussians.

Besides following England, loyal Royals' eyes were on the tournament in Germany for other reasons – Bobby Convey became the first-ever Reading player to appear in the World Cup Finals, when starting for Bruce Arena's USA side in a 3–0 Group E defeat to the Czech Republic. Convey also featured in a 1–1 draw with eventual champions Italy and as a substitute against Ghana, but Marcus Hahnemann remained a spectator as Kasey Keller stood between States' sticks.

Back in Berkshire, with the pitch half torn up, the Red Hot Chili Peppers rocked Madejski Stadium. As soon as the de-rig was complete the re-dig could begin, and extensive preparations started to transform the arena into a stage fit for Premier League football. The pitch was relaid and grass regrown, North and South Stand concourse refreshment kiosks were extended to accommodate for full houses and the previously red ash-coloured running track circling the pitch was recoated in royal blue. The dugouts housed brand-new Recaro seats and the players' tunnel was adorned with a new photo montage celebrating the Royals' achievements of the previous season. The Reading FC crest was also written into the floor for the players to step onto before running out under a new extendable tunnel canopy.

Wage bills almost tripled as bonuses and promotion clauses kicked in but, after becoming part of the worldwide television rights deal sold by the Premier League, the Club's finances were able to cope, and more structural changes to a now non-smoking Madejski Stadium included a grand brand-new reception area. Further plans included a renovation of the previously fairly basic Hogwood Park training ground – a gymnasium was installed in a marquee, dressing rooms were rejuvenated, a press portakabin

Chairman John Madejski was preparing to welcome top flight football to Madejski Stadium.

appeared for pre-match press conferences, landscaping of the grounds began, a dining facility was upgraded and plans were actioned to relocate some of the club's football-based administration staff to permanent offices at the training ground. An automatic blue entrance gate was also erected, with every player given key fobs that would 'open sesame' upon arrival every morning.

Elsewhere the matchday programme added 50p to its price tag by growing to 84 pages, and the press gantry grew too – provision for more seats was made at the top of the Upper West Stand and overflow seating was allocated to account for the increased interest in Reading's football and footballers. Mini video screens were installed to play replays in the gantry,

ensuring no journalist had any excuse for misidentifying a goalscorer or wrongly reporting an assist. A new Media Suite was created at ground level, while photographers' movements were restricted, as two layers of perimeter advertising took priority in view of the TV cameras.

A section was set aside for the erection of a temporary Sky Sports studio next to the video screen in the South Stand, and a full time press officer, Simon Heggie, was added to the staff, helping the club's media department to cope with the heightened global media interest and a sudden but seemingly endless influx of interview requests for our previously little-known players.

To capitalise on the Club's growth a new women's team was launched and,

with the Princess Suite upgraded and most of the hospitality areas recarpeted and redecorated, a new hospitality suite was born – the 106 Club, named after the record-breaking number of points the Royals amassed in 2005–06.

The fixture calculator worked its magic and pitted Reading against Middlesbrough at Madejski Stadium on the opening day, giving fans the home-game opener they had hoped for, although eyes were naturally drawn to a series of games starting at the end of September that would see Manchester United, Arsenal and Chelsea all visit Madejski Stadium in the space of a month.

It was all becoming very real. Suddenly you could pick Reading players in your Fantasy League and sticker-book collections. Reading's

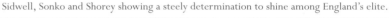

Sidwell, Sonko and Shorey showing a steely determination to shine among England's elite.

name moved into the Premier League category on Ceefax and the BBC's website, while the badge soon appeared alongside the others in all the Premier League branding. A newly remodelled ticket office soon sold out of their full allocation of 18,000 season-long seats. A change in emphasis tried to persuade more fans to buy their tickets online, and the Royalty Points system continued to control the obvious demand for tickets.

Meanwhile, security was being tightened: the players were allocated a special secure parking compound in Car Park Three; matchday wristbands were given only to staff who needed tunnel access; and matchday hospitality guests were introduced to a new swipe-in system. A Premier League requirement led to a secure coach compound for visiting teams being introduced outside the players' entrance, and solid panels were put in place to discourage crowds from building up and avoid overspill into the roads. Kitchens were upgraded and extended, an 'urban traffic control' system was installed in the control room to aid traffic management on the A33, and new matchday bus services were introduced. Most poignantly perhaps – the trophy cabinet had to be made bigger. No wonder that stadium manager Ray Booth recalls 'I remember being a bit busy!'

The megastore invested in an off-site warehouse in a bid to cope with higher demand for stock, and a mail order service was securely set up. Worldwide interest from the US, Australia, Japan and South Korea coupled with much higher demand

Seol Ki-Hyeon became Reading's record signing and soon stole the limelight with his South Korean skills.

domestically, with countless Premier League badges printed onto home strip shirt sleeves, and, of course, a few new names were being heat-sealed onto the back.

Somewhat surprisingly, though, no wholesale changes were made by Steve Coppell as the Royals boss showed warranted faith in the squad that had earned such a glorious promotion. However, 27-year-old South Korean idol Seol Ki-Hyeon was the big signing of the summer, the exciting right-sided international being signed for an initial fee of £1 million from Wolves. 'When Reading made an offer to me I was very happy, they've just had a fantastic season and they have a good squad of players,' Seol said in broken English upon penning the deal. 'The first thing is to stay in the Premiership and I'll do my best, that's my aim.'

Sam Sodje joined for a more modest fee from Brentford to add defensive cover and, before the transfer window was slammed shut, Ulises De La Cruz was signed to offer a little more top-flight experience to a Royals squad that, besides Glen Little's brief loan stint at Bolton and John Oster's time with Everton and Sunderland, had virtually no knowledge of Premiership football. Steve Sidwell's refusal to sign a new deal dominated the pre-season transfer talk, but Steve Coppell seemed happy with his settled side as they returned for the start of training.

On the coaching side, former Watford defender and coach Nigel Gibbs was added to the staff and a full time ProZone analyst was employed, meaning an intricate set of cameras were installed across Madejski Stadium's roof. Our kit man, Ron Grant, was also afforded an assistant for the first time – Selby Armstrong. Selby's first contribution was to make a cameo pre-season appearance as a player – Aaron Brown's broken ankle at Bromley forced Coppell to field reserve keeper Adam Federici up front and expend his final substitute, and Shane Long picked up a knock near the end to allow the kit man a brief run! His impact was not as great as Federici's, as the Aussie stopper scored the only goal of the game to everyone's surprise.

Didcot and Rushden & Diamonds were duly dispatched, as were Northampton (4–1) and Millwall (1–0). Swindon held Reading to a 1–1 stalemate before a three-game unbeaten tour of Sweden. Returning to Madejski Stadium, the final pre-season fixture served up a big name at home – Dutch giants Feyenoord paying the last pre-Premiership visit to Reading. A far post Dave Kitson header was fast followed by Ivar Ingimarsson's close-range stab home and, despite substitute Benjamin De Ceulaer's second half consolation, Reading won 2–1 against the Dirk Kuyt-led Dutch. Unbeaten throughout the build-up, the Royals' confidence was sky high.

The scene was set. As always seems to be the case, the sun shone on the opening day of the season and Madejski Stadium made its debut as a Premier League venue bathed in swathes of warm sunlight. Even disregarding the physical changes to the perimeter advertising, the sponsored stands and the newly blue running track, the sense

A long wait for Premier League football was about to end in dramatic style.

of occasion that afternoon seemed to reinvent the stadium. Followed by cameras throughout the opening day preparations, Chairman John Madejski did a sweep of his stadium, receiving an impromptu round of raucous applause as he passed through the hotel bar, where fans had arrived early to bask in the history of the day. Unsurprisingly, every seat was occupied when the eponymous creator of the stadium, the man who can claim to be the pioneer of Reading's unparalleled success, strode onto the dewy turf to soak it all up himself. Amid hasty rumours he was about to step aside, Madejski was not going to miss this afternoon for anything and announced:

Having been Chairman for the past 16 years and helped guide us into the top flight, I feel in many ways that my task is completed, but this doesn't mean that I will abandon the Club immediately – indeed, I would like to enjoy the Premier League. I have immensely enjoyed the last 16 years at Reading Football Club, working with my exceedingly good and professional staff. We've built this club brick on brick, we have a magnificently run club and the future looks incredibly bright. Everything at Reading Football Club is extremely stable and we are very much looking forward to the new season in the Premier League.

Skipper and former Middlesbrough trainee Graeme Murty added: 'I'm buzzing – I'm running about like a little kid! The guys have said that they need to calm me down, rather than me calming them down! It's been building up and building up and it's going to be good, it's going to be special.' And the magnitude of Middlesbrough's opening afternoon visit even had the level-headed Steve Coppell stimulated. 'Oh, beyond 10!' he told the pre-match press conference when asked how he'd gauge his excitement levels as the game approached. He continued:

But all that's in my mind now is the preparation process. We look at Middlesbrough, look at ourselves and make sure we get things right. I don't sit and think about how excited I am – it is work, it is preparation…we've no indication yet of how we will do. Most experts say we're going down, but that will only spur our challenge to prove them wrong. I might have the odd word to the players before the

game, but they've been in the process for long enough to know what they're doing. Players are much more professional than they used to be and they have to prepare for the top end of the scale. If they don't they're exposed. This is for real now.

The first fixture had conjured a quaint story, as Coppell locked managerial horns with a man he once managed as an apprentice; Gareth Southgate was beginning his coaching career by taking over from newly appointed England boss Steve McClaren to steer Middlesbrough's young side through another Premier League season.

Finally the waiting was over and, after changing ends at the coin toss, Kevin Doyle kicked-off Reading's first-ever top-flight campaign. After half an hour, fledgling boss Southgate – opting for the polo shirt and tracksuit-bottomed ensemble – stood relaxed on the edge of his technical area, while his former Crystal Palace employer, Coppell, nervously watched with

Reading start to find their feet.

scraps of paper in the directors' box, grimacing at a first half hour that had not exactly gone according to plan.

Murty had preached the importance of not being afraid to play 'our brand of football' before the momentous match had begun. 'We have to play the game and not the occasion, because if we get caught up in the occasion everything else will pass us by,' the captain forewarned. But, a little like startled rabbits stranded in the middle of a very busy road, Reading froze and paid the price.

Eleven minutes in, George Boateng fed powerful Nigerian striker Yakubu, who cut back onto his left foot to swing in a deep cross from the right side. Murty's eyes bulged as he realised the pinpoint delivery was floating over his

head no matter how fast he backtracked, and the lively Stewart Downing was timing his run from the left flank to perfection. He drilled a sweet, low, first time volley past Marcus Hahnemann to shock the feverish home support. And when

Hahnemann could not swallow Fabio Rochemback's powerful free kick, Yakubu pounced to stab home the rebound from a free kick he had earned, doubling the deficit 10 minutes later. The script had been followed to the letter last season, but suddenly

But Boro double their advantage through Yakubu's poached second.

Reading respond in style – Kitson scoring our first top flight goal.

Southgate's side were lodging a sizeable spanner in Madejski Stadium's works.

Murty also made this comment before the game had begun: 'I think we'll know how good a team we are if something goes wrong, because that

Sidwell levels before the break and Madejski Stadium reaches fever pitch.

will test the fabric of the team. It'll test how tight we are together, how close we are as a team.' What a prescient remark that proved to be, and the skipper certainly got his answer in what remains the most dramatic comeback

ever to grace Madejski Stadium.

Memorably, a barnstorming run forward from Nicky Shorey seemed to galvanise the crowd and team alike and, although the move ended in Mark Schwarzer saving Kevin Doyle's first effort on target, the belief that had been so prevalent in 2005–06 began to trickle back into Reading's veins. Their confidence was flowing so fast it was threatening to burst blood vessels.

Shortly after Shorey's run and Doyle's shot had breathed new life into the home team's day, Dave Kitson became the first-ever Reading player to score in top flight football two minutes before the interval. Seol Ki-Hyeon skipped past Julio Arca on the right to

Kitson is scythed down by Chris Riggott and hobbles off at half time.

fizz a low cross into the six-yard box and, after skidding past Doyle's desperate near-post lunge, the ball cannoned off Kitson's standing shin. The striker was first to react, stretching out his left leg to toe the loose ball past Schwarzer from close range, and Reading were back in it. Incredible scenes followed seconds later as Steve Sidwell restored parity – Ivar Ingimarsson peeled off to collect Shorey's pass down the left channel, and the Icelandic centre back blindly cut the ball back for influential midfielder Sidwell to brilliantly slide a first-time shot past Schwarzer for 2–2.

Sidwell had come under some criticism for delaying contract talks, but all the angst was released as he threw himself into the crowd to celebrate in

sheer joy. 'I had a wonderful 10 seconds – you could tell that from my celebration! I had some blue face paint in my hair afterwards from the guy in the crowd. He was buzzing and he must have got himself on *Match of the Day*. The crowd were superb. They played a big part in the comeback,' Siddy

revealed after the final whistle.

There was a sense of inevitability that the comeback would be completed in the second half. It was. Leroy Lita's last first team appearance had ended in a freakish ankle break at Burnley, but having replaced Kitson – the subject of an outrageously unpunished horror

Kits' replacement, Leroy Lita, seals the dramatic victory by lashing home a scrappy second half winner.

Reading hold on to collect their first three top flight points.

tackle from Chris Riggott – the pacy £1 million man returned in style to banish memories of his Turf Moor accident. 'I won't be completely happy until I score with my left foot, I'll feel better then,' Lita had revealed after bagging a hatful in a pre-season parade at Didcot. So when he ruthlessly lashed Seol's low cross, which had bobbled free from a bundle of bodies inside the six-yard box, high into the roof of the net, Madejski Stadium rightly erupted. 'You see in the Premiership every week that there are players who are like magnets in the box,' Coppell told the press. Lita had just become one of them.

Royals fans have largely chosen to forget the fact that Mark Viduka had a late goal wrongly ruled out for offside, and TV pundits chose to gloss over that let-off too. Another equaliser would have got in the way of a fantastic underdog story. 'This team just staggers me! We take our belief from the manager; he's not signed many players, he wants us to prove ourselves. And we're finally getting it into our thick skulls that we're not a bad team!' Murty summed up.

Saturday 19 August 2006. Reading 3 Middlesbrough 2. Madejski Stadium magic!

Gareth Southgate congratulates his former boss at the end of a memorable afternoon.

DAVE KITSON

Reading appearances: 121 (+26)
Reading goals: 60

What a bargain! Twenty-three-year-old Dave Kitson was a relatively unheralded signing when he was snapped up for a modest initial fee of £150,000 from Cambridge United on Boxing Day 2003. But, four years later, he was the leading English goalscorer in the Premier League and being tipped for an England call-up.

None of that could have been foreseen when he arrived at Madejski Stadium at a time when, nearly three months into his job at Madejski Stadium, Steve Coppell had pinpointed strengthening the striker position as a priority – and Kitson's arrival came three days after that of Lloyd Owusu.

Kitson was a late entrant into the professional game; having famously been employed as a Sainsbury's shelf-stacker, he finally earned a contract at the Abbey Stadium in 2000–01 and rapidly became a regular in the U's first team, scoring 10 goals in his first full season – including one against Reading in a 2–2 draw at the Abbey Stadium. By the time Coppell came calling, Kitson had recorded 47 goals in 123 appearances for Cambridge and, over the next three months, he eased his way into the Reading team. His full debut was marked with the second goal in a 3–2 victory at Cardiff City, but it was an impressive all-round performance that allowed him to keep his place in the side.

Famously, Kitson properly announced his entrance as a force to be reckoned with within a fortnight of that debut at Cardiff, by recording a well-taken brace in a 2–0 victory over West Ham United as Alan Pardew made his first return to Madejski Stadium. That fixture is well chronicled in chapter six and needs no further elaboration here, but it certainly earned Kitson an immediate place in the hearts of all Reading fans – and provided a natural heir to Jamie Cureton's 'what a bargain' chant!

The following weekend Kitson netted his most spectacular goal for the club with an astonishing overhead volley at Bradford, but his goals were too few to earn a play-off spot at the end of the season. The same end result materialised at the conclusion of the following campaign; Kits was named Player of the Season and boasted an impressive tally of 19 goals – even though he had missed two months through injury – but the Royals missed out on the play-offs with a final-day defeat at Wigan.

Finally, glory came at the third attempt in the never-to-be-forgotten 2005–06 campaign, and the Royals' strike force of Kitson, Leroy Lita and Kevin Doyle, supplemented from the bench by Shane Long, was a major factor in the team's success. After an opening day loss to Plymouth, Kitson helped get the ball rolling with a goal that secured a 2–0 victory at Brighton. The goals continued to flow, including a hat-trick against Brighton and braces against Coventry and Cardiff, and the Royals racked up victory after victory in an astonishing march to the title. By the end of the season he had totalled 22

goals, narrowly edging out Doyle (19) and Lita (15) to top the scoring charts as Reading FC entered the previously uncharted waters of the Premier League.

The opening fixture of the Club's first season in the Premier League paired the Royals with Middlesbrough and Kitson was to play an historic part on an historic day, scoring the Club's first top flight goal. Sadly, Kitson was not on the pitch to enjoy the conclusion of the staggering 3–2 victory that ensued; on the stroke of half time, visiting defender Chris Riggott, frustrated by his team's capitulation, launched into a disgraceful knee-high challenge on the striker. Riggott was very fortunate to escape with just a yellow card, but Kitson was not so lucky – he was stretchered off with knee ligament damage and would play no further part in that year's football.

After a number of irritating minor setbacks, Kitson finally got himself back into the starting line up five months later in a fourth-round FA Cup tie at Birmingham, promptly scoring the opening goal with less than three minutes on the clock. He was gradually eased back into Premier League action over the final weeks of the season, making his relief and joy plain to see when he netted a stunning volley to defeat Newcastle United towards the end of April.

The task he was set by Steve Coppell at the beginning of the 2007–08 season was to stay injury free throughout the campaign – something he had never managed to achieve before. He met that target, missing just four Premier League games over the course of the season –

and three of those were forced upon him by an opening day red card at Old Trafford. He was also a regular on the goalscoring charts in the early months, with a particularly strong run of form around Christmas (a goal at West Ham on Boxing Day and two more at Spurs three days later), prompting speculation that he would be named in Fabio Capello's first England squad. He was, after all, the Premier League's top-scoring Englishman. But those rumours proved groundless, and Kitson was unable to make the same impression in the new year as the Royals slid towards relegation.

As a striker, Dave Kitson is capable of conjuring up the spectacular, most clearly demonstrated by that overhead special at Bradford and a curling 20-yard missile in a 2–1 Madejski Stadium win over Newcastle. Although such a tall player is naturally regarded as a big threat in the air, Kitson is also more than capable with the ball at his feet, possessing a deft touch and an incisive range of passing. He has also fulfilled a vital role at the other end of the pitch, by both intercepting stray passes in midfield and nodding away countless corners and set pieces that have been flung into Reading's own penalty area. But more than anything, Dave Kitson is a goalscorer and his primary asset is his ability to be in the right place at the right time to score goals. He has that unteachable instinct to do whatever is necessary to get the ball between the posts and across the line – and he did it with impressive regularity throughout the second half of Madejski Stadium's opening decade.

David Kitson, what a bargain indeed.

More Than A Game:

In Community We Trust

James Harper poses for pictures with youngsters at Madejski Stadium.

Ever since the earliest moments in his leadership, throughout the development of the new ground and during seasons among the country's elite, Reading Football Club's Chairman John Madejski – the founder and financier of Madejski

A Young Royal enjoys his day out as matchday mascot.

Stadium – has stressed repeatedly the importance of the 'community'.

Since 1992 Reading FC has supported a football in the community scheme. It began with a modest bunch of two full-time coaches and six casual staff plus one part-time administrator focusing on the growth of a network of soccer schools across the Reading area. Awarded FA Charter status in 2004, the community trust now employs seven full-time and more than 50 part-time coaches – each one fully UEFA qualified, first-aid trained and Criminal Record Bureau checked – who, assisted by one full-time office manager and two administrators, operate in areas as far flung as Hungerford, Slough, Wallingford and Farnborough while

sustaining a dominant presence within Reading. Leading soccer schools, in-school PE sessions and after-school clubs, developing players on the early rungs in our academy ladder as well as providing training for coaches and managers, the trust also supports initiatives such as Kickz – a nationwide government-led scheme aiming to draw underprivileged youngsters off the street and away from crime through football. 'Care. Develop. Educate' is the trust's motto.

The community department also takes charge of our Girls Centre Of Excellence, and a women's team stemmed from that in 2006 – a side who have now gained back-to-back promotions in their first two campaigns without losing a League match and who will travel the length and breadth of the country to strive for another move up into the ladies' top flight in 2008–09. Plus, the hard-working community staff have become well-travelled in recent years, building strong links overseas by providing their expertise throughout Europe and in a thriving American market.

The facilities for our multi-age academy sides and four seasonal soccer schools were very quickly improved by the building of a £1 million on-site

Reading Women celebrate their second successive automatic promotion.

indoor training dome. The 60m x 40m fibreturf pitch allows football to continue undisturbed by the cold or wet weather conditions, and besides acting as a back-up training venue for the first team during the winter months, it caters for hundreds of young footballers every week, as well as being hired out for children's birthday parties and to the general public when the busy calendar allows.

The Club has never underestimated its powerful position within a community that has become intrinsically affected by the team's performance, and Reading have always been keen to help as many local causes or charities as possible. Since moving to Madejski Stadium and with demand

Anti-racism events are just some of the initiatives the Trust run.

naturally linear to Reading's rise through the divisions, the number of signed shirts, programmes, photos and footballs requested and provided has risen dramatically, and in 2007–08 the

squad happily took part in more than a staggering 200 club-organised player appearances to schools, fêtes, hospitals and presentations. Furthermore the players' wives and girlfriends launched

Brynjar Gunnarsson and Emerse Fae make an appearance at one of many soccer schools.

their own charity, The Royal Families, in 2006 and by staging fund-raising events, often at Madejski Stadium, such as a fashion show, a celebrity darts evening, race and quiz nights and more, they have raised more than £200,000 for a variety of local worthy causes.

Investing in the future, a junior supporters' club has been engaging youngsters ever since the stadium opened, with the Young Royals gloriously relaunched in 2007 to see almost 2,500 junior fans sign up for an exclusive welcome pack and even more eye-widening opportunities to visit the first team during a training session,

become mascot for a matchday, fire questions at the players in a Young Royals fans' forum and win loads of signed items.

On a more educational level, the stadium's Study Support Centre is effectively a school classroom based in the north-west corner and run in conjunction with Reading Borough Council since 2003. The aim is to help provide an alternative learning environment for local youngsters by running a wide variety of educational activities that are often actively supported by the football club. James Harper, for example, has backed

Bobby Convey voluntarily helps out in the children's ward at the Royal Berkshire Hospital.

initiatives by appearing in person at no less than 20 different Study Support Centre events, with Marcus Hahnemann and Ivar Ingimarsson not far behind.

Michael Duberry trains with kids from the Royal Blind Society.

Kalifa Cisse is mobbed at a local school.

Chapter 9

A Top Flight Adventure

A memorable victory over Middlesbrough had set the tone. Three points were secured in the most dramatic fashion as Reading announced their arrival as the newest club, of 40 in total, to take on Premier League competition, and Steve Coppell's men had crucially retained the boundless confidence that had seen them race to a runaway Championship title.

The town's football fever had to be temporarily subdued as two away trips delayed a return to Madejski Stadium, when Reading would host Manchester City live on Sky Sports. And, despite early promise, the party could not continue on the road. Against Aston Villa, Kevin Doyle gave the Royals an early lead by nodding Seol Ki-Hyeon's fourth-minute far post cross past Thomas Sorensen and the honeymoon period showed no sign of ending, until Ibrahima Sonko's ill-timed challenge on Luke Moore earned the Senegalese centre back a sending off and gave Juan Pablo Angel a chance to level from the penalty spot. Villa pressed home their advantage and Gareth Barry snatched the winner with a powerful header on the hour. Having

Seol rises to challenge in the air at Villa.

played for 60 minutes with 10 men at Villa Park, the Royals fortunes got no better at Wigan; Emile Heskey's close-range finish was enough to separate the sides and somewhat realign Reading's bold ambitions. It had been the first time Reading had lost twice on the trot since the disappointing end to 2004–05, but the Royals had started their campaign well and arguably deserved something from all three fixtures, and thousands poured into Madejski Stadium's North Stand to meet and congratulate their newly termed 'top-flight' heroes on a summer's open day at the end of August.

Returning from an early season international interruption, Stuart Pearce's City side were the first to visit the top-flight Royals under lights, but Ivar Ingimarsson was too busy seeing stars to celebrate his match-winning goal with the fervour it deserved. Midway through the first half, Leroy Lita was wrestled to the ground by Sylvain Distin, and Bobby Convey delighted in whipping in a left-footed set piece. The Icelandic vice captain bullishly beat Distin to a diving header and nodded a great effort past a helpless Nicky Weaver to send the home crowd crazy. Distin managed to connect cleanly with Ingimarsson's head, however, and it was up to James Harper to let his dazed colleague know that his header had given the hosts the lead. 'For him to come out and play on in the second half was brilliant,' Coppell told the post-match press. 'You want a player to be brave, but you also want him to be honest about whether he can continue. He is a very sensible man so I know if it was going to be harmful for the team he'd have said he was ready to come off.'

Ingimarsson was needed at the other end to help the returning Sonko in keeping Reading's first Premier League clean sheet, and Doyle came closest to adding to the score sheet only for debutant Hatem Trabelsi to slide in and clear an injury-time strike off City's goalline. Physio Jon Fearn revealed that although Ingimarsson had been groggy 'there was no loss of consciousness and there were no balance issues', so he was fine to take to the field at Bramall Lane

Ivar is out cold seconds after scoring the only goal against Manchester City.

Doyle proved early on that he was capable of stepping up to the top flight.

five days later as the previous season's top-of-the-table rivals battled for Premier League supremacy. Amazingly, Doyle took just 16 seconds to start Reading's journey to their first away win in the top tier, racing onto Bobby Convey's ball forward and slotting past Paddy Kenny to convert a stunning opener. Seol scored his first in a Royals shirt before the break – a breathtaking drive that whizzed past Kenny for 2–0 – and although Rob Hulse pulled one back, the points were heading to Berkshire.

A couple of long-term loan deals were agreed before the transfer window was slammed shut. We had already been introduced to the 'occasional madness of Andre Bikey' when, in a relatively unprovoked fit of rage, he headbutted an opponent while on trial during the pre-season tour of Sweden – a rash red card warranting reaction that seemed to hammer a large nail into his coffin in terms of earning a deal under the level-headed Steve Coppell at Reading. The Royals boss remained open-minded though and captured the centre back on a loan switch from Lokomotiv Moscow. Peter 'The Mammoth' Mate was also borrowed from Hungarian side Debrecen and both made their bows in

Doyle racing toward the East Stand in celebration.

a kid-for-a-quid Carling Cup clash at Madejski Stadium.

'We don't know a lot about the opposition, mainly because the post office lost a couple of videos they were sending us!' the Royals boss explained ahead of Darlington's visit. 'We've had reports, obviously, and I know from their staff it will be a hard, gritty game. If we think otherwise we'll be making a big mistake.' And Reading almost slipped up. Perhaps with their eye on the visit of Manchester United at the weekend, a much-changed Royals side crawled over the line to see off the Quakers…eventually.

Darlington's Darren Holloway earned Simon Johnson the chance to open the scoring from the penalty spot in front of the North Stand but then headed wide of his own onrushing keeper at the other end to allow Leroy Lita an open goal and an equaliser. Ex-Leicester and Aston Villa strike star Julian Joachim was rolling back the years when he put the League Two side in front again, but Lita ensured that lead lasted for less than a minute by springing the offside trap to slam home John Oster's through ball. Joachim again gave the visitors the advantage seven minutes after the break, and Coppell's hand was forced sufficiently to see the introduction of Doyle. The Irishman's impact was immediate – David Duke committing a professional foul on the pacy striker to earn an early bath and reduce David Hodgson's side to 10. Mate's debut impact was memorable; the Hungarian converted from an 86th-minute corner with his hand, but the goal stood and extra time beckoned. There was no way through

during the added half an hour, so a dramatic penalty shoot-out graced a late night at Madejski Stadium. Stephen Hunt missed but converted after being allowed to retake it, and Kevin Doyle saw his strike saved, but Graham Stack watched three Darlington penalties fly high and wide before Bikey calmly slotted home the winning spot kick. Sadly that was to be Mate's only appearance for the Royals – a cruciate ligament injury sustained in a reserve game a few weeks later meant the rest of the season was spent rehabilitating.

Meanwhile, the true impact of Dave Kitson's knee injury, suffered on the opening day, was starting to sink in. At first the prognosis suggested a few weeks of rest might rectify the problem, but his return was repeatedly deferred and it became apparent that Lita, Long and Doyle would spearhead Reading's front line for much of the year. 'It's going slower than slow. It's a nightmare!' the flame-haired frontman said. 'I came to the Darlington game in midweek – it was entertaining but I just couldn't watch any more than the first half. I was so depressed at not playing I had to leave. I've not been able to do anything faster than walk for the last two or three weeks, and it's not easy to come in to training and watch your mates kicking the ball around.' Not one for sympathy, the Royals striker continued 'Words won't heal my knee. I want results, not comforting. It's my right to be depressed as long as I don't annoy anyone! I try to stay out of the way and not be a bad vibe.'

Those who were fighting fit needed no firing up ahead of an appetite-whetting meeting with Manchester

United. Over a long and, to be honest, largely mediocre history, loyal Royals had needed to whip up a storm of excitement ahead of away trips to Millmoor, snowy evenings at Gresty Road and visits of the likes of Scunthorpe, Rochdale and Bristol Rovers. But when the 2007–08 fixture list was announced, this was a month of mouth-watering proportions – Sir Alex Ferguson's champions elect would walk through the doors first, and Chelsea and Arsenal would famously follow them down the tunnel as Reading were due to host three of last season's top four within the space of four games.

'For the fans it is special to have Manchester United here but we'll play it like we do every game,' Sonko remarked in the build-up to the United game. 'It doesn't feel any different to the other games.' Despite towing the party line, Sonks was not kidding anyone – this was going to be exceptional. Especially for a former Manchester United wing wizard – Royals boss Steve Coppell. 'This one is bound to mean more to me. I was blessed to have nine years at United and in my heart it is a little special,' he professed.

The clash had understandably attracted the attentions of the live TV cameras once again, and a late kick-off only helped to build an electric atmosphere at a jam-packed Madejski. Earlier in the week, it had been revealed that wheels were in motion to extend the stadium with planning application for a 14,000-seat expansion being prepared and a consultation period with fans and local residents due to be held. This game showcased the need for a bigger arena.

Sonko times a tackle on Wayne Rooney to perfection.

Marcus Hahnemann was the busier keeper for the opening half an hour, saving from Cristiano Ronaldo and Wayne Rooney as Manchester United heaped pressure on the home side. But 'Superman' Sonko was particularly immense in shackling England's star striker, and Reading grew in confidence. Confidence that was rewarded three minutes after the interval. Seol and skipper Graeme Murty combined down the right, and the full back swept a cross into the box. After seeing the ball skim past a number of men in the middle, a startled Gary Neville nervously intercepted the bouncing delivery with his arm, and referee Peter Walton pointed to the spot. Exultation turned to tension and, although there were few complaints from the visiting side, it seemed to take an eternity for the spot kick to be taken. Long-time Manchester United fan Doyle took charge. He placed the ball, knowing he had missed from 12 yards in the Carling Cup shoot-out only

Gary Neville's handball is punished by penalty-taker Doyle and Reading lead!

Cristiano Ronaldo's true class tells with the equaliser.

days earlier, stepped back, waited and struck the ball low under Edwin Van der Sar's right glove and into the bottom-left corner of the goal. As teammates sped to his side in celebration before the North Stand, Doyle thanked the heavens as the pressure was visibly lifted from his shoulders. Reading were beating Manchester United!

As expected, United pushed forward and pressed for a route back into the game. For a long period, it seemed the gutsy Royals might continue to repel attack after attack and earn a very unlikely victory. But a moment of individual class drew Sir Alex's men level – Ronaldo was to be crowned the PFA Player and Young Player of the Year later that season, and he demonstrated why by skipping

inside Murty from the left to earn half a yard of space and drill a low swerving strike hard into the far corner. 'The big clubs simply have the best players. You can't stop individuals with tactics. If you know how to stop them then tell me because I don't!' Coppell had openly admitted before kick-off, and it was a supreme solo effort to share the spoils. A point against the might of Manchester United was something to behold, but a mark of how far Reading had come in recent seasons was that the Madejski Stadium crowd departed tinged with a little disappointment that their seventh-placed side had not held on for a famous win. 'In terms of possession and shots at goal we were a bit unlucky, but you have to admire Reading. They played a survival game, they fought for every ball, worked their

tails off and made it difficult for us,' Sir Alex opined.

Before another international break, winning ways were vitally restored courtesy of a blistering second-minute Seol strike and an acrobatic last-gasp Steve Sidwell goalline clearance that thwarted Alan Pardew's West Ham side in torrential rain at Upton Park. But the tricky fixture quartet had been added to – Reading had been drawn away to Liverpool in the next stage of the Carling Cup, meaning the Royals' first-ever trip to Anfield would come 10 days before their first League trip to the same venue. However, Chelsea came first – a game that stole all the headlines.

The reigning champions arrived very aware of Reading. Having seen United drop points only a fortnight earlier, manager Jose Mourinho paid

Reading grapple with Chelsea's £30m striker, Andriy Shevchenko.

tribute to the Royals' 'winning mentality'. But another stimulating Madejski Stadium atmosphere was dampened by an early injury that was to spark fiercely hyped-up debates about goalkeepers' safety in football. Petr Cech's evening lasted little more than a minute – sliding out to cut out a through ball, Cech gathered the ball just ahead of Stephen Hunt, who accidentally collided with the Chelsea stopper in his follow through. Replays and sheer logistics answered any questions about any intent, but a hot-headed Mourinho stoked the fire with a post-match attack on our innocent winger. Even after the fiery Portuguese manager had calmed down, he remained desperate to lay blame at Reading's door, accusing the Club and the local ambulance service of sub-standard medical provision. The Club released a statement pointing out their version of events, and after the FA had backed Reading's matchday facilities and refused to charge Hunt, Chelsea slowly reined in some sort of control over their 'loose cannon' of a manager. Thankfully, Cech recovered fully, but Madejski Stadium had been at the centre of one of the biggest media storms in Premier League history.

Petr Cech lies injured by the byline after colliding with Hunt in the opening minute.

The game itself saw Reading leave the pitch feeling a little robbed. The only goal came courtesy of a double deflection from a Frank Lampard free kick – the last touch coming from Ivar Ingimarsson's ankle to divert the ball wide of the wrong-footed Hahnemann just before the break. Kevin Doyle had earlier beaten Cech's replacement, Carlo Cudicini, only for the post to deny him, and when John Obi Mikel was issued with a second yellow card for cynically hauling down Sonko, the Royals felt they might be in with a chance of upsetting one of the 'big boys'. Soon after, though, referee Mike Riley evened things up by dismissing Andre Bikey for a second bookable offence, and the Blues found a new resilience. Reading piled men forward to push the ball over the line through sheer weight in numbers and they almost did in the dying seconds, only for play to be stopped with Cudicini laying spark out in his six-yard box. Another accidental collision, this time with Sonko as an inswinging corner was contested, meant John Terry had to pull on the goalkeeper's jersey for the final few minutes, but a defiant Chelsea held on and celebrated bare-chested in front of their thrilled travelling support. It was very evident how much this victory meant to Chelsea – they knew they had been tested to the full.

As a result, the delicate commodity called confidence was still untainted. The top two had been more than matched in recent encounters and a top half position looked sustainable. As players and management alike kept quoting, nobody had 'embarrassed' Steve Coppell's top-flight fledglings. Arsenal came to town in mid-October though and, with arguably the most stylish footballing display ever delivered to Madejski Stadium, emphatically demonstrated how good the best can be.

Incredibly, no visiting side had scored in front of the North Stand since Andy Johnson equalised in Crystal Palace's 3–2 defeat at Madejski Stadium more than a year previously, but it took Thierry Henry just one minute to destroy that record, racing onto Cesc Fabregas's cut back to sweep first time between Sonko's backtracking legs and past Marcus Hahnemann for an early goal. With an early lead, the Gunners set about picking their opposition off at will. Alex Hleb slammed a second through Hahnemann before the break, and Robin Van Persie completed a sublime move to touch home a third after the interval. Fabregas earned a penalty near the end, and Henry – the starter of the procession – duly converted.

Some suggested that the emotional and physical battle with Chelsea a week earlier may have had an effect on the

Royals stars, but in truth the class of Arsenal was simply too much. 'There's no disgrace for us, they were fabulous,' Coppell admitted. 'I want to pay a huge compliment to one of the elite teams. We're both in the Premiership, but they're not in our league. What can we learn from a game like that? Only how to run after people! It's not a case of admiring them because you want to be competitive. But I would say that they are inspirational.'

'That's the worst game I've been a part of in my life. I don't think any of us played badly, they were just unbelievable!' ex-Arsenal youngster James Harper revealed. 'I've never seen anything like that. They would beat national teams and all-star XIs playing like that! Before the game I thought "we can win this". Once you cross the white line, reputations go out of the window. But it was just frightening. It doesn't matter what system you play or how you try to combat that – they had such a rhythm and flow.'

Shorey holds off Arsenal's Julio Baptista.

Henry and Van Persie are too good for the shadow-chasing Royals.

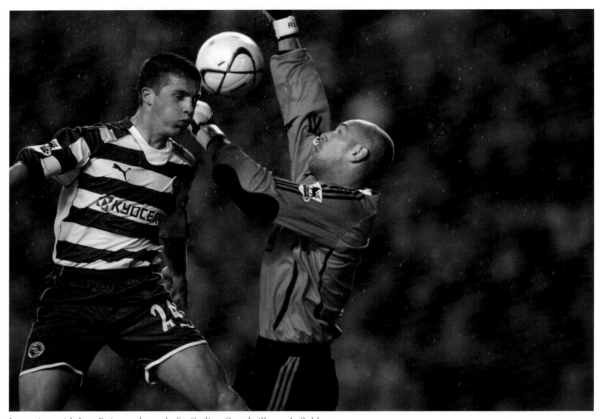

Long rises with Jose Reina at the end of a Carling Cup thriller at Anfield.

Two trips to Anfield followed, making history as Reading faced Liverpool for the very first time. The first saw a much-changed Royals side narrowly edged out in a 4–3 thriller – goals from Leroy Lita, Andre Bikey and Shane Long rattling Rafa's men with a late comeback but not enough to halt Reading's exit from the Cup competition. The second fixture saw Reading experiment with a 5–4–1 formation, but Dirk Kuyt – who had skippered Feyenoord in a pre-season defeat at Madejski Stadium in the summer – bagged a brace in another Liverpool victory. Sandwiched in-between was a difficult trip to Fratton Park and, for the first time since sealing

Harper battles with Liverpool maestro Xabi Alonso.

promotion to the top flight (and arguably since a 3–1 defeat at Wigan on the final day of Reading's unsuccessful 2004–05 Championship play-off campaign), Steve Coppell's men flattered to deceive. Brynjar Gunnarsson had needed some dental work after an aerial clash with Peter Crouch earlier in the week, and his first Premier League start did not go much better – his near-post own-goal was followed by a Kanu stab and Pedro Mendes' sweetly struck volley as Pompey took a three-goal lead. Mendes handled on the line to prevent Gunnarsson pulling one back and Doyle eventually did scramble one past David James, but the Royals were well beaten.

Five consecutive defeats meant questions were being asked of Reading's self-belief. Their season was threatening to be thrown off track – live on Sky for the fifth consecutive home clash – when Tottenham stormed into a Madejski Stadium lead with a calmly taken Robbie Keane spot kick. The home team's resilience was plain for all to see, and a new stadium attendance record of 24,110 saw the Sunday afternoon encounter come to life with a Nicky Shorey 'screamer'. Receiving the ball 25 yards out, the left back spotted a gap and unleashed a swerving left-footed thunderbolt that bulleted low past Paul Robinson's desperate dive and inside the right post. 'Shorey for England' chants rang around the stands as the campaign to get the full back into the international set-up quickly gathered pace. Coppell, not keen on losing more players to international duty, praised Shorey's

importance while playing his England chances down. 'He's very, very important to us. He's a hell of a good player. His use of the ball is top quality. He's a foundation for us in getting from defence to attack. But I'm not going to campaign anyone for international recognition. I'm reminded of the prayer "to labour and not ask for reward". Football does its own talking.'

Shorey's equaliser inspired a dramatic return to full confidence for Reading, and before the break the hosts had the lead; Glen Little's inswinging corner was missed by an unmarked Doyle at the near post, but a similarly unseen Steve Sidwell took advantage of some woeful Tottenham defensive work to poke home the loose ball from close range. Madejski Stadium was rocking again. Games and seasons can turn on fine margins and, had substitute Jermaine Defoe struck his second half on-the-swivel effort on target, a lot of things might have been different. But with Defoe firing wide, Leroy Lita flicked Hahnemann's goal kick into

Doyle's path and the Irish strike star brilliantly held off Ledley King to drive wide of Robinson and low into the bottom-right corner to seal a 3–1 win.

A sense of excited anticipation ran through the club as Royals fans were routinely treated to new opponents. There was a freshness to their first top flight season that is so rarely experienced (perhaps a contributing factor to the team's 2006–07 success and its absence being a possible excuse for the season that followed), so even the clashes with lesser names drew interest. After Iain Dowie's departure, the inexperienced Les Reed led Charlton to Madejski Stadium and a familiar feeling swept through the home crowd. In a runaway title-winning season, fans and players became accustomed to expecting three points to come their way as soon as the 11 self-assured players stepped onto the field. And a 2–0 triumph over the Addicks seemed so pleasantly routine. Starting as a striker, Seol nodded Shorey's chipped cross past Scott

Carson only 18 minutes in. After opening his Irish account in a 5–0 thrashing of San Marino earlier in the week, Doyle added a second goal 18 minutes from time, as Sidwell's mishit effort fortuitously spun into Doyle's path and the striker instinctively touched it home. For the first time in the Premier League, it never seemed as though the result was in any doubt – Reading had calmly and quickly settled into their top-flight life.

Doyle continued his outstanding goalscoring form at Fulham – the Irishman drawing the foul from a red-carded Ian Pearce and converting from the spot to separate the sides. Doyle revealed afterwards:

I was reading something over the summer on why the Germans score and why the English miss. The Germans went through everything they did, analysed everything, even counting the number of steps back they take. It was the same for every penalty whether in training or in a match. Now I have a routine which I practise in training a lot. I take a lot of deep breaths to relax and I know what I am going to do beforehand. It is not perfect – I missed one in the Carling Cup against Darlington and I will probably miss the next one now! But I don't leave anything to chance.

He was the man on target again when Bolton came to town, rising high to plant his head onto John Oster's delightfully dinked cross and power home the only goal of the game with his fourth in four. 'When Kevin first came to the club, we didn't know about him,' teammate Sidwell admitted. 'He got his chance when Dave Kitson was injured last season and, since then, he has played in virtually every match. There are often strikers who burst on to the scene and Kevin is one of those. He's proving what a real handful he is. Off the pitch, he is down to earth, gets on with his training and is always willing to learn.'

Four straight wins had seen the Royals climb the table and achieve astonishing heights for a side almost entirely new to top-flight football. A win over Newcastle at St James' could have catapulted Steve Coppell's high-flyers into third place at the start of December, and they led thanks to a

Seol wheels away after scoring in a routine victory over Charlton.

Harper scores the second of two to thrust Reading into the lead at Newcastle.

Hunt scampers away against Blackburn.

James Harper brace before the break. But against the run of play, Obafemi Martins earned a dubious penalty and slotted home from the spot before an Emre wonder strike dealt Reading a long, pointless trip home. Reading's desire to attack and search for the win had possibly gone against them at Newcastle, and as a reaction a goalless draw and a much grittier display followed at Watford. A winnable Madejski Stadium double header ran Reading into Christmas, so hopes were high for a continued rise. Europe was slowly becoming a word strongly associated with Reading FC, as the qualification places did not seem an unreasonable ambition.

Sadly the pre-festive fixtures did not go according to plan. Harper's 41st-minute finish against Blackburn marked his third goal in three games and sparked some touchline tangoing with kit man Ron Grant – the pair had first shared their fancy footwork at St James' 10 days earlier. But Benni McCarthy finally converted the last of a host of chances to level, and another 25-yard stunning strike by David Bentley – bizarrely virtually the same 84th-minute strike as Emre's 10 days earlier – denied Reading points. Looking for a reaction against Everton the following weekend, the home fans were disappointed. Andy Johnson stabbed home Mikel Arteta's cut back early in the opening half, and any hopes of another Royals comeback were quashed when James McFadden added a second two minutes after the interval.

The fragmented festive period threw up mouth-watering matches at Chelsea and then Manchester United, the first of which took place with the events at Madejski Stadium earlier in the season providing a backdrop that added extra bite. Stephen Hunt received a brief torrent of abuse while warming up at Stamford Bridge on Boxing Day, but the Blues fans were truly hushed as Reading twice bounced back from Didier Drogba-dealt leads – former Chelsea trainee Leroy Lita stooping to head home Glen Little's cross for the first, and Ashley Cole's clearance hitting Michael Essien and dribbling over the home goalline for 2–2 late on. 'Little Reading' were having an impact on the title chase and, after

all the accusations issued by Chelsea over the last few weeks, the Royals left London with a smug sense of pride…and a point. There were no such heroics at Old Trafford, although the majority of the 75,910 at the Theatre of Dreams were nervously whistling for referee Mike Dean to blow up at the end, with Lita again threatening a similar comeback in a 3–2 defeat to United. And this was not to be the two teams' last meeting in 2006–07.

'We've had two tough games and come through unscathed,' Doyle remarked ahead of 2007's curtain-raiser against West Ham. 'We've changed

formations and shown we can do that, but now we're back at home. Hopefully we'll be back to 4–4–2 and out for all three points.' The games had come thick and fast, and Reading had been handed the hardest possible double header over Christmas, but back at home Coppell's men were simply out of this world, kicking-off the new year with a scintillating 6–0 romp against Alan Curbishley's demoralised Hammers.

Gunnarsson began proceedings in a simple opener for the Icelander's first top-flight goal, cunningly ghosting between bodies to glance Shorey's inswinging free kick past Robert Green. Hunt followed suit by breaking

Doyle skips over a challenge from United's Wes Brown.

Anton Ferdinand is the unlucky man to score an own goal and notch the third of six to fly past Robert Green.

his duck only three minutes later, heading Sidwell's floated cross across Green. The lively Irishman scampered down the East Stand touchline jumping high into the air as if his bouncing body had been possessed. 'It's a dream come true – my first goal in the Premiership! It was great and I hope there are more to come. I was a bit surprised by my celebration, though. It was shocking!'

Reading were rampant and West Ham were imploding; an injured Lee Bowyer bowed out before Anton Ferdinand turned a delightful Shorey free kick into his own net at the near post. Shorey's outstanding impact was further emphasised by a scintillating solo run down the middle that led to the fourth goal, as James Harper crossed for Doyle to tap in at the far post. The scoreline read 4–0 at the break. New Year's Day had never felt so good! 'Once we got to half time it was a case of stopping it getting to 8–0,' Hammers boss Alan Curbishley forlornly explained. 'We were not going to turn it around – it was just a question of not letting in a lot more.'

Despite West Ham's second half defiance, two more flew past Robert Green. Lita first slid in to scramble Sidwell's low cross inside the near post, and Doyle notched his second by calmly heading Shorey's inswinging corner past the desolate Hammers keeper. Having hit the relegation-fearing Londoners for six, a flourishingly offensive Reading recorded the biggest

Brynjar Gunnarsson starts the rot against the Hammers.

Doyle rubs salt into West Ham's wounds.

victory of the top flight season and scored six at Madejski Stadium for the first time in one game. 'That was terrific for us, and an occasion to enjoy.

To have that energy and flow was a tremendous compliment to the players. They'd put in such application and discipline to prepare for this game

and today things went our way,' Coppell calmly commented. 'They had enthusiasm, pace, shape, aggression and above all hunger,' a glum-faced

The inspirational Shorey in a New Year's Day massacre.

Curbishley agreed. 'I look at Reading and I see a lot of the things you need in your side. Our team last year was playing like the Reading of today, with commitment and confidence.' It was certainly an afternoon to behold for all Reading fans.

Expecting the morning papers to be filled with colourful images of Doyle wheeling away to celebrate his second, Hunty bounding down the touchline as all the pent-up tension was released with his first Premier League goal and Leroy saluting his fans after adding his name to the scoresheet, Reading fans were a little disappointed as the headlines dwelled on West Ham's sorry demise instead. 'We don't need recognition, we're just not bothered,' an unconcerned Coppell commented. 'We've had

enough praise this year and we've got no thirst for headlines or the desire to be on the tip of people's tongues. We get on with things very, very quietly and hopefully efficiently.'

After the thrills of West Ham, a huge anti-climax followed when the Royals' first FA Cup hurdle fell foul of the weather and, for the first time in Madejski Stadium history, a fixture was postponed before a ball had been kicked. Despite thunderous torrents of rain falling on the sodden turf, referee Rob Styles was hopeful the third-round tie between Reading and Burnley could be played. But with the players warming up in puddles and the downpour so relentless, the decision was soon made for the man in black. No one could argue and the tie was fast rearranged for three days later. For the

first time ever, Reading were a potential top-flight scalp instead of a plucky lower-League team looking for a giant-killing. This giant was not ready to topple though and, before an hour had been played, in front of 11,514 fans who had returned for the tie, Coppell's changed side were three goals to the good. Lita and a stunning Shane Long strike had given Reading a healthy half-time lead before Sam Sodje's towering header added another. Although Ade Akinbiyi pulled one back and substitute Gareth O'Connor scored an injury-time consolation, Reading were comfortable winners and would meet Birmingham in the next round.

Sylvester Stallone was the unlikely centrepiece when Reading travelled to Everton's Goodison Park the following week. The Rocky star was a high-profile Toffees supporter that afternoon but could only inspire David Moyes' side to a 1–1 draw. A true tussle more commonly found in one of Sly's boxing bouts took place when Sheffield United visited Madejski Stadium in late January. Neil Warnock has never been one to shy away from a confrontation, and the Blades boss made headlines while earning himself a tidy fine for some more sideline antics. On the pitch, it was eventful enough. Sidwell's momentum and sheer desire seemed to get the ball into the six-yard box, and Shane Long popped up to score his first Premier League goal on the stroke of half time, joyously flattening Kingsley by the corner flag. A much less likely scorer added another with an unstoppable break from the left back that ended in Ulises De La Cruz opening his Royals account with a stunning virtuoso goal. Warnock was riled – again his side were being systematically undone by Reading – and when Keith Gillespie received a red card after elbowing Hunt only seconds after coming on as a substitute, his mood failed to improve. Whether asking his players to battle hard in the challenge or complaining about a Sidwell tackle that had upset him, the Blades boss's touchline gesture did not look good and Wally Downes took exception to it. The handbags were out as the two benches tussled momentarily before being banished to the stands, where they watched Hunt, ironically, end the game as a contest by acrobatically hooking a third home.

Handbags ensue on the touchline.

The Royals were making light of key injuries by consistently picking up points and consolidating their top half status. Sidelined by knee and hamstring injuries, as well as an appendix operation, Dave Kitson's long-awaited return coincided with a hamstring injury for Kevin Doyle. Kitson's first goal back came in a 3–2 FA Cup fourth-round win at Birmingham City. And returning to Berkshire, January ended with a fifth win from six when Wigan were easily swept aside thanks to Long, Ingimarsson and Lita goals cancelling out Emile Heskey's third-minute opener and rendering Denny Landzaat's injury-time goal a mere consolation.

Before kick-off against the Latics, Greg Halford became the Royals' latest January transfer window signing, following Cork City's Alan Bennett, teenage Aussie Oliver Bozanic and young goalkeeper Mikkel Andersen to join the Madejski Stadium ranks.

Experienced defender Michael Duberry was also added as cover for Ibrahima Sonko, who was ruled out for the remainder of the campaign with a cruciate knee ligament injury sustained during the win over Sheffield United.

Despite the injuries to Doyle and Sonko, Coppell's men felt invincible. Lita bagged a brace to stun Manchester City and his under-21 boss Stuart Pearce in a 2–0 win at Eastlands, before Sidwell followed suit in dismantling Aston Villa by the same scoreline in an early afternoon kick-off at Madejski Stadium, which was fuller than ever (24,112). The golden 40-point mark had been surpassed so swiftly that even Coppell was prepared to admit that top flight status had been safely negotiated.

Drawn away to Manchester United in the FA Cup, the dream kept getting better. Adam Federici's patience as understudy to the immoveable Marcus Hahnemann was being richly rewarded with Cup starts and outrageous saves

Lita thrilled with brace in front of his under-21 boss at Eastlands.

from Burnley's Ade Akinbiyi, and Birmingham City striker Cameron Jerome touted the Aussie as a potential successor to Mark Schwarzer on the Aussie international scene. After a similarly spectacular reaction stop to deny Henrik Larsson a winner at Old Trafford, the unheralded young goalkeeper was thrust into the limelight and awarded the FA's Player of the Fifth Round accolade. Reading secured a famous 1–1 draw in the Theatre of Dreams thanks to Gunnarsson's brilliant second half header, but the Royals stalled to disastrous effect in the opening minutes of the replay, only days after a long League trip north to a victorious Middlesbrough.

Live on the BBC Federici fast went from hero to zero, letting Gabriel Heinze's 25-yard drive skim under his sprawling dive to gift United a second-minute lead. Louis Saha raced onto Rio Ferdinand's punt forward to squeeze

another past Federici only two minutes later, and a previously raucous Madejski Stadium was almost completely silenced when Ole Gunnar Solskjaer converted a one-on-one to make it 3–0 in only the sixth minute. 'It was just crash, bang and then wallop! A real sloppy start. We were all at sea for those 10 minutes,' the Royals boss recalled. He reacted though, abandoning a five-man back line and reverting to a more familiar 4–4–2 formation. Reading's unbelievable character again began to shine through. Federici made amends with an excellent save from Kieran Richardson, and Edwin Van der Sar saved from Sidwell, Seol and Oster at the other end. He could do nothing about Dave Kitson's far post header though, reducing the deficit to 3–1.

Reading dominated the second half and Kitson was denied a second goal by Van der Sar's superb save, only for Leroy Lita to send a superb diving

header past the Dutch stopper to make it 3–2 in the 84th minute and set up a grandstand finish. It was electric and Sir Alex was forced to introduce Wayne Rooney and Cristiano Ronaldo to proceedings, as he feared one of the greatest Cup comebacks. Seconds remained when John Oster fed the hero from the first fixture – Brynjar Gunnarsson. From just outside the box, the Icelander unleashed a fearsome unstoppable drive that fizzed through Van der Sar's flailing palms and hammered against United's crossbar.

Ferguson's team held on but the veteran manager later admitted 'I thought we had to get ready for extra time. The game was with Reading, there's no question about that. I told Scholesy to go and get himself ready for extra time because it was going that way.' Coppell told the post-match press: 'Just put yourselves in their situation, being 3–0 down in a game

against debutant Greg Halford – and only pick up goalless points in a drab home meeting with Portsmouth and an away trip to relegation-threatened Charlton. Liverpool frustratingly took all three points at Madejski Stadium too, with substitute Dirk Kuyt nodding home fellow sub Jermaine Pennant's far-post cross to prevent the home fans celebrating Gunnarsson's stunning right-footed drive as a deserved point-winner.

The defeats did not excuse Coppell from having to field countless questions about his side's chances of a European qualifying spot. 'Our objective is to finish as high as we can, not just to make a brief foray into Europe which may not be of help to this club,' an honest boss repeatedly revealed. Coppell had penned a two-year contract, breaking his regular one-year rule, to commit himself to the long-term cause at Madejski Stadium. Knowing he had the Club's best future interests at heart, his words held even more gravitas: 'We're not geared up for Europe yet. It would be too heavy a load in our development, which would not be good for us. Europe has been a burden to a lot of clubs, and we can't afford to have that burden. Our concern is just playing our Cup Finals every weekend in the Premiership.'

Meanwhile, the reserve team were plying their trade against top-flight opposition for the first time too and with astonishing success. Madejski Stadium attracted huge four-figured

that you're desperate to do well in. Coming back from that was just terrific. It's not often I say there's honour in defeat, but I can compliment them all. They were warriors, they never lay down and died. They kept getting up again and again, and that has to be one of our best qualities.'

Reading's Cup ambitions were over for another season, but an unlikely European berth remained up for grabs. A tough run of fixtures saw the top flight newcomers beaten by penalty kicks at Arsenal and Tottenham – the second of which was awarded for an extremely harsh handball decision

Kitson nods past Van der Sar to give Steve Coppell's men hope.

crowds on midweek Soccer PM evenings, and after Brian McDermott's side had surged to the Barclays Premier Reserve League South title, the stadium welcomed more than 4,000 for the Final against North Division winners Bolton. Alan Bennett and Alex Pearce scored the goals to prompt scenes of jubilation, which included some dramatic pyrotechnics as the Chairman celebrated with the squad and the silverware on the podium at full time.

The women's team had also secured promotion in their first season in existence, and Eamonn Dolan's under-18s had only missed out on a title of their own by the narrowest of margins – Leicester pipped our Academy starlets, who had entertained Madejski Stadium crowds with successive 5–1 FA Youth Cup victories over Coventry and Blackburn earlier in the year. Talk about strength in depth!

As the first team season sauntered into its final five fixtures, a gaggle of photographers gathered to focus on a newly appointed Premier League manager under immediate pressure, as

Lawrie Sanchez's furrowed brow led a lowly Fulham to Madejski Stadium. The full house that crammed into Madejski Stadium took the total number of fans who had watched the Royals in 2006–07 to more than a million, and they saw Irish midfielder Stephen Hunt ruin the former Northern Ireland manager's afternoon with a close-range 15th-minute finish. An astonishing late comeback at Bolton followed, in which Kevin Doyle (twice) – who had recently received a PFA Young Player of the Year nomination – and Hunt overturned a Nicky Shorey own-goal to earn the Royals an amazing 3–1 win in a six-minute-long final flurry.

The next side to visit Madejski Stadium were Newcastle, and again the hype surrounded a famous face that formed part of the visiting side. Michael Owen ended his latest injury lay-off with a bright performance, but it was Dave Kitson who stole the headlines with a second home goal, following up his opening-day strike against the Magpies' north-east rivals. Kitson spotted Seol's cross and read

John Oster's dummy to control and smash an unstoppable volley past Shay Given for the only goal of the game early in the second half. Jumping into the East Stand fans, Kitson's outpouring of emotion was a thank you to the fans for the support he had received during an injury-hampered campaign. 'I finally got one in the League again, it's fantastic and I'm on top of the world! Some people say they lose their head when they celebrate, but I knew exactly what I was doing, and I knew I'd get booked! I jumped into the fans because when it wasn't going the way I wanted there was not one bit of criticism – they were always behind me. It was a way of saying thank you, even if it might have been a bit feeble!' Kitson's goal meant that Reading were in prime position to secure a UEFA Cup spot!

In playing down his side's European chances, Coppell had said 'It might sound like I'm protecting my handicap by scoring two eights on the last two holes, but that's not what's happening here. Wherever we finish, we will accept the consequences of that.' However, to everyone's immense dismay, he double bogeyed when Watford came for Madejski Stadium's curtain call. A hapless Watford were already well relegated when they arrived, but Marlon King had his own injury nightmare to end and he did so in style by sealing a 2–0 win for the Hornets. It was a strange end to a fabulous campaign – the lap of honour came after one of the most disheartening results of the nine months, but fans still applauded what had been an

Shorey battles with David Bentley in an entertaining 3–3 on the final day.

historic Madejski Stadium campaign.

Drama unfolded at Blackburn on the final day, as Reading came from behind three times to draw level with Mark Hughes' men in a desperate bid to nick seventh spot from Bolton. Wanderers could only manage a point against Aston Villa, but the Royals needed to better Bolton's result to secure a route into the UEFA Cup. And as a last-gasp Ivar Ingimarsson header was ruled out for a push, Reading's plucky efforts won them immense pride, widespread admiration and global recognition – but no UEFA Cup slot. Chairman John Madejski summarised:

I have to say that in my wildest dreams I didn't think we'd be spending the season in the top half of the Premiership. It's beyond my expectations and everyone else's as well. It just goes to show the grooming and professionalism of Reading Football Club, from the manager and players through to the backroom staff and the rest of the people who work here behind the scenes. It's been a great season which has rewarded all the hard work that has gone on. And we must not forget the fans, who have played a huge role in the achievements we've enjoyed over the last few seasons.

'Whatever we do, we're making history,' was the sentence Steve Coppell (voted the League Managers' Association Manager of the Season for the second consecutive year) continuously quoted throughout the campaign. 'Everyone questioned whether we had the ability to meet the test this season, and maintaining our status here is a much bigger achievement than we made last season with 106 points. Last season was magnificent, but this has been even better.'

2006–07 Barclays Premier League – in and around us:

		P	W	D	L	GD	Pts
6	Everton	38	15	13	10	+16	58
7	Bolton W	38	16	8	14	-5	56
8	**Reading**	**38**	**16**	**7**	**15**	**+5**	**55**
9	Portsmouth	38	14	12	12	+3	54
10	Blackburn R	38	15	7	16	-2	52

Champions: Manchester United
Relegated: Watford, Sheffield United, Charlton Athletic

FA Cup: Fifth round (v Manchester United)
League Cup: Third round (v Liverpool)

Top scorer: Kevin Doyle (13)

Most appearances: Marcus Hahnemann (38), Ivar Ingimarsson (38), Nicky Shorey (37)

Kevin Doyle

NICKY SHOREY

Reading appearances: 296
Reading goals: 12

A reserve team friendly against Bristol City at Palmer Park is not the most salubrious of surroundings to start your Reading career, especially for someone who would become the club's first England international for more than a century, but that is exactly how Nicky Shorey's time in Berkshire got underway. The 19-year-old was spending a brief trial spell from Leyton Orient in February 2001 and quickly impressed Alan Pardew sufficiently to prompt the manager to fork out the modest sum of £25,000 for a permanent transfer.

He had only played 16 games for the Os and spent the remainder of the 2000–01 season quietly settling into life at his new club with a series of impressive performances for the reserves. His first team bow came in a hugely impressive 4–0 demolition of Luton Town in the League Cup on 21 August 2001, and he was soon applying great pressure on the first team's incumbent left back, Matthew Robinson. Finally, with Pardew's job under threat following a series of disappointing results, Shorey helped the team to an important 2–0 victory at Northampton and there was no looking back. He enjoyed a seamless introduction to the team, starting every game as the Royals went on a superb run of form to claim promotion from Division Two.

MEN WHO MADE THE MADEJSKI

Shorey remained a constant automatic selection throughout the remainder of Alan Pardew's tenure, and there was never any doubt that he would retain a starting slot once Steve Coppell took over. Shorey's greatest asset was his consistency – a superb passer of the ball, he was also a very reliable defender who hardly ever seemed to make a mistake. He was never flustered in possession, and his wicked crosses were another impressive aspect of his play, along with vicious shooting ability from set pieces, which yielded memorable goals against Sheffield United and Queen's Park Rangers among others.

By the time of the 2005–06 Championship-winning season, Shorey had developed into one of the team's most potent creative forces, despite being a defender. His cultured left foot was a constant source of dangerous crosses and incisive passes, and it was no surprise when he was named in the Championship PFA Team of the Season. But the best was still to come.

Despite all the spectacular goals and brilliant assists, arguably Shorey's most significant moment in a Reading shirt was neither of those. On the opening day of the Royals' opening Premier League game, Coppell's men found themselves 2–0 down against Middlesbrough and in desperate need of a spark. Shorey provided it, receiving possession in his own half, cutting inside past a challenge and embarking upon a winding run before releasing a perfectly weighted throughball to Kevin Doyle. The Irishman's shot was saved, but the mood inside the stadium was completely changed and Reading were lifted. They went on to complete a famous come-

from-behind 3–2 victory, and boss Coppell frequently cited Shorey's run and pass as the turning point.

The left back's exceptional form continued as the Royals enjoyed a memorable first season in the top flight, and chants of 'Shorey for England' regularly rang out around Madejski Stadium. That was never more the case than on New Year's Day 2007 when a superlative Shorey display inspired the team to a stunning 6–0 victory. He later admitted that it was probably his best performance in a Reading shirt, and it did his growing case for international recognition no harm whatsoever.

England boss Steve McClaren could not ignore those claims, and shortly after the season's conclusion he selected Shorey in his B squad for a friendly against Albania at Burnley's Turf Moor. Although Michael Owen's return to the England fold stole the headlines, Shorey was quietly impressive and within days he had been called into McClaren's senior squad. An international debut beckoned, and the timing could not have been better as England prepared to take on Brazil on Friday 1 June…in the very first international fixture at the new Wembley Stadium.

With regular selections Ashley Cole and Wayne Bridge both injured, speculation was mounting that Shorey would be named to start, although in truth the pre-match build-up was dominated by another 'new' name in the squad, as former skipper David Beckham ended his international exile. To the delight of Reading fans everywhere, the news was confirmed when McClaren handed in his teamsheet – Nicky Shorey was starting for England! It seemed too

good to be true and would have reduced most people to a gibbering wreck, but Shorey turned in a typically calm and composed performance to play the full 90 minutes (one of only five players to do so) in a 1–1 draw. For Reading fans, it seemed the perfect way to end an unforgettable first season in the top flight, but Nicky himself had no time to relax and celebrate because the following day brought another rather important event to his attention – his wedding.

Shorey remained a regular fixture in the England set-up for the remainder of McClaren's ill-fated regime, making his second international appearance in a 2–1 defeat against Germany, but he seemed to suffer after McClaren controversially overlooked the Reading man in favour of Everton central-defender Joleon Lescott for a decisive Euro 2008 qualifier in Moscow. Like many of his Royals teammates, Shorey suffered a dip in form during the second season syndrome experienced in 2007–08 and was powerless to prevent relegation, but his place in history was already assured – a £25,000 left back from Leyton Orient had become Reading's first full international for more than a century.

More Than A Game:

Just as the move to the new stadium meant huge changes to the way the football club operated, so it led the Supporters' Club (RFSC) to rethink just what its role was. For decades, its focus had been on fundraising and maintenance work, together with social activities, a souvenir shop and running the away coaches, all carried out by a core of hardworking volunteers.

In the wake of the Hillsborough disaster and the hooliganism era of the 70s and 80s, a new government-funded organisation called Supporters Direct (SD) had been established 'to help people who wish to play a responsible part in the life of the football club they support'. SD's role was to encourage the formation of supporters' trusts 'to deliver responsible, democratic representation at football clubs to help promote the highest standards of governance, financial accountability and community re-orientation'.

By 2001, there were more than 100 trusts throughout England, with wide representation in the Premier League. The RFSC Committee, led by Chairman Martin Brailli and his predecessor Roger Titford, decided that it was time to adopt this wider, more accountable and professional approach and create Reading's own supporters' trust. So, after a lengthy legal process, on 28 March 2002, Reading Football Supporters' Society Limited, a democratically-run Industrial and Provident Society with its own legal constitution and regulated by the Financial Services Authority, was born

The nunber-13 shirt is proudly displayed before kick-off at Madejski Stadium.

— we, of course, all know it by its trading name, STAR, 'Supporters' Trust at Reading'. RFSC was absorbed into STAR and several existing committee members were voted on to the initial STAR board. Chris Witcher, a finance director in the financial sector and an active Reading supporter since the 1950s, was invited to be the first Chairman.

'One of the first things we had to do,' Chris says, 'was to look at STAR's constitution (you can see it on our website at www.star-reading.org.uk) and decide just what our priorities

were going to be. We quickly decided that RFSC's core activities, much valued by supporters – especially the away coaches, the shop (or "STAR base", as it's now known!) and the popular Fans' Forums where members get the chance to quiz and to meet the manager and players, for example – would continue.

'There are 13 trusts who own and run their football club and many more that are associated with clubs that are badly run or which have dubious ownership. We had the luxury of being

able to focus our efforts on the one thing that we all have in common: a passionate desire to see Reading FC succeed at the highest level. There's a lot in our constitution about promoting football in the local community and strengthening the bonds between the Club and the community and representing the interests of the community in the running of the Club.

'So we felt that the key role that STAR could perform was to do all we could to persuade as many people as possible to come along to matches – to convince the people of Reading that supporting the Royals is easy, enjoyable and safe; that everyone is equally welcome to be a part of what we are doing – and that remains our core objective.'

STAR has tackled this in various ways. Here are just a few examples.

- Liaison between supporters and the Club: regular, monthly meetings with the Club's senior management have been of great benefit to both supporters and the club. Fans' day-to-day concerns are raised with the club and vice-versa.

- Relationships with other Clubs' supporters and the police: rivalry between supporters is what the game is all about, but STAR has worked hard to ensure that it is friendly rivalry and it has excellent relations with trusts and supporters' organisations throughout the country, as well as with the police.

- Disabled supporters: the interests of

Happy fans brave the cold.

disabled supporters are looked after, both at the stadium and for away travel.

- The 'exiles': STAR has branches for its members living away from Reading, both in the UK and abroad, and helps obtain match tickets for them when needed.
- Publicity: dealing with the media, locally, nationally and worldwide has been a big part of STAR's role, particularly since 2005.
- Social activities: these include occasionally working with the Royal Families in joint charitable fundraising activities.

The Club's success in recent years has seen a huge increase in all of STAR's activities, especially the number of coaches needed for away games and the demands of the media. The Communications team is headed by STAR vice-Chairman Jon Keen: 'When we set up the team, we couldn't possibly have imagined just how our role would take off. It's been quite mind-blowing!' And life's been pretty

The Readibus crew parked up by the East Stand.

hectic for long-time supporter Colin Bishop who runs the coaches – not to mention his wife, Melanie, who keeps the membership records and has coped with an increase in membership from 1,800 in 2003 to 3,800 in 2007, making STAR (according to Supporters Direct) one of the most successful trusts in the country!

Chris completed his five-year term of office in August 2007 and he reflects on that period. 'It seems strange looking back that, in 2002, hardly anyone knew what the letters of STAR stood for or what the organisation was. We were so

fortunate that STAR's creation coincided with the most momentous few years in the Club's history and it's been a real privilege to have been involved at a time when all of our impossible dreams have come true. We know from the reaction to the Club's successes and failures that both the Club and its supporters are highly regarded throughout football, and we hope that STAR has played its part in that.'

STAR's new Chairman is Paula Martin, known warmly to many supporters for her tireless work as STAR's Goodwill and Liaison Officer. Looking to the future, she says, 'STAR's future is very dependent on its members; as an RFSC committee member I stood for STAR's first election and have seen board members come and go, as they have to if the organisation is not to stagnate. New people mean new ideas and new directions, so where we go is down to those of our members who contribute effort.'

Chapter 10

Second Season Syndrome

Minutes after the final whistle sounded the end of the Royals' 2006–07 campaign, time was, almost inevitably, called on a distinguished Reading career. Steve Sidwell's contract negotiations had stalled the previous summer but, remaining loyal to the cause throughout, the bullish midfielder manfully helped the side through their first season in the top flight before arranging a glamour move to Chelsea. 'Steve Sidwell has been magnificent for this football club,' director of football Nick Hammond remarked. 'He's a top player and a tremendous professional who sets a fantastic example for any youngster. Everybody at Reading loves him and we wish him every success in the future.'

Steve Sidwell's departure was not unexpected.

Understandably, a pre-prepared Steve Coppell took no time in trying to fill the ex-Arsenal youngster's boots. Almost £1 million delivered French-born Malian midfielder Kalifa Cisse from Boavista to Madejski Stadium and, as the new smiling face strode with a Vieira-esque elegance through the doors, worries that the departure of an inspirational character would upset Reading's balance were somewhat allayed.

With the surprise success of the campaign still soaking in, Coppell was rightly decorated with his second successive Manager of the Year gong from the League Managers' Association. The modest manager stressed:

I'm not one for awards; I'm not one who thinks I need some kind of verification by anybody to know if I've done a good job. We've done well this year, I know that. But it's so much more pleasing when other people from your own profession say 'given the resources, given the people around, he's done a terrific job'. I appreciate that... The job of a football manager is an absolutely wonderful one. If you strip it down to the bare bones: going into training, preparing the training, preparing the team, going to games, having that camaraderie, all of that is absolutely magnificent. When you win a game, it is the best feeling ever, but the reality is that you don't win every game and when you are beaten the pressure that is placed on managers now is cruel. If you are losing, it's a lonely job.

Coppell probably already suspected that such scrutiny would be fiercely focused on his attempts to immunise Reading against the potentially fatal second season syndrome. Two more players to see the spotlight fall in their vicinity were Nicky Shorey and Leroy Lita. For an age, loyal Royals fans had bellowed the words 'Shorey for England' from Madejski Stadium's stands and his consistent displays were finally rewarded when he became the first Reading player to pull on an England shirt since Herbert Smith in 1904–05.

Meanwhile, Lita had revealed to the Club's matchday programme in the previous season that he did not think he was eligible for under-21 duty any longer. A little research discovered that he was still able to feature in the upcoming European Championships, and the Reading striker shone in Holland to earn Stuart Pearce's side a semi-final spot and the lead in their meeting with the hosts. A ludicrously long penalty shoot-out knocked England out, and Lita could only watch the spot kick drama from the bench after being substituted late on. The striker was also rested during the Club's pre-season tour to South Korea.

Back at home, the Madejski Stadium pitch had been relaid and lengthened by three metres in the process – to comply with UEFA standards – and Reading Borough Council had also granted permission to proceed with plans to increase the ground's capacity to around 38,000. Artists' impressions were updated, but a date for the start of construction was to be considered and delayed to suit.

Swapping the annual low-profile pre-season schedule spent in European backwaters for a trip to South Korea,

Stephen Hunt battles with his former teammate Sidwell in the first home game of the season.

the Peace Cup saw Steve Coppell's world-renowned outfit battle it out with River Plate, Lyon and Shimizu S-Pulse for a place in the Final. Despite 1–0 wins over the French champions and Japanese outfit, goal difference (crucial not for the last time in 2007–08) was to send a starry-eyed Royals squad home a few days before finalists Bolton lost out to Lyon in Seoul. But it was a very worthwhile tour – the 'Reading brand' was being circulated, new partnerships were being forged and the Royals had been idolised since the start of their 10-day stay. Ironically, the link that prompted Reading's invitation to the competition was winger Seol Ki-Hyeon who, having barely featured in the tournament due to an ankle injury, was soon on his way out of Reading – Seol's swap sale with Fulham's Liam Rosenior sparked some deadline day activity at Madejski Stadium.

With the signature of Nantes and Ivory Coast midfielder Emerse Fae also secured, Brentford, Brighton and

Andre Bikey celebrates the opener against Chelsea.

Stephen Hunt battles with his former teammate Sidwell in the first home game of the season.

Wolves were all comfortably beaten as pre-season edged to an end and, despite the fixture machine spitting out the most daunting of starts at Manchester United, it all started relatively promisingly. Marcus Hahnemann was fit to begin the campaign despite needing 16 screws to fix a shattered hand, fractured in a final-day collision with Benni McCarthy at Ewood Park in May, and the big American marked his return with an impressive clean sheet at Old Trafford as a resolute Reading side repelled the inevitable United attacks and held firm for a point – even with 10 men for the final 18 minutes, after substitute Dave Kitson's start to

the season lasted just 37 seconds courtesy of a lunge on Patrice Evra.

Having picked up their first point at the home of the champions, the Madejski Stadium curtain-raiser saw runners-up Chelsea revisit Madejski Stadium for the first time since Petr Cech's unfortunate injury and the controversy that ensued, with Steve Sidwell starting against the side he helped pilot to an eighth-placed finish the previous season. But by the time a lacklustre Sidwell was replaced at half time by Claudio Pizarro, Reading rightly led – Cech's mistimed punch saw the ball bobble loose and substitute Andre Bikey slid home into an empty net before somersaulting towards the fans. Chelsea were freezing under the early season scrutiny, but Stephen Hunt – the

Hunt wheels away after scoring the only goal against high-flying Everton.

man inescapably under the most ruthless examination – was thriving. The livewire Irishman provided the cross that almost led to 2–0, as John Oster spurned a glorious chance by agonisingly lashing an effort against the woodwork.

Seeing the Royals dominate against Jose Mourinho's star-studded Blues, a packed Madejski Stadium crowd was in full voice, but the furore was quelled in a five-minute flourish from the visitors after the break. Frank Lampard ran onto an innocuous flick on and, beating Nicky Shorey to the ball, he touched it wide of the onrushing Hahnemann to restore parity. With Reading still catching their breath, Didier Drogba arced a superb edge-of-the-area effort inside the right post for a relatively undeserved lead. After Kalifa Cisse's home debut had come to an abrupt end

with a very harsh second yellow, Chelsea – as the top four teams tend to – held on.

Everton's opening week had earned them the early top spot in the table, and the Toffees visited Berkshire looking to build on confident victories over Wigan and Spurs. But, one minute before the break, the Merseysiders' unbeaten streak came to an end and Madejski Stadium welcomed its first three points of the 2007–08 campaign; Kevin Doyle held Alan Stubbs off to allow Ulises De La Cruz's long throw to drift into the box, where the in-form Hunt nudged ahead of Tony Hibbert to control and deftly finish with his right foot from close range.

Coppell was impressed, 'I don't like singling players out but if there's a better left-sider in the Premier League

than Hunty at the moment, he must be playing fantastically well. He used to be known as a hard-working player, but he's added so much. Hunty's matured quickly and his leadership is coming through more and more.' Everton had their chances, but it seemed Madejski Stadium would continue to be a place even the best sides feared to visit.

An international break saw Shorey star for England against Germany and Shane Long score a superb brace for Ireland against Denmark, but when club football resumed, a leg-weary Reading were harshly handed a long trip to Bolton, where they were soundly beaten by Gary Speed, Nicolas Anelka and Daniel Braaten goals. Another journey to Swansea City's new Liberty Stadium was next in the Carling Cup, and Steve Coppell's 10 men (with Sam Sodje

Hunt's fury is eased by Harper after taunts from Craig Bellamy.

becoming the third Royals player to receive a red in the opening five matches) could only edge over the line in extra time courtesy of a scrambled Leroy Lita finish.

When West Ham lined up for a Madejski Stadium clash at the start of September, memories of the six-goal New Year's Day drubbing were swiftly replaced by a rampant Hammers outfit, who gained ample revenge. Craig Bellamy's pace carved out a simple opener after just six minutes and, as Reading floundered, Alan Curbishley's men doubled the advantage through Matthew Etherington soon after the break. Etheringon scored his second breakaway goal in the dying stages to condemn Reading to their second 3–0 defeat on the bounce.

Suddenly questions were being asked, and they were questions Steve Coppell was struggling to answer. The transfer window had slammed shut, and Reading looked exposed in a number of areas. Seol had signed for Fulham, John Oster was struggling with an ankle injury and Glen Little was still some way off returning from a long-term achilles injury, so the right side of midfield was a major source of alarm. At the back, Ibrahima Sonko was still missing with his cruciate knee injury, and, in midfield, Scott Brown's decision to opt for Celtic as opposed to a £4.4 million switch to Reading had left Brynjar Gunnarsson holding the fort; Emerse Fae and Kalifa Cisse were taking time to adapt to Premier League football. Up front, matters were starting to settle down — Leroy Lita had

Lita scores an extra time winner at Swansea.

returned to action after a freak leg injury had ruled him out of the opening encounters, Long and Kevin Doyle had each found the net on the international scene and Dave Kitson's three-match suspension had elapsed to allow the flame-haired frontman to open his account with a consolation goal in a 2–1 loss at Sunderland.

Kitson bagged the opener and his 100th career goal as the Royals returned to winning ways against Wigan, but the victory was only sealed with an injury-time strike from James Harper after Marcus Bent's second half headed leveller. Racing onto Kitson's sublime reverse pass, Harper slotted the first of his six strikes for the season past Chris Kirkland to send the stadium into raptures. 'You can't underestimate the importance of this win,' Kitson remarked. 'There's an amazing change in everybody's persona when you win. It lifts everyone and you all feel 10ft tall.'

That result tempted a near full house to a second consecutive Carling Cup clash with Liverpool – this time at Madejski Stadium. In 2006–07 the Royals had been knocked out 4–3, and now a characteristically much-changed Cup outfit twice pegged their big-named opponents back but eventually suffered the same fate. Yossi Benayoun began proceedings with a well-taken opener before a stunning left-footed volley from Bobby Convey dramatically levelled things up and, although Fernando Torres elegantly nudged Liverpool back into the lead after the interval, John Halls stabbed home from

a scramble to make it 2–2. This was turning into another crowd-pleaser but £26.5 million Torres spoilt things by ensuring class finally told, with the Reds' Spanish striker scoring his second with 18 minutes remaining and then rounding Adam Federici to secure their progress on the Cup trail.

If, in League Cup defeat, Reading were proud to have taken part in a 'crowd-pleaser', excited smiles turned to confused frowns when total mayhem exploded upon Premier League resumption at Fratton Park in a game that got into the history books – for all the wrong reasons from the Royals'

point of view, as Pompey ran out 7–4 winners. 'Seven goals…I don't know what to say,' Marcus Hahnemann conceded. 'We've not become a bad team defensively overnight. We've got to figure out what we're doing. If we go down a goal we seem to go crazy. Everything is going forward – there's no caution. I don't know what's going on…seven goals is a joke.'

Ironically, that craziness was followed by a clean sheet and three much-needed points against a Derby County outfit that already seemed resigned to their bleak fate. Goalless at half time, many feared another lack of concentration could gift the Rams a lead after the break – Reading had conceded during the 10 minute post-interval spell in their last five games. That hoodoo was broken and, as Derby were shut out, Kevin Doyle's headed finish proved the difference just after the hour.

Steve Coppell's double century as Royals boss was brought up at Blackburn, but Reading once again felt the effects of a long trip north after another international interval, and the leaky defence returned to ruin his Ewood afternoon as Blackburn ran out 4–2 winners. Home form was keeping the Royals out of trouble and, when Newcastle United arrived low on confidence in late October, Madejski Stadium sensed another scalp was to be had. After the interval Dave Kitson provided the opening goal with a spectacular edge-of-the-area swipe that arrowed into the top corner. Joyously jumping into Wally Downes's arms, Kitson celebrated equalling Nicky Forster's record for goals scored at Madejski Stadium with a stunning effort that made a mockery of comments in the matchday programme, suggesting he enjoyed 'tap-ins' just as much as he did 'screamers'!

Michael Duberry's thigh cruelly deflected Emre's threatening cross past Marcus Hahnemann and it seemed the Magpies might steal a point, until super sub Shane Long came to the rescue. Long was ordered off the bench to replace Leroy Lita in the 83rd minute, and the young Irishman trotted straight

A gleeful Dave Kitson races away to celebrate his stunning strike against Newcastle.

into the box to collect Ibrahima Sonko's flick on and lash the winner past Shay Given from yards out at the far post. 'Things couldn't have gone any better for me,' a beaming Long remarked with more than a degree of understatement. 'The gaffer said to go on and grab a goal. I was ready to hit it, then I saw the keeper come out and I moved it on. I knew I just had to hit the target because the keeper was out – luckily it went in off the post.'

The winless away run continued at Fulham when late goals from Clint Dempsey and David Healy gave the Cottagers a win, and the away form was becoming such a problem that the players donated a sizeable sum towards travel for STAR members to Manchester City. Sven Goran Eriksson's high-flyers had not dropped a point at the City of Manchester Stadium, while Reading had lost five straight on their travels. Those sequences were so nearly ended after Harper's curler cancelled out Martin Petrov's early goal, only for Stephen Ireland to volley an unstoppable 20-yard effort into the top corner.

Sandwiched between those losses at Fulham and Man City was a rare Monday-night spectacle, when Arsenal were the visitors on Remembrance Day. The Royals almost held Arsene Wenger's star-studded side until half time, but once Mathieu Flamini had slid in to break the deadlock in the 43rd minute, Arsenal took full control and strolled to a 3–1 victory that amply demonstrated the gulf between the top and the bottom in the Premier League. 'They are better than us,' Coppell honestly admitted before setting about trying to concoct a plan to undo the next Madejski Stadium visitors, Middlesbrough.

Unsurprisingly, the clash with Gareth Southgate's side could not match the drama, excitement or atmosphere that took place on the opening day of the previous season – and with other results not going Reading's way, more pressure was evidently being piled onto winnable Madejski Stadium fixtures such as this one. When Kitson coolly swung out a

leg to loft the ball over the onrushing Ross Turnbull, three points looked likely. 'That goal held special significance for me,' the scorer revealed after the match. His input against the Teesiders last season had been cut horribly short after a reckless challenge from Chris Riggott, and a striker out for revenge admitted 'I thought about running past their dugout, but I thought better of it. I was over the other side in the far corner and it was a long way to run to make a silly point.' As Boro probed, fit-again Ibrahima Sonko and keeper Hahnemann momentarily squared up to each other after a misunderstanding almost gifted Jeremie Aliadiere an equaliser. Reading were losing their cool, and they were duly foiled by another late goal; Luke

Doyle glances Reading into the lead to set up victory over the mighty Liverpool.

Young crossed into Tuncay from the right and the Turkish sub striker glanced it calmly over the line.

On such fine margins can seasons turn, and a relatively goal-shy Tuncay went on to score winners against Arsenal and Derby in the weeks that followed. Precariously placed Reading could not

afford a dip in home form and, characteristically, Steve Coppell's side responded by upending one of the 'big four' for the very first time. 'I hope we have a real go, with non-stop, in-your-face football. For that to happen we need the fans,' the Royals boss explained before Liverpool's visit. 'We really need the supporters pumping us up to get the atmosphere going. That will help us maintain the tempo, and that's the only way we can get a result.' Madejski Stadium responded and so did the 11 men on the pitch. Seventeen minutes in and Bobby Convey touched a bouncing ball into Brynjar Gunnarsson's surging stride. Jamie Carragher clumsily came across and clattered into the Icelander, who was further emphasising his 'big match' player status after goals against Liverpool and Manchester United in 2006–07. Despite fervent appeals, referee Andre Marriner conferred with his linesman and stuck by his point to the penalty spot. 'We had discussed penalties during the week and said that if one came up it was between three of us –

Kits, Doyler and me,' Hunt revealed. 'It was just a matter of whoever got the ball first, and I got there ahead of them.' The winger stepped up and sent Jose Reina the wrong way to give the hosts an unlikely lead.

A typically slick passing interchange saw Rafa Benitez's men level less than 10 minutes later — Steven Gerrard supplied the slotted finish to restore parity — and honours remained fairly even until the hour mark. Gerrard scythed down a barnstorming Hunt, and Nicky Shorey supplied a sumptuous inswinging free kick that Kevin Doyle got the faintest glance to, sending it skimming past the helpless Reina for a home lead once again.

Trying to single-handedly drag his side out of strife, Gerrard lashed a brilliant long-range dipping effort against the crossbar, but his excellence was usurped by Reading's own central

midfield maestro a minute later. James Harper scampered into space and, looking to set up a quick attack, Convey threaded a pass through Liverpool's high-lined back four. Driving towards goal, Harper carried it almost 40 yards before calmly rounding Reina and tucking a cool left-footed finish inside the left upright. Joined by his teammates, Harper gleefully sprang down the touchline to celebrate with a delighted dugout, who knew his solo effort had sealed three famous points.

Peter Crouch struck the woodwork late on, but this was a day for Reading Football Club to remember. 'I'm absolutely over the moon, it was a great performance,' Chairman John Madejski remarked. 'It was a tremendous result, and everybody did the business. It was like the Reading of old. They all played out of their skins, everybody was together.' Perhaps the unity displayed in

that victory was no coincidence; every member of the starting 11 against the Reds had played a large part in the title-winning Championship season two years earlier. Now those tried, tested and trusted players had inflicted Liverpool's first League defeat of the campaign — a £50 million-plus starting side had been exposed by an 11 costing less than £3 million!

The Royals travelled to Birmingham to earn a road point with a 1–1 draw, and the same result came with a gutsy 10-man performance at West Ham on Boxing Day. In between those trips, Sunderland had visited Madejski Stadium and left with a bitter taste in their mouths. Ivar Ingimarsson gave Reading the advantage by shinning home the rebound following a Sonko header, but Sonko's mistimed challenge on Kenwyne Jones at the other end handed Michael Chopra the chance to

Ivar Ingimarsson is pumped up after his goal against Sunderland.

level from the spot, which he did eight minutes from the end. But, in the depths of injury time, sub Shane Long accelerated past his marker and shot a cross to the far post, where Hunt scuffed goalwards. Craig Gordon clawed it away but the linesman's flag signalled a goal. Chaotic home celebrations began and a fiery-eyed Roy Keane was left fuming – the controversial last-gasp winner sparked a moody response from the Black Cats manager, but no amount of prowling the Madejski Stadium corridors could alter the result.

Christmas festivities had officially been sidelined, 'We'll be in every day over Christmas. "Forget Christmas" is the policy this year, regardless of results,' Wally Downes explained. But the year ended with another high-scoring defeat (6–4) at Tottenham – the Royals had suffered defeat in the highest scoring Premier League game already this season (at Portsmouth) and now they were playing a beaten part in the second highest.

Back at home, loyal Royals hoped to see the defence atone for their frailties and see in the new year with a clean sheet against a Portsmouth side who were winless in four. In only the third minute, Sonko clumsily tripped Benjani to concede a penalty and receive a straight red card. Supporters' hearts sank as Sonko's heart was broken and, although Nico Kranjcar struck his spot kick against the base of Marcus Hahnemann's right post, Reading could not regroup in time to stop Sol Campbell bundling home Hahnemann's fumble a few minutes later. The 10-man Royals toiled, but it came as no surprise when John Utaka outpaced Nicky Shorey to calmly side-foot a second past Hahnemann and seal the points.

Another trip to Tottenham came in the third round of the FA Cup, and Reading earned a deserved replay, as Stephen Hunt and Dimitar Berbatov both notched braces (Hunt's opener was notable because it came courtesy of Paul Robinson's bizarre backpedal over his own line). But after a resounding League defeat at free-flowing Aston Villa, Reading bowed out of the Cup when Juande Ramos's men edged themselves into a fourth-round tie at Manchester United, overcoming an outstanding display of goalkeeping from Adam Federici to squeeze through with a Robbie Keane winner.

As the January transfer window swung open, Coppell snapped up two foreigners – Czech midfielder Marek Matejovsky from Mlada Boleslav and Malian international winger Jimmy Kebe from Lens. He also prevented the highly regarded Hunt from joining Sunderland and kept Shorey at Madejski Stadium but opted against making further additions to the squad, although funds had been made available. Injury-troubled loanee Peter Mate returned to Debrecen, and Simon Cox was sold to Swindon on deadline day, while a flurry of loan deals gave younger members of the squad some first team experience, but besides that it remained 'as you were' at Reading.

Despite Emerse Fae (Ivory Coast), Andre Bikey (Cameroon) and Ibrahima Sonko (Senegal) jetting off to Ghana for the African Cup of Nations, the Royals squad repaid their manager's faith by valiantly holding Manchester United for 77 minutes in a thrilling game at Madejski Stadium. Sir Alex's side had been restricted to a goalless draw on the opening day and this time, with Kalifa Cisse starting and starring at centre back, a crucial point looked likely once again until a classy flick from Wayne Rooney separated the sides late on. Ronaldo raced away to score a meaningless second in the fourth minute of injury time but performance-wise Reading were fearing nobody. A trip to Chelsea yielded no reward but

Dave Kitson and Marek Matejovsky battle hard to no avail against Bolton.

Reading's gutsy display was similarly encouraging and, with a tough string of games over, February held much promise.

Boosted by those performances and a contract extension for Player of the Season-to-be Stephen Hunt, Reading still boasted confidence when Bolton arrived in Berkshire. After they had left, it was a different story. The relegation-threatened Trotters had scored just three goals in eight games and had not won away all season, but Kevin Nolan latched onto Kevin Davies' flick to sweep the opener past Hahnemann after half an hour, and Heidar Helguson scrambled home a second to quash any sort of revival. Only a last-gasp equaliser from Derby's Emanuel Villa at Birmingham prevented the Royals from slipping into the bottom three, but the home fans took little cheer after such a lacklustre display. 'After a very difficult

January, we saw this as a new month starting against a team in our part of the division,' the boss remarked. 'We thought we could put some ground between us and them, but as it turned out they gained ground on us. We didn't look sharp from the first whistle. We huffed and puffed but never really looked like scoring. We're getting very close to the bottom three, and we need to improve in all departments. We're not firing up front and we're looking a long way off keeping clean sheets. We will be asking harsh questions of ourselves this week.'

Amid Premier League suggestions that a global 39th game could be incorporated into the season, Reading fans were starting to worry that their season might be stretched to 46. That fear grew with a slender defeat at Everton the following week and then another loss to Aston Villa at home.

Madejski Stadium had become a nervy place, radiating an anxious atmosphere that only heaped more pressure on the men the fans were desperate to inspire. Huge efforts had been made to lift the supporters and players alike for the visit of Martin O'Neill's men. Chief executive Nigel Howe called for an attitude of 'positive defiance' to resound around the ground, while the Chairman asked the fans to make Madejski Stadium a 'cauldron of optimism' in his programme notes. *Reading Evening Post* launched a 'Keepy Uppy' campaign, Nick Hammond asked us to 'rise to the challenge', Wally Downes pleaded with every season-ticket holder to 'nudge their mate' and get them singing while Murts was willing to 'battle for it, scrap and sweat blood'. Coppell stated 'It's time for action. It's the time to stand up and be counted' but, despite the best of

intentions, Reading's strenuous efforts on the pitch could not match the confident attacking prowess of Villa, who elegantly dispatched the Royals with second half goals from Ashley Young and Marlon Harewood. A vibrant Madejski Stadium fell flat.

'Something's got to change. Something has got to break the cycle we're in at the moment, because it's non-productive and we need to do something else,' Coppell admitted after the Villa defeat. On the back of an 11-game winless run, Reading had not picked up a single point since the turn of the year and had scored just two consolation goals in seven straight League defeats. Changing three of the back four for a trip to Middlesbrough at the start of March, Coppell stuck to his word. And it worked gloriously. The defence kept their first clean sheet since early October, and James Harper scored another vital goal, racing onto Stephen Hunt's injury time cut back to side-foot the ball past Mark Schwarzer

in the dying embers of a match that seemed destined to end in a draw. In the same way a stirring result against Gareth Southgate's men had reignited Reading on the opening day of their inaugural Premier League season, the shackles of second season syndrome were gleefully shrugged off with a pressure-releasing victory at the Riverside.

The Royals soon had a home victory to savour too – Manchester City had robbed Reading of a point with the last kick of the game at Eastlands, but the Royals got their revenge by taking full advantage of an injury-ravaged and consequently unbalanced visiting back line. Already without the injured Micah Richards and Nedum Onuoha, Sven's men were stuttering and City had to reshuffle yet again, when skipper Richard Dunne was forced to depart after his hefty challenge on Stephen Hunt resulted in an ankle knock. Andre

Kitson and Harper rejoice as Reading re-find their scoring boots.

Bikey swivelled to crack an angled effort against the crossbar on the hour and, two minutes later, a slick move saw Kevin Doyle outfox Michael Ball and slide a low cut back into Shane Long's path. The Irish youngster made no mistake, with an expertly taken opener.

Despite taking control, nerves were still jangling, and not until Dave Kitson jinked his way through a hesitant City defence to prod home a second could the loyal Royals rejoice. Most of the teams at the foot of the table were still to play that weekend, but for the meantime Reading were comfortable in 13th and had recorded their first back-to-back wins of the campaign.

Having refound their scoring boots and more importantly winning ways, a disgruntled Leroy Lita was allowed to leave on loan to Charlton, but Marek Matejovsky stepped up to the goalscoring plate to startle Anfield with one of the strikes of the season the following week. Driving John Oster's fizzed, square free kick high into the top-left corner with a first-time

Matejovsky scores one of the goals of the season at Anfield.

thunderbolt, Reading had a surprise lead over Rafa's troops. 'He's different,' the Royals boss had said about his midfield acquisition. 'We are fairly straightforward and simple in our approach but Marek is totally different. He's inventive with his passing, he's mature, he's bright – he could play for anybody.' Sadly, his extraordinary strike was cancelled out by a 25-yard equaliser from Javier Mascherano, and Fernando Torres pounced to stab home a scrappy winner after the break. A frustrated Long threw his shirt to the ground when he was substituted – not a sign of arrogance or disrespect, just a petulant way of expressing how upset the Royals were to have been beaten by

a side they knew they had matched for most of the 90 minutes.

Coppell called for the Madejski Stadium crowd to lift their side once again for a 'massive game' when Birmingham paid a visit. 'At Liverpool we had a very small but noisy band. It's been like that all season away from home, terrifically punching above their weight. At home this weekend, they can be our extra player. Against Manchester City, the crowd took it upon themselves to make the difference. That always registers with the players – we feel it. I always say that the atmosphere at the Madejski can be as good as some of those places with 40, 50, 60 or 70,000.'

That atmosphere did help the Royals to a vital 2–1 win over the drop-threatened Blues. An unlikely scorer aptly broke the deadlock; since Andre Bikey's return from an eventful African Cup of Nations trip with Cameroon, his defensive solidity had bred confidence in a leaky back four, and the loveable centre back rose high at the other end to glance John Oster's free kick past Maik Taylor for a 31st-minute opener. On the hour, Bikey's desperate last-gasp slide was not enough to prevent a stubborn Birmingham levelling through Mauro Zarate, but the enigmatic Cameroonian was not going to let the spotlight over his dreadlocked head fade. It was discovered afterwards

Madejski Stadium campaign late in the game; but, with 10 men, Reading conjured up their best football and created their best chance, as Long picked out Hunt with time and space in the middle, only for the winger to totally miss his kick and glance a shinned first-time effort well wide of the goal. Bolton had thrown away a two-goal lead to lose at home to Arsenal, so Marcus Hahnemann's 100th clean sheet had edged Reading closer to safety, and a point was pleasing.

March had been the Royals' most profitable month, but they travelled to a resurgent Newcastle at just the wrong time in early April. The rejuvenated Magpies made no mistake in dispatching a lifeless Reading team, as Obafemi Martins, Michael Owen and Mark Viduka found the net. So all eyes fell on the visit of Fulham and one of the biggest games in Reading Football Club's history. 'This is an opportunity for us to prove that we are more than capable of handling the pressures that come with playing in the Premier League,' the Club's injury-sidelined skipper Graeme Murty announced. 'The media spotlight will be on us and I have no doubt that our players will raise their game accordingly.'

Watching in anguish from the stands, Murty witnessed quite the opposite. An atmosphere intended to inspire the hosts ended up heaping pressure upon Reading, and the home side crumbled. Knowing only a win would really do, Fulham conversely revelled in a new-found freedom and simply outplayed Steve Coppell's men.

that Bikey had chosen to play on despite suffering the loss of his mother-in-law only days earlier. And after glancing Nicky Shorey's beautifully delivered free kick inside the near post, he followed up his trademark somersaulting celebration with a poignant point to the heavens, dedicating the winner to his 'mum wife'. 'I came today with a big motivation,' he said. 'It was not for me

only, it was for the whole family. My wife said it was better if I played because her mother would be happy for me to play, she loved to see me play.'

The following weekend, a tightly contested Madejski Stadium tussle with Blackburn yielded more reward, with a gutsy goalless point that kept the points tally ticking over. Matejovsky was harshly shown two yellow cards, prompting the third red card of the

Brian McBride set the sorry wheels in motion by sliding in to convert Simon Davies' low cross, and Erik Nevland finally put Reading out of their deepening misery in injury time. In between, Hahnemann fingertipped a stunning McBride volley and a thunderous Brede Hangeland header onto his crossbar, and the instrumental Jimmy Bullard struck the woodwork for a third time with an arced free kick late on. Fulham were brilliant, Reading were hapless and thousands poured out of the stadium knowing that the 2–0 home defeat to the Cottagers could well be the result that would condemn Reading to relegation. At the time, though, few realised that Roy Hodgson's men themselves – miraculously reignited after recording their first away win in 33 games – would be the ones to upset the odds and push the Royals down by the slenderest of margins.

Sweeping changes saw Coppell rest a number of first team stars for a tricky trip to the Emirates, and Arsenal did enough to saunter to another victory over Reading. First half goals from Emmanuel Adebayor and Gilberto ensured that the Gunners would remain the only side to claim maximum points since Reading's shift into the top flight. Lita was drafted back in, and a valuable point kept Reading's head above water on an arduous afternoon at Wigan which saw scores change so alarmingly elsewhere that only at the final whistle could the goalless draw be truly evaluated. Bolton and Birmingham leads against Spurs and Liverpool had been lost, but Fulham had astonishingly bounced back from two goals down at Manchester City to win. The results meant that, no matter what happened in Madejski Stadium's final game of the season, Reading's destiny would

not be decided until a final-day trip to Derby.

Again, effort was thrown into creating a positive vibe, hoping that a powerful Madejski Stadium input would will Steve Coppell's men to a victory over Tottenham. The team had trained at the stadium days beforehand, and on the day of the game signed t-shirts were shot into crowds of fans, who were celebrating the sunshine by sporting the home strip and filling the stands with blue-and-white hoops of hope. Tottenham began brilliantly, though, and slick passing soon saw the visitors open Reading up, with Robbie Keane finishing from Darren Bent's breakaway after only a quarter of an hour.

Steve Coppell made his way pitchside and reshaped his Royals to accommodate for the surprise 4–3–3 formation Juande Ramos had sprung, and slowly Reading began to adapt. The second half was

Lita scores only his second goal of the season in a 4–0 win on the final day at Derby.

Kitson's joy soon turns to despair.

Reading's, but Tottenham's defence had tightened since the 10-goal debacle in December, and there was no way through. Urgency crept in a little too late and after Kitson had seen a low effort well saved, Long set up Liam Rosenior for the last top flight chance in front of goal at Madejski Stadium. The right back stabbed his effort sharply towards the top-right corner but, unlike Paul Robinson earlier in the season, Radek Cerny was not going to gift Reading anything and the Czech stopper pulled off an astonishing clawed save to preserve his clean sheet. Defeat meant Reading were in 18th place, now behind Fulham on goal difference, with only one game to go – a trip to rock-bottom Derby. Control of their own destiny had been ripped from Reading's hands.

Almost exactly one year previously, Steve Coppell was accepting his LMA Manager of the Season award as Paul Jewell was stepping down as boss of Wigan Athletic. The Latics had survived on a climactic final day but, after fast recharging his batteries, Coppell's fellow Liverpudlian counterpart was about to become the man trying to ruin Reading's season finale.

Having taken charge of a hapless and disconsolate Derby outfit earlier in the season, Jewell was hoping to rally his downbeat Rams for one final hurrah at home. And although the 11 men he fielded happily capitulated once again,

Steve Coppell thanks the raucous fans for their unparalleled support at Pride Park.

Kitson and Convey reflect on a horrible end to 2007–08.

Shorey upset as the Royals are relegated.

for the first time all season County fans could revel in others' misfortune.

James Harper's left foot scored Reading's first goal in six games with 14 minutes on the clock, after controlling Dave Kitson's pass with his right foot before curling a precise effort wide of Roy Carroll's outstretched right glove and high into the net from 20 yards out. Rampant celebrations ensued on and off the pitch; Harper raced to the bench gleefully while an unbelievably raucous following of

3,000 away fans went mental at the other end. A vast array of colourful inflatables had provided the loyal Royals with the pre-match entertainment, but the opening goal markedly changed their fun-filled party mood into one of sheer ecstasy and honest belief that three points were about to spark a heavy night of revelry.

With the goalscoring drought at an end, the floodgates were threatening to burst open. Leroy Lita dallied over a couple of excellent opportunities and

should have been awarded a penalty after being clattered by Carroll inside the box. Derby supporters had awarded themselves the Player of the Season award before kick-off, but even their loyalty was being tested as frustrated groans greeted every misplaced pass. At the break it was only 1–0, but with radio pieces rammed deep into every ear in the away fans' enclave, everyone knew that with Portsmouth still foiling Fulham's search for a goal, 1–0 would be enough.

Just before the hour, Dave Kitson made sure of the only result Reading could command, sliding in to stab Lita's squared cut back into a gaping net, and the strikeforce that had found no way through six different defences suddenly came alive to end their barren run. Kevin Doyle hooked a scrappy effort inside the far post from the floor with 20 minutes remaining and Lita headed a fourth in injury time, but every attention had already been turned to news that was filtering through from Fratton Park. No news had been good news but the FA Cup finalists, who had fired a total of nine goals past Reading, but whose focus was perhaps turned towards their approaching Wembley date, could not find the impetus to notch even one against Fulham and, just as Harper's opener had changed the provisional bottom three 14 minutes in, Danny Murphy's headed

2007–08 Barclays Premier League – in and around us:

		P	W	D	L	GD	Pts
16	Bolton W	38	9	10	19	−18	37
17	Fulham	38	8	12	18	−22	36
18	**Reading**	**38**	**10**	**6**	**22**	**−25**	**36**
19	Birmingham	38	8	11	19	−16	35
20	Derby County	38	1	8	29	−69	11

Champions: Manchester United
Relegated: Derby County, Birmingham City, Reading

FA Cup: Third round (v Tottenham Hotspur)
League Cup: Third round (v Liverpool)

Top scorer: Dave Kitson (10)

Most appearances: Marcus Hahnemann (38), James Harper (38), Stephen Hunt (37)

Marcus Hahnemann

winner 14 minutes from time meant the Cottagers would complete an incredible escape at Reading's unbearable expense. Level on points but three goals behind Fulham, Reading were relegated. Floodgates of a different kind caved in as tears freely streamed down cheeks.

'We're obviously bitterly disappointed – that's a huge understatement,' a down-mouthed Royals boss told the press after the stunning 4–0 win that felt worse than a 4–0 defeat. 'The dressing room is a very sad place at the moment and it's difficult to know what to say to ease their pain. There's no comfort in words at the moment. It's just a numb feeling. I think we've brought some good stuff to the Premiership. It's just a shame it has ended this way.'

This was not the 10th chapter in Madejski Stadium's history that anyone wanted to see written. Many can claim to suffer from regular Monday morning woes; after the freedom of a weekend, millions across the country find it hard to drag themselves out from under the covers and into work for the start of another week. But, although the sun was shining brightly and beaming heat into Berkshire, this was going to be a low very few had experienced before. Still in a state of shock, staff reluctantly sidled through their respective entrances to re-begin life as a Championship football club. It was a sad feeling but one that saw a harsh reality slowly sink in. Of course countless companies adapt or downsize but very few – upon the scoring of one Sunday afternoon goal on the south coast – have to alter everything they do so dramatically. Madejski Stadium, somewhat in mourning, was at its most sombre.

Reading FC felt a little directionless for a brief period as the dust inevitably began to settle but, after a few days of reflection, the tone changed. A new challenge lay ahead and no amount of moping would help the club address that. Reading had achieved their success through quiet, thoughtful, positive vigour and intent. Now those qualities were needed again. Steve Coppell took time to decide his next move, and after receiving an unprecedented level of support from the Chairman, the board, the staff, the players and the fans of the football club – the latter staging a vigil in Coppell's car park spot at the stadium, begging him to stick with their club – the experienced thinker finally vowed to lead the charge in re-establishing Reading as a top flight force.

In its first decade, Madejski Stadium has played host to some fairytale moments: impromptu celebrations after Curo's magical promotion-winning equaliser; the gradual rise up the divisions, culminating in Graeme Murty's last gasp record-breaking spot kick against QPR; top flight football welcomed with a memorable three-goal comeback to oust Middlesbrough on a very special afternoon; and Liverpool being beaten in the Premier League. There are many more – we have been spoiled! And despite this story not ending as happily as we would have hoped, a fresh and fierce hunger is about to be channelled into capturing a catalogue of new tales.

KEVIN DOYLE

Reading appearances: 106 (+15)
Reading goals: 38

Picking the final man 'who made the Madejski' was no simple task. So far, there has been no place for a number of worthy candidates. Marcus Hahnemann, for example, joined the Royals at the start of the Division One/Championship odyssey and has remained an absolutely central figure in the Club's progress ever since. The American has also more than played his part off the pitch, becoming immensely popular with supporters. And then there is the engine room duo of James Harper and Steve Sidwell, a pair of former Arsenal trainees who formed arguably the best central-midfield partnership in the Club's history as they provided the driving force behind the 2005–06 title-winning team.

Also worthy of significant mentions are Ivar Ingimarsson, who has barely missed a single game of the Steve Coppell era, and Glen Little, the source of some special moments of wing wizardry. Others such as Leroy Lita, Bobby Convey, Ibrahima Sonko and Stephen Hunt were also integral members of the most successful Reading squad in history and would fully warrant their own entry in these pages, as would the two men whose astute management has taken the club so far – Alan Pardew and Steve Coppell.

But it has to be someone, and Kevin Doyle presents a pretty persuasive case – if only for the fairytale nature

MEN WHO MADE THE MADEJSKI

of his story and the sheer impact of his arrival in Berkshire. Like Hahnemann, Sonko, Kitson and Shorey among others before him, Doyle was a virtual unknown when he was signed by Steve Coppell in the summer of 2005 on the recommendation of his former manager at Cork City, Pat Dolan (who just happened to be the brother of the Royals' academy manager, Eamonn). Doyle had scored sufficiently with Cork and the Ireland under-21s to attract a modicum of interest from English clubs, but none were prepared to make a commitment until Coppell, urged on by Dolan, chief scout Brian McDermott and director of football Nick Hammond, took the plunge by forking out a modest transfer fee on a player who was regarded as 'one for the future'.

When Doyle arrived in England, Coppell quickly realised that he had a bargain and a half. His first outing in Reading colours came in the pleasantly low-key surroundings of a pre-season friendly at Staines, where Doyle showed touch, strength, awareness, pace and ability. In fact, he did not seem to have any real weaknesses. And so, when Dave Kitson was injured against Burnley less than a month into the season, Coppell had no hesitation in throwing his 'one for the future' into the present fray. He responded by scoring the winner and added another in an exciting 1–1 draw at Coventry. Then he scored his third in three games as the Royals defeated Crystal Palace in one of the best games to take place at Madejski Stadium.

Kevin Doyle was here to stay and, remarkably, less than two months into his Reading career, it seemed as though he had been there all his life. With the minimum of fuss he continued to go about his business – working hard, creating chances, scoring goals – and the rest of the League scratched their heads and wondered just how Coppell had managed to unearth him. The manager was quick to hail his new strike sensation for the ease with which he had adapted to life in England, reserving particular words of praise for the 'low maintenance' nature of Doyle's personality. The Wexford-born striker was no sensitive soul and did not need pampering or cajoling. No eye needed to be kept on his off-the-pitch exploits, he just came in, did his job (very well) and went home – nothing flash, just a damn good footballer.

Inevitably, it did not take long for others to sit up and take notice, and when he was appointed Ireland manager in January 2006 Steve Staunton's first act was to come to Reading to watch Doyle in action. An international debut soon followed as Staunton's new charges demolished Sweden 3–0 and, in a similar vein to his arrival at Reading, Doyle was suddenly a regular starter for his country.

At the end of his first fairytale season in English football, Doyle received the considerable accolade of being named Player of the Season – to be regarded as the best player in that record-breaking team, you had to be pretty good! And the story continued as the Royals announced themselves in the top flight in spectacular fashion. For a while during the autumn months, Doyle led the Premier League's scoring charts, having netted after 16 seconds against Sheffield United, converted a penalty against his boyhood favourites, Manchester United,

and scored in five consecutive games in November – including his first goal at international level. Yes, the boy from Ireland had enjoyed a successful year and a half.

After that sensational rise, Doyle was long overdue a more difficult spell and it arrived in the second half of the 2007–08 season. He had started the campaign well, scoring five goals by early December despite helping out the team by filling the problematic right-wing berth on a number of occasions. But after netting with a glancing header to help the team to a remarkable 3–1 victory over Liverpool, he went through the longest barren run of his career – a scoreless sequence that lasted right until the final game of the season at Derby when, to much relief, he scrambled home an ultimately meaningless strike.

But Doyle's career is still in its early stages, and there can be little doubt that he will bounce back from that disappointing half season. There can also be little doubt that his contribution helped transform Reading FC from a club that hoped to mount a realistic promotion challenge to one that broke countless records in a title-winning campaign and then took the Premier League by storm.

Behind the Scenes

7:00am

The groundsman's day starts at 7am, when the whole pitch is cut with cylinder mowers (the grass in the goalmouth and on the touchline, needing to be a different length to the rest of the ground, is cut with rotary mowers the previous day). The process lasts a little longer than your average back garden – approximately two hours!

8:00am

A van driver reverses onto the pavement outside Gate 1, delivering the matchday programmes, and with the help of one of the operations staff the crates are offloaded, ready for a team of 20 programme sellers to count up and allocate to programme-selling points around the stadium.

9:00am

The megastore opens and telephone and counter sales begin as the ticket office opens for business, while preparations for hundreds of hospitality guests start with the organising of packs – each one with seating plans and additional match-specific information – for a team of between 15 and 25 hostesses. The afternoon's hospitality tickets are put in order ready for a swift collection from midday onwards. The pitch is marked out with white lines, a process that takes another couple of hours, and the ice baths in each dressing room are filled with cold water which is refrigerated to 8°C.

10:00am

The hospitality areas are all unlocked, the lights and air-conditioning is turned on and company names are pinned up on executive box doors, while sponsorship signage, Reading FC backdrops and welcome banners are all displayed in suites and the main reception. The stadium's LED screen is started up and the sales team check that the correct perimeter advertising boards are in position and undamaged. At 10:30pm the PA system is sound checked as boxes of programmes are divvied out to satisfy the needs of those who can keep their £3 in their pocket; both dressing rooms receive a programme per player, the match officials, mascots, PA team, journalists and photographers all get a free read, as does every scout and hospitality guest. Even Kingsley gets to paw through the pages! Meanwhile, the megastore are printing names and badges onto any new first team kit that is required by players who have swapped, given away or sometimes torn their kit in the previous match.

11:00am

The away kit arrives four hours before kick-off, but ours has usually been laid out since Thursday. If, when the manager writes his starting eleven on the board, there are any name changes, kits are quickly whipped and new numbers laid out – usually after any morning ground tours have strolled by

to ensure the starting eleven is kept a secret. The two head groundsmen have been joined by four or five matchday groundstaff, who help erect the goals, pitch the corner flags, wheel out the portable goals for the warm-up and fix the stop nets in place to protect the crowd behind. The Puma banner is also draped over the centre circle. Press and photographers begin to filter through their entrance and sign in and the PA team also arrive, collecting pre-written scripts and playlists before preparing their on-screen graphics and filming snippets of footage outside the stadium. Scouts from an array of league clubs and often other countries begin to arrive at main reception, as do some of the players for a pre-match meal. In the tunnel, the kit man is pumping up the balls for the warm-up, while two floors above signed gifts are being supplied to the match and matchball sponsors' suite, where the tables are being laid and the hostesses are being briefed before they begin welcoming and directing guests to their tables at midday.

Midday

Hotel staff are now being swamped with pre-match pint-suppers as crowds start to build in the Atrium Bar. Kingsley arrives and changes into his kit – tucking his tail down one leg of his shorts to make sure it doesn't drag in the mud – before heading over to the Young Royals kiosk that has been wheeled out in front of the megastore. The Recaro dugout seats are installed and volunteers begin wandering the complex by starting any charity collections that have been pre-arranged with the Club. The ticket telephone lines close, the final ticket batches for the last seats sold via the internet and over the phone are arranged in collection boxes and the full complement of counters are opened. As the morning drifts into afternoon, national and local press filter in for a feed, and photographers sign in, collect numbered bibs, purchase wireless connection codes and head pitchside.

1:00pm

The pitch is watered and the head groundsman meets with the coaching staff of both teams to explain where best to warm up. Passes are issued to any new stewards and the turnstile monitoring system is started up. Outside megastore units open to relieve the tills inside and the matchday mascots arrive and are welcomed into the Players Lounge with their families. At 1.30pm the gates are opened to the public. A network of radios are constantly monitored for any supporters having problems accessing the stadium, while in hospitality lunch

is served before the guests receive a visit from two of the non-playing Royals squad. Match officials arrive and are shown to their changing room and players stroll in suited and booted, delivering their complimentary tickets to the Admin staff, who transfer them to the Players' Guest Entrance for collection. In-tunnel activity steadily grows with the under-18s arriving after a Hogwood battle of their own; those 'on duty' help the kit men and the nutritionist by preparing tailored energy drinks and recovery bars. A team of 16 ball boys and girls meet their supervisor and head pitchside, but

before the players run out for a warm-up the mascots are escorted into the dressing room to meet their heroes ahead of a community coach-led kick about.

2:00pm

The goalkeepers are soon followed by the rest of the squad out onto the Madejski Stadium turf at about 2:20pm and the completed teamsheets have been photocopied for the match officials and, in a smarter form, distributed in their hundreds to all corners of the stadium - the Chairman receives the first! The PA team leap into

action with news of any presentations or upcoming events relayed to the supporters via the on-pitch microphone. Hospitality guests are treated to a pre-match quiz by their MC and tables have their photos taken by a team of snappers. Meanwhile, a bookmaker makes her way to each suite to offer the guests the latest odds.

After the warm-up is complete, the stop nets are dismantled, the goals are carted off and the banner folded up before the pitch is 'divotted' just before the teams emerge from the tunnel with the mascots. The host cameraman plugs into the stadium feed so the matchday TV channel can broadcast the footage throughout the complex and after a Club photographer snaps the centre-circle formalities the big screen's countdown clock is started and the record button is pressed; DVD copies of the match are made for immediate post-match analysis by both managers, the referee and the FA.

3:00pm – Kick off

As the action entertains thousands in the stands, the work doesn't stop for many. Up to 250 stewards line the stands and patrol the concourses, throngs of catering staff man the drinks pumps and warm the pies in preparation for the half-time rush, ball boys and girls adopt their watchful positions on stools at the foot of each stand and the media team report on every kick for readingfc.co.uk on the gantry. The PA team watch eagle-eyed ready to announce scorers, pump goal-celebratory music into the bowl, or cut the big screen's feed if a controversial incident is replayed.

3.45pm – Half time

At the interval the team of groundsmen aerate the soil with forks, replace divets and sprinkle water across the surface, while the concourses fill and any half-time entertainment takes place. And the half-time performances have sometimes earned headlines of their own. Jake the Dog, the ball-juggling hound, first mesmerised fans at Madejski Stadium and competed with human tricksters Mr Woo and Dan Magness for the keepy-uppy crown in Reading. Acts including an Elvis Presley tribute band and Lawrence Robinson's operatic rendition of Nessun Dorma have serenaded the stands, while drum clubs, dance groups and the occasional brass band have also performed. Santa has swept in on a zip line, toddlers have waddled for charity, parachutists have floated in from afar and a helicopter

even hovered within Madejski Stadium's bowl before bowing to the awestruck crowd. 'Who Wants Pizza' was the cry as a partnership with Domino's saw the Club present rows of fans with a half time feast and a Masterblaster gun has fired signed shirts into the stands. 'Play Your Shirts Right' asked fans to guess higher or lower, while a Gladiators challenge saw opposing supporters batter each other with pugel sticks. It has all happened during an often action-packed 15 minute spell.

The Golden Gamble competition was running successfully at Elm Park and the half time draws continued to thrive when the move to Madejski took place. Between 15 and 19 yellow-jacketed ticket sellers prowl the grounds, giving fans the chance to win cash prizes that reached a high of £2,000 in 2006–07! Winning tickets have been drawn out by a host of famous faces and former Royals greats and more than £250,000 has been given away during Madejski Stadium's decade - with more than £60,000 raised for the Club's 'Football In The Community' scheme.

4:45pm – Full time

Minutes before the end of the match, the Club's Head of Communications races from top to bottom - the gantry

to the tunnel – where he is ready to chaperone the manager into a post-match press conference, before guiding him through a host of TV and radio interview requests. Other members of the media team conduct internal interviews with the Royals stars for the Club's official website and online TV station Reading World.

A restocked and tidied megastore re-opens for a short period and, without interrupting his post-match shower (some take longer than others to groom every tuft), Club representatives wait at the tunnel's exit for the nominated man of the match to emerge, before leading him to a champagne presentation with the match sponsors.

The pitch is undressed, the watering system is set and often brush cassettes are attached to the lawnmowers to clear debris off the surface. The kit is often cleaned and folded by 6pm and the stadium starts being locked up. The fast-emptied car parks follow suit at 7pm. If a London Irish game follows the megastore is re-merchandised and after press conference comments are typed up and a post-match video edited, the media machine can wind down too.

Chapter 11

The Future

There was a strange and unexpected reaction to Reading's relegation from the Premier League in May 2008. Even though the Club had won just 10 games out of 38 and thereby failed to achieve the objective of prolonging their stay among the country's elite, there was a surprising lack of bitter recriminations. No 'board must go' demonstrations from the supporters, no anger, no finger pointing, no blaming. Of course there was intense disappointment and a great deal of downbeat analysis and pondering on what went wrong and why. But, on the whole, the main emotions directed towards the Club from supporters and outsiders alike were sympathy and solidarity.

Among the players and staff as well, there was a devastated but realistic acceptance of the situation. The frustration and sadness could not be hidden, but there was none of the 'his fault, not mine' petulance that so often follows failure.

The mood was summed up by captain Graeme Murty, who manfully faced up to the press in the immediate aftermath of the final day tears at Derby to admit:

The table doesn't lie. We were top of the League in the Championship and the manager said 'judge us at the end'. We were flying in the top flight and he said 'judge us at the end'. Unfortunately the harsh reality is that now we are judged at the end of a season in which we've not been good enough…we've not scored enough goals, we've not kept enough clean sheets and ultimately it has cost us. Fulham had a fantastic run – they deserve to be in the Premier League and we don't. I'm going to sulk for two weeks but I'll come out of it, because I want to be back in the Premier League. Mentally it's going to be very difficult but we have to make sure that, as a squad, we get together and deal with it properly. We can't allow this to linger on and we've got to make sure we're ready to bounce back. It's hard to take, but we have to acknowledge why this has happened and learn lessons from it.

And then there was the Steve Coppell issue. Immediately after relegation was confirmed, Coppell strode onto the Pride Park pitch to salute the supporters. Was he waving goodbye? He later admitted that even he didn't know. He wanted to take some time to consider his position and objectively decide his future in the cold light of day, but he made it clear that there was every chance he would resign. Immediately, the local radio airwaves were besieged by callers begging the manager to stay. To emphasise their faith, a few hundred fans even turned up to the manager's empty car park space to pin supportive notes and sing cheery songs. Unusual, but it worked – Coppell was swayed by the affection directed towards him by the supporters and by the Chairman, John Madejski, who had made his feelings equally plain. And eventually, the manager agreed to stay to spearhead Reading's challenge for a swift return to the top flight.

At many clubs, the reaction to relegation – or even a few defeats – is much more severe. Sack the manager, sack the board, sell the players…but that is not the 'Reading way'. A mentality of considered and thoughtful contemplation and a policy of steady sustainable growth…that was responsible for getting the Club into the top flight in the first place – and that will be how we set about getting back up there.

Underpinning all that is a quiet but firm belief that the club has the credentials to become a long-term success. Everybody has to go through their ups and downs and it has to be acknowledged that we have just experienced a major down. But if we keep on doing the right things in the right way, we have a heck of a lot going for us and the overall trend of upward movement need not necessarily be broken. In the greater scheme of the Club's long-term progress, this relegation could prove to be nothing more serious than a sizeable blip. As chief executive Nigel Howe notes:

Relegation might turn out to be not too much of a bad thing because sometimes you need a bit of a checking of your speed to make sure you're not taking too many chances or growing too fast. Perhaps our ambitions have got ahead of us a bit. This will give us a chance to examine

ourselves and go forward again in the future. We've continued to see strong support from the fans, strong use of our hospitality, a very busy use of our hotel and conference centre – and we're in such an affluent and dynamic part of the country with little serious competition around us. Those factors can combine to provide the momentum to carry on and go forward.

At the heart of that belief in Reading FC's long-term credentials is Madejski Stadium. Even though they will not have the pleasure of competing alongside the nation's elite in 2008–09, fans, players and staff alike can all clearly see that this club has the right infrastructure to sustain Premier League football in the longer term. Of course, the same can be said of many clubs who currently find themselves outside the top flight – Wolverhampton Wanderers, Norwich City, Ipswich Town, Derby County, Sheffield sides United and Wednesday and many others. But Reading now has a fighting chance of mixing it with the big boys – in the past, that was never the case. And even if we never get back into the Premier League (a future no one involved with the Club is even contemplating), at least we have had those two seasons – better to have loved and lost than never to have loved at all.

Much has already been achieved since the stadium first opened its doors on 22 August 1998. It has already served the chief purpose for which it was designed, by allowing Reading Football Club to compete in the Premier League for the very first time. That in itself is a massive achievement and cannot be overestimated. It had never happened before in more than 130 years of the Club's existence. Try to imagine Reading playing in the Premier League at Elm Park and surviving not one but two seasons…no matter how rose-tinted your nostalgic glasses are, it simply would not have happened.

Yes, the Club did come close on one occasion before, in 1994–95, but on reflection that season takes on the appearance of a brilliant and unexpected flash in the pan, a glorious one-off that was neither preceded nor followed by any kind of consistent performance. Before the move to Madejski Stadium, it was the only time that the Club had even finished in the top half of the second flight, whereas the promotion of 2006 had been anticipated by three consecutive top half placings. The Club's last three seasons at Elm Park delivered Division One finishing positions of 19th, 18th and 24th; had they remained at the old ground, the probability is that Reading FC would still be shuffling around the lower two tiers of the Football League, just as they had done for the vast majority of their first 130 years of existence.

Aside from these most easily evident achievements in the sphere of

professional football, in its opening decade Madejski Stadium has also displayed its versatility by hosting top-flight rugby union and a series of successful one-off commercial and community events ranging from rock concerts to religious gatherings, as well as becoming one of the Football Association's favourite venues for under-21 internationals. The site has seamlessly integrated the introduction of a luxury 200-room hotel and houses a thriving modern conference centre along with a local radio station and an indoor football pitch that is nearly always fully booked. And, perhaps most significantly on a wider social level, the stadium has acted as a catalyst for the regeneration of a previously neglected area of Reading, leading directly to the development of a hugely popular business park and retail park.

So where does the stadium go from here? Ironically, control of the long-term future of Madejski Stadium is likely to largely rest away from the man whose vision was responsible for its construction in the first place – John Madejski. If it is true (and it is) that there could have been no sustained period of top flight football in Reading without Madejski Stadium, it is equally true that there would have been no Madejski Stadium without John Madejski.

Since taking up the position as Chairman in 1990, Madejski has surrounded himself with talented, determined, ambitious and dynamic people who have made huge contributions to the success of Reading Football Club and its new stadium – including Mark McGhee, Alan Pardew,

Steve Coppell, Phil Parkinson, Adrian Williams, Jamie Cureton, Marcus Hahnemann, James Harper, Nicky Shorey, Graeme Murty and Dave Kitson, along with unsung (in some cases completely unknown) heroes like Nigel Howe, Nick Hammond, Ian Wood-Smith, Bryan Stabler, Sue Hewett and Ray Booth. But always at the centre of it all, pulling everything together and providing the overriding vision, has been one man – John Madejski. But that will not always be the case, and John Madejski will not always be the Chairman of Reading Football Club. For the past two years he has repeatedly stated his willingness to listen to serious offers regarding the ownership of the Club (and, with it, the stadium). At the moment he is still here and there are no signs that a change in Chairmanship is imminent, but the reality is that even if Madejski never sells the club, he cannot go on forever.

So who will be the owners of Reading Football Club and the Madejski Stadium complex when the time comes to celebrate the next 10-year anniversary in 2018? An

Abramovich-style Russian billionaire? An American NFL owner who has seized the opportunity to branch into British sport? An oil tycoon from the Middle East? Reading FC's Supporters' Trust? Maybe still Madejski himself or perhaps one or both of his daughters, Helen and Camilla? The truth is, nobody knows – not even John Madejski – but, whoever they are, they will be inheriting a football club and a site that is rich in potential.

The man who has looked after the day-to-day workings of the site ever since its opening 10 years ago is stadium manager Ray Booth, and he firmly believes there is no more active stadium in the country:

> There can't be a busier site than ours. Nowhere else does football, rugby, conferencing and a hotel on the same site. Watford have rugby but no conferencing or hotel. Bolton have a hotel but no rugby. Somewhere like Arsenal has Champions League, Premier League and conferencing – but

they don't have hotel issues or rugby! When you look at the schedules for our season, we had 55 major events here last season, in addition to all the conferences which take place more or less every day. I look at other places and think 'what an easy job that must be!' So I think if you add up the number of people who go through this place in a year it must be one of the busiest stadiums in the country. At Elm Park all we ever had was a football match every two weeks!

The success of the stadium and the component businesses is largely due to the one factor that made it the overriding choice of John Madejski and Nigel Howe when they were first planning the move in the mid-1990s – location, location, location. With its proximity to the M4, Heathrow Airport, London, Oxford, Birmingham and the south coast, it can be strongly argued that Madejski Stadium enjoys the best location out of any football ground in the entire country –

and this is something that gives Reading FC an edge over many of its rivals.

Look at a map; the closest League club to Reading is Aldershot, who have only just regained their status in the 92. And, aside from the Shots, you have to travel to Swindon (west), Oxford and Wycombe (north), Brentford (east) and Southampton (south) to find the Club's nearest geographical rivals. That relative isolation within a large, well-populated and wealthy catchment area is an advantage that very few clubs enjoy – Wolves are directly competing with Aston Villa, West Brom, Birmingham and Walsall for example. Preston have to jostle for fans and investment with Wigan, Burnley, Blackburn, Bolton and even the Manchester and Liverpool clubs. Madejski Stadium is very fortunate to be located in such a powerful position.

Relegation has not stopped the stadium from growing – the summer of 2008 saw the completion of a new £2 million media and office block in the south-west corner, while plans were drawn up to double the size of the

megastore, and a refurbishment of the hotel's Cilantro restaurant got underway. Of course, the future development that will have by far the biggest impact on Madejski Stadium are the plans to increase the capacity of the stadium to 38,000. Planning permission has already been received and, although relegation has led to an inevitable postponement of the expansion work's commencement, the most significant fact is that the Club has the capability to add another 14,000 seats if the team is successful enough to warrant it.

Self-evidently, adding nearly 60 percent to the current capacity would make a fundamental change to the dynamics of the stadium. In many ways it would be like building an entirely new stadium, and the process would undoubtedly bring an interesting new set of rewards and challenges for players, staff, supporters and the local community. If the time comes to make the decision to build those additional seats, it would be a fascinating development, once again changing the very fabric of the Club and rapidly becoming another milestone moment in the history of both Reading Football Club and the town in general.

So, we can conclude that Madejski Stadium has already achieved a lot in a short space of time, but there is the potential for a lot more to come. Clearly football and, more specifically, Reading Football Club will continue to form the cornerstone of the stadium's activities as we move deeper into the 21st century. How successful the Club is depends on a myriad of factors, but it is not unrealistic to say that with a capacity of 38,000 the stadium would be equipped to cater for

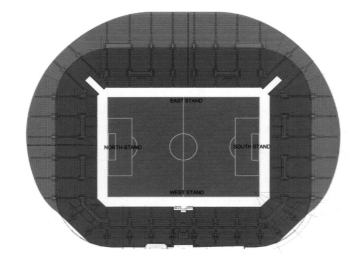

even the most unimaginable levels of success; a new owner funds a stream of superstar signings and fashions a team that becomes Champions League winners – Madejski Stadium could host it, no problem.

Equally, and to provide some balance to that outlandishly optimistic scenario, it is feasible that the recent years of unparalleled success could come to a sudden and dramatic end – Steve Coppell resigns, the new manager struggles, the team suffers another relegation, the best players leave and are not replaced and another relegation follows. It is just as likely (or unlikely) that, 10 years from now, Reading will be challenging for the newly formed European Super League title in front of sell-out 38,000 crowds every week or

clunking around in the equally all-new Football League Division Two B (South) cheered on by just 3,000 diehards. Of course, the reality will probably be somewhere in between those two extremes, but the fundamental point is that, unlike at Elm Park, the level of the Club's achievements will not be limited by their stadium.

In addition to the football, whichever level it is being played at, the next 10 years will continue to see Madejski Stadium host top flight rugby union – a new long-term contract has been agreed to extend London Irish's tenancy, and their club appears to be in a strong position to challenge regularly for national honours in years to come. We can also expect the conference centre and the hotel to continue to prosper,

with more concerts, more weird and wonderful charity celebrity kickabouts, more England under-21 internationals and, who knows, maybe even a World Cup game?

But Reading FC will be the foundation and as we have seen over these pages Madejski Stadium has already witnessed some great goals, great games, great players and great occasions. Will we ever see celebrations to rival the May 2006 promotion scenes? Will we ever again plummet to the depths of a 6–0 home defeat to Bristol Rovers? A lot remains unclear but one thing is certain, the story of Madejski Stadium has only just begun. So if you think the first 10 years have been enjoyable…imagine what the future might hold!

Madejski Stadium Statistics
Some you know and some you probably don't...

The Royals

A total of 110 different Reading players have run out onto the Madejski Stadium turf over 10 years of first team games. Twelve more only made appearances as substitutes and seven unfortunates had glory denied them at the final stage as substitutes who were never used.

Unsurprisingly, Graeme Murty, who was signed at Elm Park and actually made his Reading debut in a pre-season friendly at the old ground, has played more games at Madejski Stadium than any other player. Sixteen players have made 50 or more first team starts for Reading at the new ground, and they are:

	Starts	Sub Apps
Graeme Murty	165	6
Nicky Shorey	150	0
James Harper	139	15
Marcus Hahnemann	134	0
Ivar Ingimarsson	105	2
Steve Sidwell	90	3
Andy Hughes	89	4
Nicky Forster	88	18
Phil Parkinson	77	4
Adrian Williams	75	1
Darren Caskey	73	5
Ibrahima Sonko	66	2
David Kitson	60	15
Kevin Doyle	57	7
Phil Whitehead	56	0
Ricky Newman	54	10

Five of the seven-most unused substitutes at the Madejski were goalkeepers, with Jamie Ashdown leading the way with 56 bench-warming games. Spare a thought for the stadium's least seen players: Leo Roget, Jonathan Hayes, Ross Harrison and Tony Malessa's Madejski Stadium careers being restricted to just one game as an unused substitute.

Golden Goals

Dave Kitson heads the 61 Reading players who have scored at Madejski Stadium, with 38 strikes up to the end of 2007–08, just two more than Nicky Forster and eight ahead of Jamie Cureton. Eleven Reading players have hit double figures at the ground, with Martin Butler and Steve Sidwell both on 20 and Darren Caskey making up the top six (although Kevin Doyle and Leroy Lita, both on 17, and James Harper with 12, could catch them).

Ricky Newman, with 64 appearances in total, played more games than any other outfield player without netting at Madejski Stadium, other notable non-scorers being Matt Robinson and Linvoy Primus. On the other hand, defenders Peter Maté and Sam Sodje both scored on their only first team starts at the ground.

The Complete Record

	P	W	D	L	F	A	Attendance
Premier League (Tier 1)	38	19	4	15	48	45	899,873
Championship (Tier 2)	92	56	19	17	153	75	1,577,213
League One (Tier 3)	92	47	27	18	151	90	1,081,222
League play-offs	2	1	0	1	2	2	46,094
FA Cup	16	5	5	6	25	23	194,862
League Cup	15	6	5	4	21	17	162,797
AMC	2	2	0	0	3	1	4,286
Total	257	136	60	61	403	253	3,966,347

Manager Records

	P	W	D	L	F	A	Attendance
Steve Coppell	118	66	21	31	184	120	2,274,232
Nicky Hammond	1	0	1	0	2	2	12,594
Kevin Dillon	2	1	0	1	3	3	31,181
Alan Pardew	106	57	29	20	177	95	1,328,721
Tommy Burns	30	12	9	9	37	33	319,619
Total	257	136	60	61	403	253	3,966,347

The Visitors

82 different clubs have faced Reading at our new ground, with Wigan Athletic and Stoke City being the most frequent, both having played nine times here in the last 10 years.

Money Matters

The Chelsea starting XI that faced Reading in that controversial game on 14 October 2006 was the most expensive ever to appear at the ground, having cost an amazing £151.6 million. The following season, Chelsea's team 'only' cost £117.55 million, thanks to the inclusion of free transfer Steve Sidwell, while Manchester United's starting XI on 19 January 2008 were the only other £100 million-plus side to face Reading at the Madejski. Those three costly sides all made their value count by winning, but Liverpool paid the price of fielding a 'low-value' side for the Premier League fixture against Reading in December 2007 – their £70.3 million line up was not enough to rid them of the tag of the most expensive side to lose at Madejski Stadium.

On the other hand, six teams have come to Madejski Stadium with a team that did not cost a penny in transfer fees. Although non-League FA Cup opponents Grays Athletic and Welling United were both beaten, only Luton of the four 'free' League visitors were defeated, with Colchester United in November 2000 and Walsall in October 2003 both taking maximum points away with them.

The Arsenal starting team that inflicted Reading's biggest Premier League home defeat, featured 10 different nationalities (the double nation being France, of course). Both of Blackburn's starting XIs to play Premier League games in Reading featured nine different nationalities. You have to go back to 1 April 2002 to find the last all-English team to visit Reading, when Northampton Town drew with a Reading side that featured 10 English-born players plus John Salako who, despite being an England international, was born in Nigeria.

Frequent Visitors

Of the 1692 different players to start in opposition to the Royals at Madejski Stadium, the most frequent visitor has been goalkeeper Paddy Kenny, totting up eight games for Bury and Sheffield United. Dave Livermore and Paul McKenna have both made six appearances at the Madejski Stadium with one club – Millwall and Preston North End respectively. By way of an alternative, Steve Banks and David Brammer have both played at the ground with four different clubs.

Brynjar Gunnarsson can make the same claim; as well as his 41 games for Reading he has played against us with Stoke City, Nottingham Forest and Watford. Other villains turned heroes include Ivar Ingimarsson and Glen Little, both of whom have faced Reading four times with other clubs before seeing sense! But what has Glen in common with Andy Hughes, Dean Morgan, Steve Sidwell, Adi Viveash and Tony Barrass? The answer is that all five played against Reading before they joined the club and then again after they left. Glen Little's inclusion is explained by the fact that his two games came either side of his loan spell at Madejski Stadium in 2003. Special mention in this category also goes to Seol Ki-Hyeon, who was an unused sub before and after his year with Reading, for Wolves and then Fulham. Equally strange is the fact that, although John Halls only started one Madejski game for Reading, he has played three times against them at the ground when he was with Colchester United and Stoke City.

Loan Stars

When Southampton visited Madejski Stadium on 10 February 2006 they became the first and, to date, only club to use the League maximum of five loan players in their side.

A Cautionary Tale

The 'dirtiest' teams in Madejski Stadium's history are both Brentford and Bradford City – both received 11 bookings in three visits…an average of 3.66 per game.

Just Managing

Other regular visitors are opposition managers, and the Club's 'old friend', Neil Warnock, leads the way. He has taken charge of teams in seven matches against Reading at the Madejski. Neil is followed by Ian Holloway, Paul Jewell and Lawrie Sanchez, who have all managed five teams at the ground. Sam Allardyce, Gary Megson and Tony Pulis have all been in charge of three different teams at Madejski Stadium but are beaten by Peter Taylor who, as well as bringing his Gillingham, Leicester and Brighton teams to Reading, also managed the England under-21 side in games at the ground.

Goals Against

It will come as no surprise to Reading fans that the most feared visitor to Madejski Stadium has been Andy Johnson, who has averaged a goal a game in his five visits with Crystal Palace and Everton. Only three players have scored a hat-trick against Reading at the Madejski – Fernando Torres for Liverpool in the September 2007 Carling Cup tie, Neil Harris for Millwall in January 2001, while Reading fans eventually forgave Jamie Cureton his four-goal burst for Bristol Rovers in January 1999. 'Curo' was not the only Reading player to score while playing for the opposition. Seven former or future Reading players netted against the Royals, with Tony Thorpe scoring twice against Reading, compared with the one he scored for them.

The Referee

Madejski Stadium's most frequent referees are Paul Taylor and Rob Styles, both having officiated 11 games at the ground. Between them they hold the record for the most cautions – Taylor clearly favours the Royals as he has booked 21 visiting players and sent off four, compared to just 14 Reading cautions. On the other hand, Styles has booked more Reading players than any other ref, taking the names of 16 Royals. Equally unpopular is Mike Read, the only official to have dismissed two Reading players during 10 years at the Madejski.

By The Book

In total, 13 Reading players have seen red at the Madejski Stadium, compared to 27 visitors while the booking totals stand at 326 for Reading and 451 for our opponents. Millwall's Dave Livermore and Leicester City's Joey Gudjonsson have both received three Madejski Stadium cautions, while Graham Kavanagh has been booked with three different clubs, as has Steve Sidwell, cautioned with Brentford, Chelsea and Reading. But Kavanagh edges ahead as he also has a sending off to his 'credit', coincidentally for a foul on Steve Sidwell. As far as opposing teams are concerned, Millwall players have been booked 19 times in seven visits, making them Madejski Stadium's naughtiest guests.

Top Ten Goals

Reading fans have voted Leroy Lita's overhead volley against Crystal Palace in September 2005 as the best goal ever scored at Madejski Stadium.

With the Royals trailing 2–1 midway through the second period of a pulsating fixture, a half-cleared corner dropped towards Lita inside the penalty area. After carefully watching the ball drop, the striker leapt acrobatically to launch a ferocious overhead volley towards goal. His right boot connected perfectly, and the ball flew into the net before Gabor Kiraly could even move. It was an unforgettable moment and fully deserves the accolade of Madejski Stadium's best goal.

Leroy's wonder strike narrowly beat Bobby Convey's first goal for the Royals into the top spot – the US ace beat three challenges and sprinted 70 yards before calmly slotting home. Third place was also claimed by a goal in the title-winning 2005–06 season, with Graeme Murty's penalty against QPR claiming the sentimental vote. The top ten was as follows:

1. Leroy Lita v Crystal Palace, 13 September 2005
2. Bobby Convey v Millwall, 20 August 2005
3. Graeme Murty v QPR, 30 April 2006
4. James Harper v Liverpool, 8 December 2007
5. Leroy Lita v WBA, 17 January 2006
6. Nicky Forster v Ipswich, 19 October 2002
7. Ulises De La Cruz v Sheffield United, 20 January 2007
8. Jamie Cureton v Burnley, 27 August 2002
9. Darren Caskey v Northampton, 1 January 2001
10. Dave Kitson v Middlesbrough, 19 August 2006

Roll of Honour

Mark Adams
David Hugh Aitken
Mike Amos
Chris Andrews
Bryan Appleton
John Appleton
Jack Arlott
Mark Ashcroft
Lauren Bailey
Joel Baillie-Lane
Cameron Baker
Richard Baker
Chris Baldwin
Russell Baldwin
Michael Ball
Nick Bamford
Colin Banbury
Mrs Barry
Neil Bartlett
Lance Bates
Deirdre Benn
Dean Bennett
David Deacon Berry
Nick Bird
Colin Bishop
Andy Blake
Nick Bluring
Valerie Bolton
Mrs J M Bowtell
Malcolm Brewerton
Jeannie Brice
Brian Broad
Kerry-Ann Broad
Johan & Tom Brooke
Andrew Brown
Glenn Brown
Andrew Bryant
Graham Bryant
Steven Bryant
Helen Bullen
Jeffrey Burgess
Shaun Capel
Andrew Carpenter
Sue Carter
Ian Chalmers
Andy Charman
Mike Christmas
Keith Churchill-Coleman
Simon Clarke
Alan Clements
Daniel Cochrane
Chris & Vanessa Cook
Graham Cook
Peter W Couch
Dan Cradock
Stuart Croucher
Wendy Cullenaine

Russ Cummings
Darrell Dainton
Dave Dance
Chris Dillistone
Nick Dixon
Peter Dobson
Sam Docker
Graham Dougall
Eddie Dove
Alistair Dowlman
David Downs
Steve Duffy
Philip Duncan
Phil Dutfield
Karl Dyer
Rachel Dyson
Simon Eedle
Graham Mark Elliot
Miriam Elliot
Colin F Elliott
Paul Ellix
Paul Evans
Oliver Fitzsimons
Andrew Flatt
Ann Flatt
John Flatt
Paul Flatt
Colin Ford
Sybil Ford
Daniel & Jake Foster
Carl Freeman
Pam French
Pete Frost
Denny Fullbrook
Paul Fursman
Alan Garfield
Alan Giles
Ashley Gilliam
Ron Girdler
Jamie Glover
Kevin Goddard
Stuart Gosney
Andrew Green
Neil Green
Phil Green
Barry Greenaway
Dawn Greening-Steer
Kay & Andy Grubb
Andrew Hadland
Paul Hadland
Christina Hall
Kevin Hall
James Hammerson
Keir Hardie
Paul Harding
Dan Hare
Mark Harvey

Tim Harvey
David Hatfield
David Hawkins
Jonathan Hayward
Mark Heffernan
Frank Hickson
Chase Alexander Hill
Ivor Hipgrave
Alan Hogg
Jenny Hood
Martin Houghton
John Howarth
Graham Hughes
David Hunt
Mat Hurst
Mel Jacob
Caroline Jeffcote
Luke Jenkins
Paul Johns
Neil Johnson
Brian Jones
Daniel Jones
Richard W Jones
Anthony Kearns
Anthony 'ak' Kendrick
Louise Kersley
Owen Kilbane
Peter Kilbane
Graham King
Philip Kingdom
Alison Kingston
Luke Krauze
Samuel Krauze
Andy Lambourne
Chris Lang
Gary Leach
Dan Leahy
Malcolm Lee
Andrew Lester
Rachel Lester
Jennifer Lewis
Steve Linstead
Emma Lock
Martin Locock
Harvey Lodder
Tony Look
Alan Lovegrove
Josephine Mann
Justin Mann
Jack Mansell
Keith Marlow
Krikor Maroukian
Paula Martin
Daniel Maskell
Neil Maskell
Paul Masterman
Steve Matthews

Stephen May
Jason Mccready
Lee Mcdonald
Kenneth Mcgrath
John Mchugh
Teresa Mchugh
Matthew Miles
Petar Miljus
Mark Moody
Fiona Moore
Andrew & Ben Morris
Claire Needham
Anne 'nobby' Newbery
Stuart Nicholson
Michael North
Richard Norton
Eric Roger Nowell
Peter Jack Nowell
David Oliver
Ian, Adam, Daniel Osmond
Karen Pain
Gary Painter
Ian Parham
David Parker
Russell Parker
Cliff Patching
Rod Paterson
Sarah Payne
Stephen Peacock
David Peart
Ben Phillips
Lewis Pickett
Reece Pigden
Roy Pigden
Andrew Plimsoll
Andrew Keith Plummer
Jeffrey Keith Plummer
Douglas Pound
Robert W Pound
Win Povey
Tony Powell
Leo Pratico
Rodney Proud
Martin Raisey
Mark Reading
Andrew Reaney
Amber Louise Reed
Dave (Royal Tour) Reed
Jeffrey Reihle

Peter Rich
Ken Richardson
Paul Richardson
Sarah Richardson
Tom Richardson
Ron Roberts
Toby Robinson
Allan Roe
Chris Rose
Richard Ruffell
David Rush
Barry Salmon
David Sampson
Jim Saunders
Tony Savery
Paul Schembri
Alan Scott
Alan Sedunary
Peter Sharpe
James Simpson
Hannah Slade
John Slater
Andy Smith
Dave Smith
Jamie Smith
Janet & Holly Smith
Lorraine Smith
Matthew Smith
Natalie Smith
Robert Smith
Trevor Smith
G & M & E Snelham
Edwin Soares
Pamela Sollis
Mick South
Louise Squire
Christine Stacey
Andrew Stagg
Ben Stagles
David Stone
Ian Strange
Terry Strange
Cameron Stuart
Mark Sugar
Janice Sumner
Nigel Tandy
Anthony G Taylor
Colin Taylor
Phil Terry

Nick Theobald
Roger Thomas
Allan Thompson
Anthony Tomas
Paul Toovey
Georgina Toseland
Max Toseland
Mike Townend
Alayne Townsend
Kyle Townsend
Ian Trevett
Alan & Ben Trivette
Richard Tudor
Andrew Tull
Stuart Venn
Inga Vickery
Pete Vickery
The Wakefield Family
David Walker
Mark Walker
Rachel Warner
Bill Warwick
Neil Warwick
Andy Waters
Alan Webb
Barry Webb
Kris Weber
Colin Weller
Scott Weller
Gordon West
James West
Gemma Wheeler
Stephen W Wheeler
Raymond White
Sarah White
Andrew Whitlam
Mr A Whitlock
Richard Wilcox
Steve Wilkerson
Rob Williams
Richard Willis
Brian Wise
Alan Woodley (Wobble)
Jack Woodley
Robson Woodley
Leila Woollam
Damian Wyles
Darren Wynn
Andrew Yoxhall